34 Days

ISRAEL, HEZBOLLAH, AND THE WAR IN LEBANON

Amos Harel
AND
Avi Issacharoff

Translated by Ora Cummings and Moshe Tlamim

palgrave
macmillan

First published in hardcover in 2008 by
PALGRAVE MACMILLAN®
in the United States—a division of St. Martin's Press LLC,
175 Fifth Avenue, New York, NY 10010.

Where this book is distributed in the UK, Europe and the rest of the world,
this is by Palgrave Macmillan, a division of Macmillan Publishers Limited,
registered in England, company number 785998, of Houndmills,
Basingstoke, Hampshire RG21 6XS.

Palgrave Macmillan is the global academic imprint of the above companies
and has companies and representatives throughout the world.

Palgrave® and Macmillan® are registered trademark in the United States,
the United Kingdom, Europe and other countries.

ISBN-13: 978-0-230-61436-9
ISBN-10: 0-230-61436-1

Library of Congress Cataloging-in-Publication Data

Harel, Amos.
    34 Days : Israel, Hezbollah, and the war in Lebanon / Amos Harel and
  Avi Issacharoff.
      p. cm.
    Includes bibliographical references and index.
    ISBN 0-230-60400-5 (cloth)
    ISBN 0-230-61436-1 (paperback)
    1. Lebanon War, 2006. I. Issacharoff, Avi. II. Title. III. Title: Thirty four days.

DS.65.H37 2008
946.9204'4—dc22   2007048534

A catalogue record of the book is available from the British Library.

Design by Newgen Imaging Systems, Ltd., Chennai, India.

First PALGRAVE MACMILLAN paperback edition: May 2009

D 10 9 8 7 6 5 4 3 2

Printed in the United States of America.

CONTENTS

INTRODUCTION AND ACKNOWLEDGMENTS

HERE AND THERE you can still see them along Israel's roads and highways, car bumper stickers, left over from mid-July 2006. Some of the country's larger newspapers handed them out during those days of optimistic patriotism. On one the legend reads, "Israel is Strong!!," as if we're not quite sure and need a reminder. Another reads simply, "We'll Win." When the war ended, many drivers, frustrated and angry, scratched off the stickers. Their hopes were dashed. The media, full of praise for the country's leaders, now attacks them for their haste and stupidity in deciding to go to war.

Over a year has passed since the end of the second Lebanon war, but its signs are still clearly noticeable. As far as losses are concerned, this was not a particularly big war. An average week of Shiite and Sunni violence in Iraq causes more deaths than were recorded on the Israeli side during 34 days of war with Hezbollah (161, of whom 119 were soldiers and 42 civilians). But the war had a far-reaching effect on Israel. More than 4,000 rockets were fired at the northern towns and villages; this was the first time the Israeli home front was under constant attack for so long. The Israel Defense Forces (IDF) failed in its attempts to stop the bombing, and the end of the war did not leave Israel in a controlling position. Israel's achievements—which included the removal of Hezbollah from the border and the arrival of a multinational force (whose efficiency remains controversial)—were nowhere near the level of expectations defined by the prime minister Ehud Olmert and minister of defense Amir Peretz at the beginning of the war. Israel was badly scalded by the war, which had an adverse effect on the way in which Israelis view their leaders, their army, and even the future of the state within the hostile region that surrounds it.

In some ways, this could have been a case of overreaction. Recuperation was quick, too. A year later, Israel is enjoying an economic boom; in the North, restoration of war-damaged property is moving ahead at a reasonable pace; tourists are again arriving in the thousands. But the swift recovery did not dispel, or even dull, the national feeling. Many Israelis continue to feel mistrust, disgust even, toward the leadership and have expressed their doubts as to the IDF's ability to face up to future challenges. No less serious is the fact that our neighbors have also noted the results of the war. Hezbollah's rocket war has exposed the vulnerability of Israel's home front and its leadership's indecision in carrying out IDF counterattacks. At least some of the Arab states now believe that Hezbollah has come up with a winning strategy worthy of emulation. In this regard, the second Lebanon war could be remembered as the decade's key turning point.

As we see it, the war did not begin on July 12, 2006, when Hezbollah abducted two Israeli reserve soldiers. The story has a broader scope that goes back to Israel's decision to withdraw from southern Lebanon, a departure that was completed in May 2000. In this book we have chosen to provide an extensive description of the six years prior to this war, years during which the IDF's strength was sorely tried in an effort to curb Palestinian terrorist attacks from within the occupied territories while Hezbollah was preparing itself for another potential confrontation with Israel.

All this, of course, could be pure hindsight. Most of the intelligence we now have was not available to Israel's decision makers at the time of the withdrawal from Lebanon; when Israel showed restraint over Hezbollah's first abduction of soldiers on Mount Dov (Sha'aba Farms) in October 2000; or when the government decided to deviate from its former policy when two more soldiers were abducted. Leaders, especially those in Israel, are under enormous pressure. In the Israeli case, it is due in part to the hostile environment in which the country exists; it is also due in part to Israeli society's well-known tendency toward mass hysteria.

More than a year and a half has passed since the war. Today, too, some details remain classified, hidden from the public eye, to become known only when the archives are opened. Throughout our research and writing of this book, information continued to flow in our direction, and viewpoints and aspects sometimes changed. The book, therefore, is based on everything we knew during the summer and fall of 2007. Future developments may well shed a different light on some things. There will no doubt be those who will say that by publishing the book at this time we are jumping to conclusions. We are convinced, however, that there is enough in what we have seen to provide a reasonably clear picture of the events of the summer of 2006 in our region. In order to write this book, we interviewed more than 200 people who were involved in the war. On the Israeli side, we found a great willingness to talk. As usual in Israel, an investigative journalist has at his disposal a large amount of information that should, by rights, be classified. At times, even we were surprised at the ease with which details were made available to us. We spoke directly to the vast majority of the war's main functionaries we quoted in this book, and used many of the protocols of the government's meeting and army chief of staff discussions. The transcripts of the testimony presented to the commission of inquiry headed by retired judge Eliyahu Winograd have provided us with an important source of information.

Unlike research for our previous book, *The Seventh War*, on the Israel-Palestine conflict, access to the enemy side was harder this time. Beirut is not Ramallah. Still, we believe that, through talks with diplomats and press people, some of whom were in Beirut during the war, we have succeeded in producing an extensive picture of events beyond Israel's borders during that time. Among those we interviewed are Americans, French, and Arabs, all of whom played important roles in the war. Most of them chose to remain anonymous. We found the majority of them open, frank, and exceptionally willing to admit to mistakes; above all, we encountered frustration. However, on the Israeli side, we could not help but notice the hair-raising discrepancy between the sacrifice and devotion of the soldiers at the front and the inexplicable apathy exhibited by some of those who sent them to war. Notwithstanding the problems revealed by the war, the IDF is not a broken army.

There is no single explanation for Israel's failure, but rather an overall accumulation of circumstances: arrogance, superficiality, and inexperience among the decision makers both in government and in the army. Different decisions, before and, certainly, during the war may well have brought different results.

On the Lebanese side, despite the enormous pride in the success of a guerrilla terrorist organization's ability to withstand the same Israeli war machine that previously defeated the combined Arab armies, the loss was much greater. Over 1,000 Lebanese people lost their lives, almost half of them civilians (although figures are conflicting on this). The country is divided as it has not been since its civil war, and another conflagration between the various ethnic communities seems imminent. Repairs have barely begun on the war damage (estimated at a few billion dollars) in the South, whereas Israel's economy has made a wondrous recovery. The rift between the moderates and the extremists in the Arab world has never been more obvious. The conflict between Israel and Hezbollah took place against a background of much broader processes, including America's floundering in the Iraqi mud and the rise of Iran as an extremist regional superpower, granting patronage to states and organizations. This is an important part of the big picture; we believe it is often overlooked in the Western debate. As these words are being written, the danger of a new war hangs over Israel and its neighbors. It seems to us that an in-depth discussion of these issues is just as important today as it was right after the war.

⊷⊐   ⊏⊶

We are happy to thank all the many people who made important contributions to this book. First are those who agreed to be interviewed, who shared with us their time and their wisdom. We were lucky to have from the very beginning of this project our research assistant, Naomi Toledano, who conducted several of the interviews, scanned documents for us, and contributed a great deal of extremely useful counsel. Thanks to the behind-the-scenes readers and advisors, Arieh Neiger, Professor Eyal Susser, and Aluf Benn; special thanks to the editors on our own paper, *Ha'aretz*, David Landau and Ronen Zaretzky, for their support in getting the book published and for their infinite patience throughout the writing process.

A big thanks to our literary agent, Lynne Rabinoff, for all the time and hard work she put in on our behalf and for making this English version possible. To Ora Cummings and Moshe Tlamim, thanks for the fine English translation. To Jake Klisivitch, our editor at Palgrave Macmillan, who embraced the idea of this book.

The final and most important thanks go out to our families, which actually expanded as the book was being written: to Liat and Liya Issacharoff, Efrat, Tamar, Itai, and Eyal Harel—we know how much this book depended on the time, patience, and love you gave us so generously. We promise not to repeat the adventure too frequently.

As we wrote, we often thought about the casualties of this war: the civilians who were hit by the murderous torrents of Katyusha rockets and the soldiers who gave their lives in defense of the home front. The memory of two in particular is always with us. They were both younger than we are: Major Binyamin (Benjie) Hillman, company commander with the Golani Brigade, who was killed in the battle of Maroun a-Ras, and Captain Shai Bernstein, company commander with the 401st armored corps regiment, who was killed in the battle of Sluki. We hadn't known Benjie well. We learned about Shai from the stories of his commanders and friends. Both exhibited courage and devotion. Thousands more IDF generals, officers, and soldiers were raised on similar values. It is up to us to demand, not only hope, that, in the future, those people responsible for making life-and-death decisions will exhibit a more suitable measure of knowledge and responsibility when they send our soldiers to war.

CHAPTER ONE

THE ABDUCTION

UDI GOLDWASSER WAS 13 when his father, Shlomo, who worked for an international shipping company, moved his family to South Africa. From the beginning, young Goldwasser couldn't stand life in Durban, so his parents promised him that the family would return to Israel if he was still unhappy three months later. When the time came and Udi still wanted to go back, his parents tried to buy more time. The boy refused to let them renege on their promise. One Saturday, his mother, Micky, drove him to the weekly meeting of the Jewish youth movement, Habonim. When she went back to collect him, Udi had disappeared. Half the Jewish community of Durban turned out to help the family search for their missing son. After a fruitless three hours, by which time his frantic parents thought of involving the Israel Embassy, Udi emerged from his hiding place behind a bush very close to where his mother was standing. "Here I am," he said to her. "See, I fooled you. All this time, I've been watching you searching for me. If you don't let me go back to Israel, I'll disappear again."

Udi's parents gave in and allowed him to return to Israel on his own, where he stayed with relatives. Eighteen years later—again in Durban—when Shlomo informed Micky that Udi and another soldier, Eldad Regev, had been abducted by Hezbollah, she recalled that day in 1988 and was barely able to curb the urge to turn around again, expecting to see her son pop out from behind that same bush.

Ever since, she says, she can't stop thinking back to then, when Udi jumped up and said, "I fooled you."

HANNIBAL, SECOND TIME AROUND

It was 9:45 a.m. and Noam Schneider was only about 100 meters from the two burned-out Hummers when he saw the smoke, two large columns of fire rising to the skies on the road leading down the slope, crossing the *wadi* (valley) at the spot known over the field radio as 105 phase line. It took Schneider only a couple of minutes to understand that he and his men were too late. A count of the dead and wounded in and around the Hummers revealed that the patrol was two soldiers short. Hezbollah were nowhere to be seen. In the 45 minutes between the attack and the arrival of the first reinforcements, the abductors had had more than enough time to make a safe getaway from the Israeli side of the border and back into Lebanese territory. Hezbollah had carried out its plan perfectly: an effective attack on the patrol moving along the security fence that runs parallel to the border; a simultaneous decoy operation, consisting of heavy shelling along the border and a decommissioning of all the observation cameras that were set up near the border. Together, all these actions created the commotion necessary to provide time for a successful abduction. Schneider, the officer in charge of reserve battalion support company, looked helplessly at his commander, Lieutenant Colonel Benny Azran. All the officers in 91st Division, entrusted with guarding the Israel–Lebanon border, were told the same thing, either before taking up their positions or during their stint of reserve duty: Anything you don't get done during the first few moments after the enemy has conducted a successful abduction, you'll never get done. Next to the cut in the security fence, they found a blood-stained flak jacket belonging to one of the abducted soldiers. Nimer, 91st Division's scout, warned that the hole in the fence might be booby-trapped. There were eight officers and soldiers on the scene, clearly not a force capable of conducting a chase into Lebanon. At that point, Azran and Schneider decided that it would be no use trying to pursue the captured Israeli soldiers. From that moment on, it was a matter for the ranks above theirs.

Israel Defense Forces (IDF) slang has a term to describe the mood prevalent among the reservist soldiers in the Zar'it section—the area of the abduction—on the morning of July 12, 2006: they call it "end-of-term feeling." There is not a reservist in the IDF who doesn't know this feeling: On the last day of term after three and a half weeks of exhausting activity along the border, the main, if not only, topic of conversation during those final hours is the length of time it will take to get home. If the replacement battalion turns up on time and the quartermasters at base camp get the equipment issued quickly, there's a good chance to see the family or girlfriend before dark. The battalion's thoughts are elsewhere, and the replacements still have not acclimated to the terrain. The assumption in the army is that the enemy has identified this weak spot; by monitoring the field radios and keeping a close eye on the observation posts, it is easy enough to identify changeover days—and changeover days mean trouble.

C Company's final morning watch, set for 8:00 a.m., was delayed—not unusual for a reserve unit—by about 45 minutes. Thirty-one-year-old Sargeant Udi Goldwasser from Nahariya was the commander in charge of the patrol; his code name over the communications network was 4. Goldwasser, an amateur photographer and deep-sea-diving coach, had married Karnit the previous October and was enrolled at the Haifa Technion to begin working on his master's degree the following fall. He was seated in the commander's seat, to the right of the Hummer's driver, career soldier Razak Mu'adi. Eldad Regev and Tomer Weinberg sat in the back. The patrol left Zar'it and traveled eastward, together with another Hummer (4A) carrying three soldiers instead of the regular four: Wasim Naz'al, the driver; Shani Turgeman, the com-mander; and combat soldier Eyal Banin.[1] The soldiers were not particularly tense as they drove off on their mission, although Goldwasser had heard First Lieutenant Nir Leon, the officer in charge of the patrol he was replacing, say that a "red touch" had been identified at 2:20 a.m.: Someone or something had touched the electric security fence. Leon's patrol observed the spot, in the region of report point (RP) 105, but identified nothing. "It was a very fright-ening night. I thought at least 20 Hezbollah people had passed through the fence," said Leon. Goldwasser promised to examine the spot. Since alert had been dropped two days previously, patrols were allowed to move freely around the "red areas" considered to be more potentially dangerous, includ-ing that part of the road known as RP 105.

The attack began shortly after 9:00 a.m. Hezbollah waited patiently until the two Hummers appeared from around a bend in the road and were com-pletely exposed. As the second Hummer passed the highest point and began descending, it was attacked by heavy machine gun and antitank fire. Hezbollah's holding link, which had positioned and hidden itself among thick undergrowth on the opposite bank (on the Lebanese side of the fence), dis-abled the Hummer so that its crew could not come to the aid of the first vehi-cle, which was moving down the slope about 110 meters ahead of it. Naz'al, the driver, was killed inside the truck. Turgeman and Banin were shot to death as they climbed out. But Hezbollah focused mainly on the first Hummer. A small force that had crossed the border into Israel during the night shot two RPG (rocket-propelled grenade) rockets at short range at the Hummer, which took most of the flak on the right side. Weinberg, badly wounded, and Mu'adi, slightly wounded, managed to haul themselves out of the left-hand side of the burning vehicle and hide in the bushes. "I had already said all my good-byes," Weinberg related later. "Just a few more steps and they could have come and taken me, too." Since the two wounded soldiers were not in a position where they could see the abduction, the rest of the reconstruction is based on findings in the field. Hezbollah, it appears, went up to the Hummer and pulled out the two wounded Israelis, Goldwasser and Regev, a 26-year-old Bar-Ilan University student from Kiryat Motzkin. With the two captured soldiers, the abductors boarded the civilian jeeps awaiting them across the border and headed north to the nearby village of Ita a-Sha'ab.

Immediately after the attack on the Hummers, an artillery attack began on the border settlement Moshav Zar'it and surrounding military positions. Several civilians and soldiers were slightly wounded. At the same time, Hezbollah sharpshooters disabled all IDF observation cameras in the area. Battalion commander Azran heard the explosions from his office in the Zar'it camp. "Already, as I was walking from my office to the command and communications room I knew we'd had it. I entered the room and there were so many reports from so many places. . . . I didn't know where to turn my attention to first." The first one to really understand what was happening was Ze'ev, the sergeant major of the support company, who had heard a report over the communications network: "4, 4A, collision." Ze'ev phoned his company commander, Noam Schneider, who did not know the location of the patrol under attack. Knowing that 105 was an obvious weak spot, he decided to set out in that direction from headquarters in Zar'it. Schneider chose to take a hidden route, via a wadi that joined the road from the south rather than from the west, along the high road. Because the entire area was under fire, it took some time for communications to be checked, as some commanders were unable to immediately respond to their radios. But it was quite clear even before the check was completed that two Hummers, 4 and 4A, were not responding. Schneider had joined Azran, who announced over the network that they were in a "Hannibal" situation—suspected abduction of soldiers.

The gate into the wadi was locked. After the scout who had come with Azran shot the lock open, the small force advanced toward the burning Hummers and soon encountered the driver, Mu'adi, who jumped out from behind some bushes. Mu'adi had just managed to report the attack on his cell phone to another driver in the adjacent zone. Azran and Schneider tried to question Mu'adi, but he was too shocked to say much, and they continued to make their way toward the Hummers. Two bodies lay alongside the second Hummer and a third body could be seen inside. A quick count of the dead and wounded verified the original fear: It was an abduction—two Israeli soldiers had been taken by Hezbollah.[2]

TROJAN HORSE

The videotape captured by Maglan (a prime paratroop unit) at Mount Dov—also known as Sha'aba Farms—close to Mount Hermon in late June 2005, left little room for speculation: Hezbollah was planning further abductions of Israeli soldiers in the region of the Sha'aba Farms, around the border between Syria, Lebanon, and Israel. Three Hezbollah special force members were identified in Wadi M'rar, in Israeli territory, an area where no fence separates Israel and Lebanon. The IDF chased them for a whole day. At the end, a Hezbollah commander was killed at a range of several dozen meters in a clash with the Maglan force, but his two colleagues managed to escape back into Lebanon. In order to cover the group's escape, Hezbollah began a heavy bombardment of the IDF positions on Mount Dov. A soldier from the Golani Brigade was killed by a mortar shell. Signs in the wadi where Maglan had come across the Hezbollah section indicated that the men were professionals. The position in the undergrowth where the three Hezbollah fighters were lying in wait had been expertly prepared and perfectly hidden by camouflage nets. The location had been chosen after a thorough analysis of field conditions and maximum control of the surrounding area. The section penetrated Israeli territory under cover of darkness and used state-of-the-art night-vision equipment.

But the most interesting find was the recording, which the three Lebanese had made several hours before the attack, while they were still in Israeli territory. Apart from providing a detailed account of the area, the three had also found time to fool around. One of them filmed his two friends taking a rest, dressed in camouflage fatigues and helmets. All three had beards and appeared completely relaxed. Their commander, who was later killed, was chewing gum. "Can you see the flies?" he asked the photographer and pointed to the sky, probably at Israeli mini-RPVs (remotely piloted vehicles). "Take a picture of the RPVs." "What's up?" the photographer tested his prowess as an interviewer. "Great," the commander replied. "What could be better than this? We'll take it walking."

The recording, like the large amounts of intelligence equipment the three carried, reflects the exaggerated self-confidence of people who obviously had already spent time in Israeli territory without getting caught. Findings in the field where the three were located showed that Hezbollah had dispatched sections, experienced in spending time behind enemy lines, to collect intelligence and then assigned a team to prepare for the kidnapping operation on Mount Dov. It was unusual for the IDF to encounter a Hezbollah section at such short range, now that Israel had withdrawn from Lebanon. The Hezbollah's 30-year-old section commander—who was killed—was a veteran fighter in the special force and son of a south Lebanon Hezbollah leader. The encounter reinforced Israel's conviction that Hezbollah was determined to kidnap Israeli soldiers. The only possible change in plan would involve the choice of location.

Over the next 12 months, Hezbollah waged several rocket and mortar attacks on IDF positions on Mount Dov. On several occasions Hezbollah, Lebanese, and Palestinian subgroups also shot a few short-range Katyusha rockets in the direction of Israeli towns and villages along the northern border. At the same time, Hezbollah planned three further attempts to abduct Israeli soldiers, all of which were thwarted. Intelligence at the disposal of the Northern Command of the IDF, which was responsible for the area of the border with Lebanon, was partial and limited but with proper deployment and tactical orientation in the field, the IDF managed to foil Hezbollah plans.

The most ambitious kidnapping attempt took place at Kafr Rajar on November 21, 2005, when dozens of Hezbollah special forces crossed the border into Israel on foot and in all-terrain vehicles and tried to attack an IDF paratroop position. But, relying only on a general intelligence warning, the Israeli paratroop commander in the village adopted a devious tactic. The IDF force changed location in time so that Hezbollah stormed an empty post and were attacked in an ambush. A young sharpshooter, Corporal David Markowitz, killed three Hezbollah fighters. Even then Prime Minister Ariel Sharon was impressed. "You have saved the country from a tricky strategic situation," he wrote in his letter of congratulations to Head of Northern

Command Udi Adam and intelligence branch chief Aharon Ze'evi. But Corporal Markowitz's courage overshadowed the fact that the IDF had enjoyed a great deal of luck in thwarting the attack and that Hezbollah fighters, deployed along the border, were able to make further attempts at abducting Israeli soldiers whenever they chose.

More significant repercussions to the Rajar incident provided disturbing warnings for the future. Three days before the attack, the Northern Command observation points noticed Hezbollah antitank sections deploying near the border. Chief of Staff Dan Halutz refused Udi Adam's request for permission to launch a preemptive strike. Lacking any other way to thwart a Hezbollah attack, the Northern Command decided to turn to the media. Following this previously successful tactic, information was passed on to the Israeli press regarding the special IDF deployment along the northern border in response to abduction warnings. The Northern Command reckoned that, as before, Hezbollah would understand that its intentions had been exposed and cancel the operation. But this time, Hezbollah continued as usual. In Israel, the conclusion was that Hassan Nasrallah, Hezbollah's secretary general, was under sufficient pressure to undertake the risk.

During the abduction attempt in Rajar, Hezbollah managed to hit a number of IDF tanks with, as was later discovered, improved Russian-made RPG rockets, sold to Syria shortly beforehand. Israel went public with these facts in an attempt to dissuade Russia from transferring its state-of-the-art weapons to Damascus, from which point they went to Hezbollah. But Moscow remained unmoved, and advanced antitank rockets continued to follow the same route: final destination, Lebanon.

Late May 2006 saw a further escalation, which began with a mysterious explosion of a kind that is commonplace in Lebanon. In a bomb explosion in Sidon, Mahmoud Maj'dov, commander of the Palestinian Islamic Jihad in Lebanon, was eliminated. This set off a chain of focused reactions, with each side slightly raising the level of its activity. Hezbollah, suspecting that Israel was behind the assassination, reacted to the killing by launching an accurate Katyusha rocket attack on the Israel Air Force (IAF) base on Mount Meron, the southernmost point to be attacked in recent years. The IDF closed the round of blows with extensive rocket and artillery fire across the zone close to the border, in the course of which dozens of Hezbollah positions were targeted from the air and on land. At least three Hezbollah members were killed, and the organization abandoned its forward positions. Israel agreed to stop the attack after Hezbollah appealed to the United Nations Interim Force in Lebanon (UNIFIL) via the Lebanese government. However, the IDF's proposal forbidding Hezbollah from returning to their border positions after the firing had subsided was not taken up.

Thus the scene was set for another abduction attempt. The Northern Command and 91st Division continued to exhibit creativity and improvisation that thwarted further attempts. But according to Israel's Winograd Commission on the War in Lebanon, "The next abduction was just a matter of time and it was doubtful if it could be avoided. All available means for managing the situation surrounded the lowest target concept, in other words, removing soldiers and military objectives from places which Hezbollah could penetrate with ease."

The Northern Command approached the job of preventing further abductions with limited sources. The familiar problems—little attention on the part of general headquarters (GHQ), limited resources, relatively few forces compared to those allotted to the Palestinian front—became more acute in early June; and the Gaza Strip, less than one year after Israel's complete withdrawal, was once again demanding attention, as if the Palestinians were trying to emphasize all the disadvantages of a one-sided divorce.

HANNIBAL, FIRST TIME

The deterioration on the border with the Gaza Strip had begun about five months after the Hamas victory in the Palestinian parliamentary elections, at the end of January 2006. The constant increase in Qassam rocket attacks on the town of Sderot and the western Negev had Israeli Prime Minister Ehud Olmert's new government confused. The suffering in Sderot increased, and the government was unable to provide solutions. The attacks led Israel to question its withdrawal from the Gaza Strip. The attacks were a development that Olmert, who intended to renew the political momentum by way of his convergence plan, which included a massive evacuation of the Jewish settlements and strongholds throughout the West Bank, found difficult to ignore.[3] Israel responded by renewing IAF attacks and by dispatching small commando units into the Gaza Strip, especially in regions near the border. Dispatch of troops seemed to be limited and hesitant. Neither the public nor the government was overjoyed at having to return to territories from which Israel had withdrawn, especially if it would involve Israeli casualties; the same response would happen in Lebanon one month later. As a substitute for a major ground operation, Israel launched a furious attack from the air; achievements were only partial. The dozens of Palestinian casualties included many civilians. Each time the IDF broadcast optimistic reports on its success in reducing the number of rockets, the Palestinians would fire more, as if their purpose was to annoy. Things reached a dangerous state of escalation on the morning of June 25. A joint section consisting of Hamas, the "Committees for National Uprising," and a small offshoot known as the Army of Islam infiltrated Israeli territory via a tunnel north of Kibbutz Kerem Shalom, on the border between Israel and the Gaza Strip. The infiltrators, helped by an organized military cover of antitank rockets and mortar fire, attacked a number of positions and troops along the border. The team of a Merkava tank facing the Gaza Strip was surprised by the Palestinians as they emerged from the tunnel. Lieutenant Hanan Barak and Sergeant Pavel Slotzker were killed. A third team member was wounded and remained inside the tank. The fourth, Corporal Gilad Shalit, was wounded and led by his armed abductors into the Gaza Strip. As with the Zar'it abduction, confusion reigned. The forces in the field, busy fighting secondary terrorist groups linked to the infiltrators and noticed too late that one of the tank crew was missing. There was no real chase after the abductors.

In response to the abduction, Israel launched an extensive military operation in the Strip called Summer Rain. The air raids became even more intense and were followed by infantry attacks in the Bet Hanoun region in the north of the Gaza Strip. In a month of activity—with the number of forces drastically reduced after a second abduction on the Lebanon border—some 450 Palestinians were killed, including about 100 civilians. One Israeli soldier was killed by friendly fire. Shalit remained in captivity, and Israel's force did nothing to persuade the organizations that held him to budge so much as an inch.

The Israeli government's management of the crisis seemed to reveal some worrying trends, such as a predisposition for taking unconsidered decisions, oversensitivity to public opinion, and bombastic declarations that turned out to be groundless. On July 4, after the Palestinians fired a rocket at the southern Israeli town of Ashkelon (thus scaling up the scope of the operation), Olmert threatened to "cause Hamas to weep and whine." Unlike his predecessors Yitzhak Rabin, Ehud Barak, and Sharon during similar crises, Olmert made a number of bombastic statements. "The question of freeing

Palestinian prisoners [in return for Shalit] is not to be considered," he announced the day after the abduction. According to another of his declarations, "There will be no deal. Either Shalit is released, or we shall be obliged to free him by force." Behind the scenes, Olmert's people informed the press that the prime minister intended to change the rules of the game. Israel would no longer be so vulnerable to blackmail. Israel's response would prove to the terror organizations that the abduction of Israeli soldiers is of no benefit to them. Olmert's declarations, which included hints of disapproval of Sharon, were later repeated with regard to the Lebanon abductions. Olmert, it was said, dares to act, where his predecessors showed weakness.[4]

But the North still seemed a long way away from the battle in Gaza. In early July, the press announced that plans were under way to reopen a tourist resort on the northern coastline at Ahziv after a five-year hiatus.

With the deadlock surrounding Shalit, IDF forces advanced deep into the Gaza Strip in the early morning of July 12. For the first time since the withdrawal, Israeli soldiers entered the outskirts of the region that only a year before had housed the Israeli settlements in Gaza Strip. At the same time, Israel made attempts to dispose of the Hamas military leaders Muhammad Def and Ahmad Ja'abri in their hiding place in Gaza. Def was badly injured. His colleague was unhurt, although a number of civilians were killed. The press praised Olmert's daring. Regardless of the danger to the abducted Shalit, the prime minister had followed a hard line toward Hamas. On the morning of July 12, the head of Northern Command received a call from Major General Gadi Eisenkott, who suggested that, with things as they were in Gaza, it might be a good idea to consider possible repercussions on the situation in the North. Hezbollah might see itself obliged to respond to developments in Gaza. Adam checked with his intelligence officer. Since no danger signs were identified, it was decided to remain on low alert.

ALERT 2

Following the abduction of Shalit and with little, if any, concrete intelligence to support their fears, Adam and 91st Division commander Brigadier General Gal Hirsch decided to raise the alert level in southern Lebanon from level 2 to level 4, on a scale of 1 to 5. According to the officers, the abduction in Gaza could stimulate the appetite of Hezbollah, and Hassan Nasrallah might be tempted to grab the reins of the struggle from the Palestinians. Headquarters was party to the decision, and over the next couple of weeks the northern border was placed under high alert. All furloughs were canceled in units stationed close to the border. South of Zar'it, along phase line 105, Egoz Company commander Major Benjie Hillman set up ambushes and teams from elite units were posted at other known weak spots. But all Hirsch's attempts at obtaining concrete information on Hezbollah's intentions failed. According to the investigative committee that questioned the abduction, he had no such information, even after he'd sent the division's intelligence personnel to check out the situation for themselves.

On July 10, following continued pressure from his officers, and after GHQ had already dropped the alert from level 4 to level 3 on July 2, the 91st Division commander also announced that the alert would be lowered from level 3 to level 2. There seemed no point to maintaining a high alert, since it was not backed by additional troops and other resources. Eventually tension eroded the troops' awareness and the significance of the alert warning. As an immediate result of the lowered alert, "red zones" were reopened to military movement. At times of high alert, these zones, which the division had earmarked as potential trouble spots for abductions, were out of bounds to military patrols. On the other side of the border, Hezbollah waited patiently. "They simply sat there and waited for us to lower the alert," said Hirsch after the war. "As soon as the Hummers returned to the [security] fence, Hezbollah was back in action."

NATURE RESERVE

In retrospect, the IDF believes that, after its crushing failure in Rajar the previous November, Hezbollah planned the abduction meticulously over several months. Command of the operation was most probably entrusted to the head of the organization's terror mechanism, Imad Moughniyah. More than 20 Hezbollah fighters, divided into four sections, took part in the action. One section crossed the border during the night and carried out the abduction. The location had been picked after careful deliberation and lengthy observation. Hezbollah knew that IDF patrols rarely came to the spot and that the nearest army post, Livna, which allowed only partial observation of the abduction spot, was not permanently manned. As far as IDF observation points were concerned, it was a "dead area."[5] Here even radio reception was distorted. According to American researcher and author Andrew Exum,

Hezbollah expected the IDF's response to the abductions to be slow and clumsy due to the chosen location.

A well-equipped bunker, built by Hezbollah on a rise overlooking the road on the Lebanese side of the border, was chanced on by the IDF only toward the end of the war. As with other "nature reserves"—well-equipped bunkers belonging to Hezbollah all across southern Lebanon that Israeli soldiers happened on during the war—in this case, too, the IDF knew too little. The observation points built by Hezbollah along the border were clearly visible, but the nearby bunkers were well hidden. Several months earlier, when the soldiers in a post near Zar'it complained of "someone digging under our feet," the division brought in geologists. The soldiers, it later transpired, had been right. IDF Intelligence knew where Hezbollah was headquartered in Beirut and where it was hiding its Fajr rockets in the homes of activists, but had only scanty information as to what was happening close to the border. Hezbollah's extensive deployment had been carried out right under the noses of the IDF.

The first Israeli force entered Lebanese territory less than two hours after Udi Goldwasser and Eldad Regev were abducted. It was more a demonstration of presence than a real pursuit. The 91st Division had minimal resources available for upsetting the escape of Hezbollah from the area. Despite protests, an artillery battery was removed from the region shortly before the abduction and deployed elsewhere for maneuvers. Although fighter helicopters were rushed in (and were the first to report on the burned-out Hummers, just minutes before the arrival of the battalion and company commanders), they had not been instructed to attack on the Lebanese side.

Division commander Hirsch called in a Nahal[6] force, together with a Merkava tank from the 7th Brigade Armored Corps, for a retaliatory attack on Hezbollah's nearest posts, in an action code-named Header. The tank also had another objective. It was ordered to capture a vantage point over Giv'at Hadegel, a nearby hill on the Lebanese side, site of a Hezbollah post, and to take control of the exit roads from the village of Ita a-Sha'ab as a solution to the unlikely possibility that the abductors were still there. The tank advanced, intending to run over Hezbollah's tin huts, but one contained a huge bomb laid by Hezbollah's Shiite fighters. The massive explosion could be seen clearly on all the aerial photographs taken by the unpiloted aircraft and were broadcast in real time onto screens in all the IDF offices and war rooms. Television crews arriving in the Zar'it region managed to record it. The tank's four-man team was killed outright.

The explosion and the deaths of the four soldiers added to the shock and confusion caused by the abduction of the two reservists and the deaths of their friends. But this was not the end of the IDF's losses on July 12, 2006. In order to protect the tank's remains and to ensure that Hezbollah did not snatch the bodies, a Nahal force was posted near Giv'at Hadegel.

When they arrived, they found a huge, still-smoking crater on the spot where the bomb had gone off. Hezbollah soon started filling the area with mortar fire. Israeli soldier Nimrod Cohen was struck by shrapnel and died. The remains of the tank and the four bodies were removed only two days later. In his testimony to the Winograd Commission, Hirsch said that he dispatched the tank out of a commitment to the abducted soldiers. He also was probably thinking about Shalit's abduction, when Israeli forces remained behind the fence and made no attempt at a chase. The means at his disposal were limited and he was fully aware of the risks, but "everything I had to give, I gave in order to rescue them. Both professionally and ethically, in order to rescue Udi and Eldad."

MISSING INTELLIGENCE

After the war, Chief of Staff Halutz convened a tribunal headed by Major General (Res.) Doron Almog to examine the event. Almog was fierce in his criticism of the IDF's deployment along the border over the years and opined that insufficient troops, means, and intelligence had been invested in preventing abductions. But he placed most of the responsibility on Hirsch, who he believed had not done enough to instill in his troops an awareness of the dangers of abduction. The division commander firmly refuted all the findings. In November 2006, Hirsch resigned from his post and from the IDF. The debate focused on the quality of intelligence at the army's disposal with regard to Hezbollah plans prior to the abduction. The 91st Division had received no intelligence; the alert was raised along the northern border, based purely on intuition and analysis, and only after the abduction of Gilad Shalit in Gaza. However, an internal examination of the Intelligence Directorate while the war was still being fought revealed that the Intelligence collation system possessed preliminary information that had not been passed on to the 91st Division in time. During the two weeks prior to the abduction, Intelligence had recorded over 30 pieces and fragments of information relating to the planned abduction. According to Hirsch, had he been in possession of this information in time, he would have maintained a high alert. Without the information, he lowered the alert, patrols were resumed along the fence, and the abduction was made possible.

A Northern Command Intelligence officer testified in a postwar investigation that between seven and ten such pieces of information would have been enough, each on its own, to establish a state of "organization," if not of "alert."[7] According to the head of the Intelligence Directorate Research Division, Brigadier General Yossi Beidetz, two area heads in his department had—in retrospect—defined the information at their disposal as sufficient for declaring a state of alert. One Northern Command officer accused Almog and his people of trying to rewrite history. Another Intelligence officer went so far as to claim that an assistant of Almog's, who had made a point of examining Intelligence issues prior to the abduction, took action to clear his colleagues in collation. Almog vehemently denied the accusation. According to him, there had been no Intelligence malfunction, and later attempts to attach any significance to available snippets of information were mere hindsight.

No other officer in the IDF dealt with the threat of abduction as intensely as Gal Hirsch. The division commander initiated, improvised, and invented— and his troops did manage to thwart earlier Hezbollah attempts at abducting Israeli soldiers. But on July 12, 2006, the IDF's defense system failed, resulting in serious complications on the Lebanese front. The abduction of Udi Goldwasser and Eldad Regev provided the opening shot. In brief, the defense concept along the border and measures taken to prevent abductions resulting from this concept were riddled with problems, such as a shortage of soldiers. Hezbollah's gradual deployment along the border since Israel's 2000 withdrawal from southern Lebanon, which Israel had come to accept (and knew too little about), provided an easy platform from which to carry out an abduction—and left the IDF too little space and maneuverability for prevention. Over the years, the Northern Command had come to realize that Hezbollah was more interested in abducting soldiers and less interested in infiltrating Jewish settlements and murdering citizens. This is a legitimate conclusion, but a permanent weak spot is created when some red zones close to the fence are abandoned and Israeli civilians are allowed free movement along the fence.[8]

But even if we accept the dubious assumption that the defense concept was compatible with the circumstances, there is still no doubt that the defense concept was not compatible with the resources laid out across the zone on

July 12. The absence of an artillery battery and troops whose numbers were constantly being reduced, combined with a reserve battalion that had not undergone systematic training in dealing with the abduction of soldiers, meant that the chances of foiling an abduction by Hezbollah were slim. In fact—even though it did not admit it outright—the IDF relied on Intelligence warnings to provide sufficient time for more practical redeployment. When such warnings were not forthcoming (whether because information was stuck at the collation unit or because such information was nonexistent), it had been impossible to prevent the abduction. Actually, the attacker—Hezbollah—had more information on its enemy's movements. Hezbollah knew that renewed patrols along the red zones meant lowered alert. The removal of the artillery battery not only harmed the IDF's ability to respond, but signaled to Hezbollah that the alert level had dropped.

Hirsch's decision to conduct a chase was a noble and ethical gesture, but its chances of success were minimal while its results served only to intensify the crisis. After a day of battle, which included two soldiers abducted across the border to Lebanon and eight soldiers killed, the mood in the country provided an easy platform for belligerent declarations and hasty decisions that ultimately led to war.

CHAPTER TWO

BARAK PROMISES

T OWARD THE END of his term in office in early 1999, Prime Minister Binyamin Netanyahu had been extremely unpopular. The press poked its nose into every aspect of his life, he was at odds with his government ministers, the U.S. administration was sick of him, and the left called him a catastrophe. But two and a half months before the general elections, which were set for May 17, 1999, the campaign of the opposing candidate, Ehud Barak, still had not managed to take off. In spite of the sharp public criticism of Netanyahu's premiership, the polls continued to indicate a tie between the two men. If he was to distinguish himself from his opponent, Barak needed a new tactic that would prove to the electorate that his ideas for changing the country were practical and not merely empty words. The chance he needed was provided by the open wound of Israel's continued presence in Lebanon and the renewed public discourse following the death of Erez Gerstein, a legendary Israel Defense Forces general killed in Lebanon mere months before the election.

The possibility of a unilateral withdrawal from Lebanon had been discussed on several occasions among the advisors of the prime ministerial candidate. The polls these advisors conducted indicated growing public support for such a withdrawal, even if it was to be done without a peace agreement with Lebanon and Syria. On March 1, one day after the explosion that claimed Gerstein's life, Barak participated in Channel 2's *It's All Politics* program. Barak replied to a question by saying that if he was elected, he would get the IDF out of Lebanon within one year of convening a new government. "I mean to renew negotiations with Syria," he added, "but withdrawal from Lebanon does not depend on any Israeli-Syrian agreement. We can withdraw from Lebanon within a year, with the support of the international community and talks with Syria. We must bring the boys back home."

On May 17, 1999, Barak won a landslide victory over Netanyahu. Of all the major promises he made during his election campaign and immediately thereafter, the withdrawal from Lebanon was the only one he actually fulfilled. Barak did not manage to achieve peace agreements with Israel's neighbors during the first 15 months of his term, as he predicted. But on May 24, 2000, ten and a half months after his government came to power, the last Israeli soldier stepped out of South Lebanon. The IDF were hard put to understand how it happened.

THE PENNY DROPS

It took a while for the realization to seep through the various levels of the IDF that things in southern Lebanon were not happening quite the way they should. Even as the withdrawal drew near, only a small minority among the officers' senior ranks were in favor of such a unilateral step.

The IDF's presence in the Lebanese security zone constituted a war of attrition, undetermined and with no heroic victories. Most Israelis will probably remember it by the endless line of photographs of casualties adorning the front pages of the national papers every month throughout the 1990s. Yet Lebanon was the defining experience for an entire generation of officers and young fighters who came of age during those years. About two years after Gerstein's death, his friend Colonel Moshe (Chico) Tamir took part in a road-naming ceremony in his name in Metulla, Israel's northernmost town, across the border from Lebanon. The ceremony was attended mainly by members of the "Lebanon guard" (as Tamir coined it). On his way back from the ceremony, Tamir thought to himself that "aside from the bereaved families and the soldiers who fought here and who bear in their hearts the kind of experiences that they could never share with anyone else, this entire war will be forgotten in just a few years." According to Tamir, the IDF of the 1990s was often a clumsy, weighty army, too slow to understand what was happening in Lebanon and, time after time, choosing destructive and misguided tactics in its war against Hezbollah. The IDF was paralyzed by the fear of incurring casualties. "Public pressure from within Israel against the continued presence in Lebanon affected the army and seeped down to its lowest ranks. And there were more cases of reduced values (in terms of demands from the fighting units). To my mind, this was catastrophic. When each incident is analyzed individually, it is difficult to pinpoint the extent of the problem. Sometimes it might appear to be right to stop an operation in order to avoid complications that might result in casualties. In the long run, however, [an army's] indecisiveness and moral disintegration are [always] picked up by the enemy." This perception continued to haunt the IDF throughout the second Lebanon war.

Tamir describes several years during which the military hierarchy avoided taking any kind of initiative, even on a tactical level, for fear of incurring casualties and reactions on the home front. Senior officers gradually came to understand that their chances of dismissal as a result of an attack initiative involving casualties were much greater than when soldiers are killed in a defensive operation. A casualty caused by mortar fire is considered an act of fate, one for which his commanding officer cannot be blamed. The IDF in Lebanon did not usually punish officers for lack of initiative and combat activity, however. Although reduced combat activity meant leaving the field open to Hezbollah (and enabling further Hezbollah attacks), this was the path chosen by many of the officers.

THE MOTHERS

According to Major General (Res.) Ya'akov Amidror, former head of the Research Branch of the Intelligence Department, even before the decision had been taken on unilateral withdrawal from Lebanon, Israel had never defined its objective for overcoming Hezbollah. "We asked ourselves how [we could] achieve quiet, not how do we overcome Hezbollah. It was a very expensive strategy. Because your objective is to prevent them from stopping a situation of calm in the north, you turn yourself into a hostage in the hands of the other side. On the other hand, they achieved greater legitimacy in Lebanon because they were fighting against our soldiers in the security zone. Hezbollah continued to build itself up and improve. We fought them only on their forwardmost front, the one that clashed with us in southern Lebanon. We didn't prevent them from empowering the organization."

Shortly after convening his government, Ehud Barak paid a visit to the IDF's Northern Command. General Effi Eitam, then division commander, told him that "20 casualties a year is a reasonable price to pay of the ability to continue holding Hezbollah by the throat. We are stronger. All we need is another couple of years." Barak stuck to his guns.

The countdown to withdrawal had already begun; the soldiers in Lebanon and their parents were already aware of this. For years, whenever military commanders in Lebanon wanted to inspire their men to war, they would point to the lights of the northern Israeli towns and villages along the border behind them. "We are here, in Lebanon, so that there, in Israel, they will sleep in peace." Now, however, such slogans were no longer a sufficient incentive. Instead of a desire to face down the enemy, the soldiers aspired to something else. None of them wanted to be last soldier to be killed in Lebanon.

BARAK'S RATIONALE

Polls in 1997 revealed that 79 percent of the Israeli public opposed unilateral withdrawal from Lebanon. According to a similar poll immediately after the withdrawal in May 2000, over 70 percent of the Israeli public agreed that it had been a wise move. If you ask him, Ehud Barak will tell you that his support for unilateral withdrawal from Lebanon was galvanized long before the change in public opinion. Barak remembers that in 1985 he had already predicted the vicious circle, where the IDF builds strongholds and the terrorist organizations return fire. The IDF would reinforce its strongholds and the other side would attack supply convoys.

The result, as he foresaw it, would have the IDF continuing its presence in southern Lebanon, principally in order to defend itself, Syria taking advantage of the situation in order to put pressure on Israel, and, throughout all this, the security zone would be unable to prevent rockets being fired on the Galilee. Moreover, the vicious circle would develop another dimension. When the pressure was on, there would be no Israeli withdrawal from Lebanon because Israel doesn't give in to military pressure. And at times of little or no pressure, there would be no reason to even discuss Israel's continued presence in Lebanon.

Ehud Barak had been appointed chief of staff of the IDF in 1991. Why didn't he take action then to get the IDF out of Lebanon? He rationalizes his failure to do so as being due to peace talks with Syria, which had begun a year later, during the Rabin government. Syria made use of Hezbollah disturbances to pressure Israel into returning the Golan Heights, and the question of Israel's withdrawal from Southern Lebanon became one of many clauses on the agenda of both countries. According to Barak, he had realized then that

Israel continued to remain in Lebanon in order to defend a controversial, 10-year-old decision and to justify all the blood that had been shed there since then. By doing so, Israel had supplied Hezbollah, as the defender of Lebanese soil, with a reason to take action against the "usurper" as well as an arena in which to train and improve its military ability. Israel, in fact, became the main reason for Hezbollah's prosperity.

"As a major general in the IDF during the mid-eighties," Barak was often heard to say to his supporters after being elected prime minister, "I would never have imagined us still stuck in Lebanon at the end of 2000." He especially remembered a visit to an infantry battalion during the early weeks of the first Lebanon war in 1982. We, he told the soldiers then, have no problem being here, but what about the women and the babies waiting for us back home? Those babies, Barak said in 2000, before the withdrawal, are about to be drafted and we're still in Lebanon. As election day approached, he took a firm decision. Seventeen years later, he said, the Lebanon story will never be over until an Israeli stands up and unties the fateful knot. If this was really his conviction, there appears to be no public testimony to it prior to his television declaration, one day after the death of Gerstein. On the contrary, two years earlier, Barak had been opposed to a unilateral withdrawal. At that time, he claimed that the idea was a threat to Israel's security and an expression of "public irresponsibility."

FROM AN AGREED-ON WITHDRAWAL TO UNILATERAL WITHDRAWAL

Barak's original plan spoke of an Israeli withdrawal from Lebanon by agreement, as part of an Israeli-Syrian peace arrangement. In return for its proposed withdrawal from the Golan Heights, Israel expected to be compensated by then Syrian president, Hafez Assad, with full and secure peace between the two countries together with a commitment that all Hezbollah hostilities would cease upon completion of Israel's withdrawal from southern Lebanon. Barak believed that Syria was capable of removing Hezbollah from southern Lebanon and, later, of brokering a peace agreement between Israel and Lebanon. The belief that the conflict with Syria is basically over territory (and not national-communal like that between Israel and the Palestinians), coupled with the evaluation that Hafez Assad was a serious negotiating partner and more stable than Palestinian leader Yasser Arafat, led Barak to place his emphasis on the Syrian channel—a "Syria first" approach. Damascus, too, initially was relatively favorable to Barak's rise to power in Israel and to his declaration of intent. But the failure of his talks with Syria in the winter of 2000 forced Barak into a change of plan in the northern arena and to readopt the possibility of his less-favored option: unilateral withdrawal from Lebanon, with no partner on the other side to ensure a continued peace once the withdrawal was completed. On the political level, Barak transferred his focus to the Palestinian channel. In his eyes, there was no crack in the logic behind the decision to withdraw as a result of Assad's refusal to act according to the Israeli prime minister's grand plan. To others, the decision to withdraw without an agreement was first and foremost a political consideration. Less than one year after his electoral victory, Barak's popularity was plummeting. Were he to renege on his pledge to withdraw from Lebanon, a pledge that had contributed considerably to his election success, he was liable to lose any support he still had. It was a question of dependability; and it was dependability that seemed to have been troubling Barak from his first day as prime minister.

In a series of secret talks with the military high command, Barak instructed the officers to continue with the plans for withdrawal from Lebanon. According to one of the officers involved, "He was very clear, knife sharp. The chances of getting out with an agreement were weak—and the IDF must prepare to move out under blood, fire and columns of smoke." IDF Chief of Staff Shaul Mofaz, head of Northern Command Gabi Ashkenazi, and Intelligence officers again warned him against withdrawal without agreement, but the prime minister replied that the withdrawal would create "an invisible wall of delegitimacy" that would prevent further Hezbollah attacks on Israel. Without the support of the Lebanese nation and without the understanding of the international community, he claimed, Hezbollah would be unable to continue with its attacks. Barak predicted that Israel's withdrawal from southern Lebanon would remove the main validation for the continued presence (since 1975) of the Syrian army in Lebanon and begin the countdown to Syria's withdrawal. The first half of Barak's prophesy came true in part; the second materialized in full, but it would take five years. In order for Israel to obtain a United Nations (UN) stamp of approval that the 1978 Security Council Resolution 425 (which, among other things, called for a full Israeli withdrawal from Lebanon) had been fulfilled, Barak insisted that the IDF pull back from every single inch of Lebanese soil. Israel spent millions of dollars moving strongholds and fences back to the exact lines determined by UN mapping experts. The situation bordered on the absurd when the fence close to Kibbutz Manara was moved south because it deviated by a few inches into Lebanese territory.

The army's forecast, which Mofaz presented in talks with Barak and at government and cabinet meetings, was that the Lebanese army would not move south if the withdrawal was to proceed without an agreed accord. Instead, Hezbollah would take control of southern Lebanon and deploy along the border with Israel. Syria and Iran would help the organization build its strategic abilities, which, even before the withdrawal, allowed it to threaten a large part of Israel's north. According to Israeli Intelligence, on the eve of the withdrawal, Hezbollah possessed some 7,000 rockets, including over 100 of medium range, with the ability to reach Zikhron Ya'akov south of Haifa and the power station at Hadera. Terrorist activity along the border, Mofaz predicted, would continue, with the help of Palestinian organizations among others. At a cabinet meeting on April 27, 2000, Mofaz warned that "with the withdrawal completed and in an escalated situation [we must] take into consideration the Hezbollah's ability to use long range weapons. And if we are required to act against Syria, there is a possibility of a front opening in Lebanon." Barak's response was that the government had already decided and "the army has to present to the ministers how it was preparing to carry out the government's decision. I refuse to accept the premise that the IDF are unable to defend the state of Israel from within its borders. It's absurd. The IDF must deploy and the government does not have to be confused as to its historic task—to lead [the country] to an end to the conflict and not to bicker." Later Barak would claim that he was not angry with the officers. "I understood them. After all, not long ago I was in the same situation as they were. They are responsible for the security of the inhabitants of the north and they will be blamed if anything happens." To Mofaz's credit, he was diligent in implementing the plan, although he opposed it. The army carried out Barak's orders to the letter.

ENOUGH, WE'RE DONE WITH LEBANON

When it became clear that no accord would be reached with Syria, Barak dictated one more condition to the IDF: The withdrawal must be carried out in a way that will surprise Hezbollah and deny it the ability to muster forces. Much of the preparations were made, therefore, far from the eyes of

Hezbollah and the Southern Lebanon Army (SLA). By isolating the SLA, its nominal ally, Israel hoped to achieve two objectives: (1) prevent the approaching withdrawal from further weakening its cooperation with the Lebanese militia; and (2) prevent SLA members from leaking any information to Hezbollah, a situation Israel suspected occurred regularly. In a process that took several months, Israel evacuated most of its equipment from the outposts in the security zone. Empty trucks accompanied supply convoys to the outposts; soldiers loaded the trucks with supplies to take back into Israel. By early May, the only materiel at the soldiers' disposal was such that could be removed from the posts within a day or two. (The IDF had already decided not to abandon anything in Lebanon for fear that Hezbollah would present it as spoils of war, gathered as the Israelis were fleeing.)

However, neither Barak nor the IDF dictated the final date for Israel's withdrawal from Lebanon; Hezbollah and the SLA did. The spring months had witnessed a slight increase in the number of defectors from the SLA, and the IDF was having more difficulty assigning Lebanese colleagues to various operations. Any visit from the Liaison Unit for Lebanon, headed by Brigadier General Benny Gantz, to SLA posts had become a complex diplomatic operation and involved softening the fact that Barak was planning to abandon the security zone and to leave Israel's veteran allies to their own devices. "The locals are telling our soldiers that they are asses for continuing to man the outposts," a furious company commander told Gantz. Five senior SLA officers suffered heart attacks, and others were sent for medical examinations in Israeli hospitals, at IDF expense. Their troops watched Hezbollah secretary general Hassan Nasrallah promise on TV that every SLA soldier who went forth with a dowry in the form of dead Israeli officer would be granted a complete pardon for his sins.

In mid-May, a week before withdrawal, the SLA abandoned one of its strongholds in southern Lebanon under Hezbollah fire. The IDF decided to incorporate those forward SLA outposts that were subject to antiaircraft and mortar fire into larger Israeli positions on the assumption that this would make defending the security zone easier during the final weeks before withdrawal. The IDF also decided to transfer its Taibe stronghold to the SLA's Shiite battalion. Control of the Taibe stronghold, located in the narrow part of the security zone, was critical to the continued control of the zone, and its transfer turned out to be a big mistake. The SLA managed to hold on to the post for a week; on Sunday, May 21, 2000, hundreds of Shiites set off from their villages to the north of the security zone to the village of Taibe. Surprised by the arrival of the civilians, the SLA troops simply fled. Thus

Hezbollah was able to take control of the first stronghold in the security zone without having to fire a single shot.

The fall of Taibe set off a domino effect that resulted in the collapse of the entire security zone over the next three days. Chief of Staff Mofaz, who watched mini-RVP pictures of the march on Taibe during a visit to Major General Ashkenazi's office in Safed, pressured the prime minister into ordering a full retreat from the region. Barak had reservations but later accepted Mofaz's advice, especially after the latter informed him that he would have to send several thousand troops into Lebanon if he was required to hold on to regions abandoned by the retreating SLA. The next day, Barak went to the northern border and authorized the plans. The first to be evacuated were IDF and SLA western brigade headquarters at Bint J'Bayel. Israeli officers informed their Lebanese allies that "from now on, your fate is in your hands" and left the region. The following night, the eastern arena was also evacuated. In the confusion, the Israelis left behind equipment in the smaller outlying strongholds. They also left behind flags.

The sights at "Fatma gate," the main gateway to the security zone near Metulla, were not pleasant. According to most early predictions, the number of refugees from among the SLA and their families would not be in excess of two thousand. Deputy Defense Minister Ephraim Sneh (former commander of the security zone), who predicted a larger number, was described in Barak's office as a "serial worrywart." In fact, the number of refugees exceeded six thousand. The rapidly deteriorating situation in the security zone caused inhabitants of southern Lebanon to crowd near the gate in the thousands begging for Israel's help. For several years after the withdrawal, Shin-Bet, Israel's internal security service, had its refugee rehabilitation administration working on finding housing and employment in Israel for the Lebanese refugees. Gradually, when it became clear that the Lebanese authorities were not interested in retaliating against its citizens for their previous support of Israel, many returned to Lebanon. Their bitterness, however, remained and the withdrawal, together with the IDF's poor treatment of its Arab allies, sent a sad message to the entire Middle East: This is how Israel treats people who, for so many years, stood firmly by its side.

A NEW BORDER

Ehud Barak removed the IDF from Lebanon almost single-handedly. The prime minister forced his opinions on a stubborn military establishment that was opposed to the withdrawal and had for years undermined similar efforts on the part of previous prime ministers. It would seem that such an operation required the talents of a man like Barak, who had been chief of staff only five years before and knew from experience what generals were capable of when ordered to carry out something that was not quite to their liking. Barak dispelled a long-standing Israeli myth regarding the army's undisputed control over the country's decision-making process and the belief that Israel's politicians always did as the IDF told them to. If, in his dealings with the Syrians and the Palestinians, Barak hesitated or blinked, on the Lebanon issue he was absolutely firm, to a large extent because Lebanon did not depend on the goodwill of an Arab partner. Here he was able to behave with determination and doggedness, paying no attention to the warnings of some of his subordinates. Many still believe the unilateral withdrawal from Lebanon to be the finest, if not the only, achievement of a prime minister who managed to stay in office for only one year and eight months.

Did the path taken by Barak lead to the *intifada* (uprising) that broke out only four months later? This is a legitimate question, attractive in its all-inclusiveness. Serious people, such as former Chief of Staff Moshe (Bogie) Ya'alon and Sneh, believe it to this day. But now, more than a year after the end of the second Lebanon war, there is a large measure of logic to be found in the path that Barak chose to follow. The only major fault in the whole process is that Barak failed to fulfill his promise that Israel would retaliate with all its force if Hezbollah renewed its attacks on Israeli territory.

Ehud Barak has ostensibly untied the Gordian knot. But subsequent years were to teach Israel that the Lebanon story was much more complex than they had thought, that Lebanon continues to send out long tentacles deep into Israeli society. On the day after the withdrawal, Israeli newspaper *Ha'aretz* published a cartoon in which an IDF officer is shown locking a gate after the last Israeli soldier to leave southern Lebanon. But he leaves the key under a rock at the side of the gate. Just to be safe.

BEING A SHIITE IN LEBANON

What is the meaning of being Shiite—for the majority of Shiites at this point—and at this critical juncture?

To be a Shiite, means that you entrust your fate to the wise and infallible leadership without daring to ask any question even if just as a point of understanding.

To be a Shiite means that you watch the Al Manar channel, or New TV or NBN, exclusively and that you enjoy their inspirational songs and their exclusive news and that you look with enmity to all other channels because they are either "American" or "Zionist," as long as they refer to Israeli forces by their name and do not call them the "forces of the enemy." . . .

To be Shiite is to accept that your country be destroyed in front of your very eyes—with no surprise—and that it comes tumbling down on your head and that your family be displaced and dispersed and becomes "a refugee" at the four corners of the nation and the world, and that you accept standing up to the enemy with no complaints as long as there is a fighter out there with a rocket that he can launch at northern Israel. . . .

To be a Shiite is to keep silent and not to ask what is the purpose of liberating a country. Is it to destroy it all over again and to make it possible for it to be occupied once more? and not to ask about the leadership role: is it to preserve its military power and its men flush with arms without any care or concern for the normal human being? Being a Shiite means that you can only thank the Hizb for its heroism and sacrifice, it is not your role to contribute to "weakening" it or to "break its word" or to make him know when to back down or compromise to preserve his victory on the one hand and to preserve the Lebanese nation and its openness as well as its development on the other hand!! That means never to question whether pride takes precedence over the lives of others and whether stones take precedence over arms.

To be a Shiite means to confer to the leader of the resistance his role as a loyal hero to the cause of the Arab nation in its entirety. . . . If you are a Shiite you are not to ask this leadership how the groundwork was prepared to absorb this indiscriminate war and its "potential" consequences. Where are the hospitals, the ambulances, never mind the shelters. These are the responsibilities of a state—That was never consulted in declaring war. . . .

To be a Shiite means to incapacitate your mind and leave it to
Sayyed Khamene'i to guide you and to decide for you what he wants
for arms to "Hezbollah" and he imposes on you the meaning of a
victory that has little difference from suicide. . . .

And in this tense mood if you are a Shiite you have to listen to
your Shiite speaker who is disturbed and angry and who wants to
turn the world on top of the 14th of March, and who wants to forbid
the deployment of multinational forces. And you hear him distribute
labels of foreign servitude, treason, Americanism and Zionism left
and right, without raising your lip. You have to absorb his anger and
agree with all his opinions of which we have shared but a small
sample. This is what takes you as far as possible from thinking who
the heck you are? are you a Lebanese citizen? Is you being a Shiite
means that you have to give priority to Iran over Lebanon? Do you
have the freedom to have your own opinions? the freedom of expression? Is it possible to think calmly and to ask where are we going with
this nation, the institutions of this state, with plurality, with the
coexistence that we have to defend now?

If you are a Shiite and you dare write such writings and such think
such thinking, then you must be a foreign agent and a traitor. . . .
And that means you support Israel itself and its satanic war machine
and its extreme savagery and you justify its killing, its occupation, its
folly and you are lucky if you are not accused to be the one destroying the houses on people's heads and the dismemberment of
children's corpses and their scattering on the heaps of debris. . . .

—Mona Fayad, *a-Nahar*, 2006

Mona Fayad, a Shiite lecturer in psychology at the Lebanese University in
Beirut, published an article in the Lebanese daily *a-Nahar* one week before
the end of the second Lebanon war. Fayad described the war through the critical eyes of a Shiite with reservations about Hezbollah, at a time when the
organization had taken control of the Shiite population and, in many ways, of
Lebanon itself. Among the many anti-Israel articles in the Lebanese media
during the war, it was possible from time to time to come across one like
Fayad's. The psychology professor accused Hezbollah of serving two masters

(Syria and Iran), of creating a state within a "non-state," of deceiving Lebanese public opinion, and, especially, of imposing the organization's agenda on all the different communities in the country. The large amount of criticism for Hezbollah, voiced mainly by other communities in Lebanon, also reflected frustration at the speed (in historical terms) with which the Shiite organization had taken control of the country. In the 24 years of its existence, Hezbollah had developed from a fringe ethnic organization to a central political entity, with the most significant military capability in the country. It had managed to raise the persecuted and underprivileged Shiite community to a position whereby it dominated Lebanon with an ability, disconnected from the state, to help its people in every sphere of their lives. After the war, Hezbollah, which today has the support of most of the country's Shiites, was able to challenge the government and the entire legislative establishment in Lebanon.

THE PARTY OF GOD

The close relationship between Iran and Hezbollah was evident immediately after the organization was established. It was Iran that founded Hezbollah (which means, literally, "party of god") and directed its activity on the military and economic levels. The Iranian authorities even persuaded Lebanese Shiite religious leaders to leave Amal, the older, more moderate Shiite organization, and join the new organization. Israel's invasion of Lebanon facilitated the foundation of Hezbollah. The IDF had driven out the Palestine Liberation Organization (PLO) from southern Lebanon and created a comfortable space for Shiite organizations to fill. First Amal and, later, Hezbollah entered the region, established themselves in it, and then took control. At the same time, the war had weakened the (already frail) central government in Beirut—the army and judicial system barely had any authority there—and allowed Iran and Hezbollah to establish what was virtually a separate autonomy in the Beqaa Valley, which is located in the eastern part of the country, close to the Syrian border. For the Iranians it was a golden opportunity. On one hand, they created for themselves a focal point from which to oversee the Israel-Arab conflict with Iran spearheading the war against the Zionist enemy. On the other hand, it was a chance to actually export the Islamic revolution. The Iranian project took off because of an ongoing rift between Tehran and Amal, which led to a decision in Tehran to undermine the secular organization. By helping Hezbollah, Iran established a religious opponent to Amal, which would herald the revolution to every Shiite home in Lebanon. The immediate excuse was provided by chairman of Amal Nabih Beri's joining the newly established "National Rescue Authority," of which other members were Lebanese president Elias Sarkis and Christian leader Bashir Jemail. Hussein Moussawi, Beri's second in command and one of Amal's Iranian affiliates, attacked his decision to join forces with those who had cooperated with Israel, called on him to retract his decision, and asked for Iranian intervention in the matter. Beri refused to retract and, on June 21, 1982, when Beri attended a meeting of the National Rescue Authority, Moussawi announced his resignation from Amal and the establishment of "Islamic Amal." Moussawi was joined by almost 100 Amal members and settled in the Beqaa region. At the same time, Iran sent 1,500 members of its Revolutionary Guard to Baalbeq and Beqaa. Fearing the advancing IDF, Syria welcomed the arrival of the Revolutionary Guard contingent.

THE EARLY YEARS

Already in 1984, the Shiite districts of Beirut and the Beqaa Valley were pretty accurate replicas of Iran. Large pictures of the Imam Ruhulaah Khomeini hung at every junction. Hezbollah fighters strode through the streets with ribbons around their foreheads that bore two legends in Arabic, *Alla Akhbar* (Allah is great) and *Kaidona Khomeini* (Khomeini is our leader). A "modesty watch" patrolled the neighborhoods and villages, overseeing the dress of the women and girls. Stores selling alcohol were closed. On the anniversary of the Iranian revolution, Shiite women, dressed in the black Iranian *chador*, walked through the street and handed out pictures of Khomeini.

Iran dictated Hezbollah's three major objectives, which consisted of instilling the religious ideology of Islamic revolutionary Iran, improving the social and economic status of the Shiite community in Lebanon, and reinforcing its military power. Tehran poured millions of dollars into Hezbollah and the Shiites in Lebanon via the social institutions it established in Beqaa, Beirut, and the country's South. In Lebanon, as Shimon Shapira wrote in his book *Hezbollah Between Iran and Lebanon*, Iran tried to establish a "counter society," with the aim of providing a solution to the social, economic, and political depression from which the Shiites had been suffering for decades. In 1983 alone, Iran invested some $200 million in Lebanon. According to

Shapira the money was transferred to the country through various channels, one of the main ones being the "Shahid Fund," which supported the families of the dead, the wounded, and prisoners. The "Jihad al-Bina" was another important channel for transferring money, according to Shapira; its aims were to fund the renovation of houses, hospitals, and other structures damaged in IDF raids. The fund also paid for road repairs, infrastructure restoration, water and electricity supplies, sewage infrastructure, industry, and agriculture. It even built a power station in one of the Shiite regions. Iran oversaw the construction of a chain of clinics and hospitals in the Shiite areas, provided aid to newlyweds and small businesses, and established employment and artistic centers, a university, schools, and orphanages. Emissaries of the revolution even provided funds for school uniforms and paid for transportation to and from school. All this aid came with a price that Hezbollah was required to pay: complete obedience to Tehran.

THE TA'IF ACCORD

The Ta'if Accord[1] was signed on September 30, 1989, with the objective of ending the 14-year civil war in Lebanon and defining the principles and modus operandi of the country's future political system. According to the accord, a chamber of deputies would be convened as the legislative author-ity, to exercise full control over government policy and activities throughout Lebanon. Within this framework, all the armed militias were to be dis-banded and steps were to be taken to rehabilitate the state's army and secu-rity forces. The government of Omar Karame, consisting of 30 ministers who represented all the major political parties in Lebanon with the excep-tion of the Lebanese Communist Party and Hezbollah, was convened on December 24. The new government decided on March 28, 1991, to disarm all the militias by April 30 and approved the integration of them all in state offices. Most of the militias obeyed the directive, handed in their arms, and registered their members on the designated date, except for Hezbollah and the Palestinian organizations, which adhere to their positions to this day. The government wrangled with some of the Palestinian groups but preferred to give in to Hezbollah, which promised to use its weapons only against Israel.

The Ta'if Accord determined a new formula for the composition of the Lebanese government. Until the chamber of deputies passed an election law free of sectarian restriction, the parliamentary seats were to be divided according to these bases:

a. Equally between Christians and Muslims
b. Proportionately between the denominations of each sect
c. Proportionately between the districts[2]

This would take place in the summer of 1992, on the basis of territorial distribution. The Ta'if Accord, which emphasized the increased power of the Lebanese government, ordered Hezbollah to conform to new Lebanese laws—refraining from bloodshed—but allowed the organization to continue.

NASRALLAH

At a ceremony to commemorate the tenth anniversary of the assassination of former Hezbollah Secretary-General Moussawi in 1992 in the village of Jibshit, Sheikh Hassan Nasrallah boasted, "We have created a balance of terror with the help of the Katyusha, a weapon which is likened in military science to a water pistol." Israel, which believed that by assassinating Moussawi it had succeeded in ridding itself of a stubborn foe, has had since then to contend with one of the most highly esteemed people in Lebanon and the entire Middle East. In the Israeli intelligence community, Nasrallah is spoken of with open admiration. "Brilliant, extraordinarily charismatic" are the words used to describe him in Israeli intelligence circles. Nasrallah's son, Hadi (a member of Hezbollah's special force), was killed in 1997, during a clash with soldiers of the Golani Brigade in southern Lebanon. "There aren't that many [paramilitary] organizations in which the leader sends his own son to fight in a forward combat unit," says a senior IDF officer. "This is the kind of single-mindedness that you learn to respect." At his son's funeral, Nasrallah said that he "thanks God for turning his son into a shahid. The only consolation his mother and I have is that we did not object to his wish to join the fighting ranks."

An Israeli Arab who has had several meetings with Nasrallah in Lebanon describes him as a charismatic person, tenaciously leading the line that he himself determined for Hezbollah. "He outlined an objective for himself and has carried it out. He has a great deal more organizational skills than many other Arab leaders. He is rational, avoids corruption and loves his people and

he is straightforward and direct. Admittedly, you don't feel that you are talking with a great intellectual, but you sit facing a man with a lot of common
sense, warmth and a sense of humor." The Hezbollah leader is often
complimented for his rhetoric. Throughout the second Lebanon war, his
rabble-rousing speeches held his Arab, Lebanese, and Israeli listeners
spellbound.

Hassan Nasrallah was born the ninth of ten children on August 30, 1960.
His family migrated from the southern Lebanon village of Zariya to the
southern suburbs of Beirut. Although the family was not particularly
religious, his father, Abdul Karim, a vegetable vendor, made a point of taking
his son to prayers in the mosque. On a wall in the family home there was a picture of the "disappearing imam," Mussa a-Sadr, a Lebanese leader who had
disappeared during a visit to Libya in 1978. Like many of the founding generation of Hezbollah, Nasrallah set out on his own to study at the Shiite college in Najaf, Iraq. There he became a disciple of Abbas Moussawi, who was
only seven years his senior. Upon his return from his studies, he joined Amal
and, in 1982, when Moussawi crossed the lines to Hezbollah, Nasrallah went
with him. There was nothing to distinguish him at that time and, even on the
eve of Moussawi's assassination, hardly anything was known about him in
Israel. Nasrallah wasn't the natural choice to succeed Moussawi. In terms of
age, experience in the movement, and religious education, the previous
secretary general, Sobhi Tufaili, was considered a more suitable candidate.
However, the fanatical Tufaili, who was a passionate supporter of isolating
Hezbollah from Lebanese politics, did not conform with the more liberal
policies that Syria and Iran encouraged Hezbollah to follow in the period
after the Ta'if Accord. Nasrallah's ties with the Iranian spiritual leader Ali
Khaminai and the fact that Moussawi had been his religious and political
mentor paved his way to the leadership. He was only 32 when the Shura
Council (Hezbollah's governing body) decided to appoint him secretary
general. According to terrorism expert Dr. Magnus Ranstorp, Nasrallah
belonged to a group of outstanding young men, who, in contrast to the conservative founding generation, understood the need for change if they were to
survive within Lebanese politics. Another scholar, Nizar Hamza, claims that
the pragmatic branch that led Hezbollah from 1991 and especially Nasrallah
considered political power in Lebanon to be no less important than placing
the country under Sharia (Islamic) law. To this group, which had earned the
support of Khaminai, political power was on a par with military power.

The beginning of Nasrallah's tenure heralded no dramatic change. He continued to follow his predecessor's policy of an extreme, uncompromising line against Israel alongside a more liberal approach to the Lebanese political establishment. In interviews with the media, he emphasized the objectives in the "war against the Zionist foe," a war of attrition against Israel that would make the price of its continued presence in Lebanon unbearable and destroy Israeli society from within. Further, he planned to eliminate the power gap between Israel and Hezbollah through the use of original, state-of-the-art weapons and to bolster Lebanese society against Israeli pressure. On a local-internal level, he had to deal with several issues, which included disbanding the camps inside Hezbollah, beating Amal in Shiite public opinion, and taking care of the Shiite community in Lebanese politics. He began by purging the organization (especially the Shura Council) of the isolationist conservatives. The most critical decision he had to make involved Hezbollah's participation in elections to the Lebanese parliament. While the conservative camp utterly rejected the possibility of including an organization founded on a pan-Islamic platform in a nationalist-Lebanese parliament, Nasrallah knew that the Shiite community, especially its middle class, was eager for this to happen. Following many arguments in the organization's various offices, Nasrallah announced in August 1992 that his organization would participate in the elections and that it would cooperate with other parties on the basis of their political platform rather than their ethnic affiliation. Hezbollah would represent the underprivileged of every community in addition to its continued resistance to Israel. The decision to participate in elections, which received the blessing of Iran and Syria, constituted the most significant change in Hezbollah ideology in those years. The organization was no longer spouting promises to "uproot" the Lebanese government and replace it with an Islamic regime, as it had at its inception; from now on it would follow the state's laws. It has been said that with this choice Hezbollah crossed the Rubicon, the point of no return. It appears, however, that it was mainly an understanding on the part of the organization's leadership that, in order to survive the political war against Amal, Hezbollah would have to play according to Lebanese rules.

Unlike Moussawi and Tufaili, Nasrallah exhibited a policy of ingenuousness, even toward the media. He made use of the Lebanese media and Hezbollah communication channels in order to transmit sharp and clear messages regarding the war with Israel, the organization's identity, and its ties with Lebanon. "I wish to stress that, in Lebanon, Hezbollah is not an isolated movement, but one with deep roots in the Lebanese nation, one that fights for the land," he said immediately after being elected. He based his position on that of the Lebanese Shiite cleric Muhammad Fadlallah, who saw Hezbollah as a Lebanese movement with an affinity to Iran. "[My] loyalty to the leadership of the Islamic revolution does not contradict the fact of my being a Lebanese citizen. . . . It is no secret that we see ourselves as part of the Islamic revolution. [Our] ties are of friendship and cooperation," said Nasrallah in 1992.[3]

Hezbollah's list of candidates it supported for the election, "*qutlat al-wafa l'lmukawama*" (devotees of the resistance bloc), achieved impressive results in the 1992 general elections, when all eight of its candidates won parliamentary seats. It was a success not only for the organization but also for those of its members who supported "ingenuousness," with Nasrallah at the helm. Shortly before the elections, Naim Qassem, Hezbollah deputy secretary general, convened a special committee to examine the viability of participating in the race for parliamentary representation. Two members disagreed. The committee felt that a parliamentary presence would afford the organization a platform, legal legitimization, and the ability to promote the interests of the Shiite community in the fields of health, welfare, and a fairer distribution of the state's budget. The organization also based itself on the religious judgment (*fatwa*) of Khaminai, who granted permission to participate in the elections. To a large extent, the decision turned out to be a wise one. Hezbollah achieved legitimacy in Lebanon without the need to disarm. However, it also helped create a rift within the organization, when the a-Tufaili group broke away in July 1997.

The most substantial process to be put in motion by the policy of ingenuousness was the change Hezbollah underwent in Lebanese and international public opinion. The organization encouraged this change by downplaying its pan-Islamic approach, emphasizing its Lebanese character and ending its open terrorist activity against Western objectives.[4] Hezbollah even changed the caption at the base of its flag from "the Islamic revolution in Lebanon" to "Islamic Opposition in Lebanon." At the funeral of Hadi Nasrallah, the Lebanese national flag was flown at the organization's service. Since then, Hezbollah has been flying the national flag at all its rallies, playing the national anthem, and participating in all the national memorial days. In 1997, it announced the establishment of the "Lebanon Resistance

Forces," an initiative aimed at integrating a large group of fighters from all the communities. Many complained that the organization had abandoned its extreme ideology. Declarations on the part of Hezbollah leaders, stressing that the move into government did not cancel the movement's original strategy, were ignored. The two-sided policies propounded by Hezbollah in those years led to academic debates as to the organization's real identity: Was it Iranian or Lebanese? According to Professor David Menashri of Tel Aviv University, ideologically, Hezbollah is in every way an Iranian organization. "It adheres more to the Khomeini ideology than did Iran in the days of President Muhammad Khatami. Whereas a country like Iran required pragmatism, in Lebanon the Hezbollah could continue to be fanatical," says Menashri. According to Oren Barak of the Hebrew University in Jerusalem, however, since the 1982 elections, it is the Lebanese political system that stands at the center of Hezbollah's considerations. Barak believes that Hezbollah welcomes assistance from anyone willing to give it but is committed mainly to Lebanese public opinion. Not that the debate bypassed the Israeli intelligence community. A former senior member of the Military Intelligence Directorate admits that, at a certain stage, Hezbollah's move toward elections caused the department to think that the organization was abandoning its extreme ideologies. "The Intelligence Department found it hard to understand what Hezbollah wanted. Was it the *Hezb* (the party) or Allah? To me it was obvious that the mistake lay in the question. The party constituted a necessity, that supplied the legitimacy to pursue holy war, *jihad*."

Journalists who have met with Nasrallah on more than one occasion reckon that the enormous interest he shows in Lebanese politics, his current focus on the return of the Sha'aba Farms (Mount Dov) to Lebanon, and the release of the Lebanese prisoners are proof that he has never (nor will he ever) relinquished the dream of liberating Jerusalem.

According to Timur Goksel, a lecturer at the University of Beirut and former spokesman for the United Nations Interim Force In Lebanon (UNIFIL), despite what outwardly appears to be united ranks, inside Hezbollah there are many ideological streams and trends at work. "There are senior members in the organization who believe Hezbollah should be more religious and stay out of Lebanese politics. Others want to be more secular. Extraordinary powers of leadership are required in order to hold all these together. At the moment, they have such a leader. But if a successor were to appear in the future who does not possess this kind of control, Lebanon and to the entire region could find itself under serious threat. The organization's famous discipline would collapse and anonymous, well-armed groups would rise instead of the unified Hezbollah. The people in Nasrallah's milieu want the organization to be more involved in local politics, because they know that the armed struggle is ostensibly over and the party cannot continue forever talking about resistance, while the Lebanese nation is more concerned with its socioeconomic situation."

YOU CAN KEEP THE CAKE

In many ways, the 1990s were the most successful period in Hezbollah history. The organization enjoyed the growing admiration of the Shiite public in Lebanon, which saw it as the only group with the courage to challenge the military supremacy of Israel and to face that country with honor. Unlike the other factions in Lebanon, Hezbollah continued to hold on to its weapons. At the same time, it developed, undisturbed by the government, its chains of welfare and educational institutions in the country's south. Relations with the Lebanese government remained complex. In 1996, Prime Minister Rafiq Hariri admitted that he was "unable to disarm Hezbollah, whether we agree with their political platform, or not. . . . If we begin to disarm Hezbollah at a time when the occupation is still in force, we shall be seen in public opinion as aiding the occupiers."

Hezbollah was back on form after the violent conflict with the IDF in 1996, the operation dubbed Grapes of Wrath by Israel, and continued its attacks on the IDF and SLA in the security zone, which sometimes escalated into rocket fire on northern Israeli settlements. Thus tension with the Lebanese government peaked and Hariri believed that Hezbollah's activity in the south was jeopardizing the entire country. In October 1998, the pro-Syrian politician Emile Lahoud was elected president of Lebanon. Severe differences of opinion between Lahoud and Hariri resulted in the resignation of the latter, who was replaced in December by another pro-Syrian politician, Salim al-Hus. The government reshuffle improved relations between the Beirut government and Hezbollah and provided the organization with free rein to act against Israel. Encouraged by the growing support of Israeli public opinion for a withdrawal from Lebanon, Hezbollah intensified its attacks in the security zone and responded as it saw fit to IDF operations.

THE FARMS

As the Israeli withdrawal drew close, so Lebanese support for Hezbollah increased. Hezbollah was seen as the first Arab military organization to have beaten Israel by force, without having had to pay a very high price for doing so. However, Nasrallah was also aware of the dangers awaiting Hezbollah in the aftermath of Israel's retreat. Once Israel was out of Lebanese territory, Hezbollah no longer could claim that it had to remain armed and to maintain independent military policies, free of the authority of the government in Beirut, in order to continue its resistance to Israel's occupation.

Hezbollah's secretary general came up with a new claim: the Sha'aba Farms. A few days before the withdrawal, Nasrallah announced that his organization would continue to fight Israel, if Israel did not include the area of the farms in its retreat from southern Lebanon. At that time few people in Lebanon knew anything about the farms. Nabih Beri, who had met with a UN representative a few months earlier, was unable to explain the location of the area under discussion.[5]

The farms constitute an area on the western foothills of Mount Hermon, close to the border between Lebanon and Israel, which, until 1967, served Lebanese and Syrian farmers. According to UN maps, the Sha'aba Farms were part of the Syrian Golan Heights, captured by Israel in 1967. But Nasrallah was never too bothered by the United Nations. At a Hezbollah rally on May 16, he said: "We did not intervene on this issue when talk begun of a withdrawal because our mission is to liberate the land. We shall fight until [we have] liberated the last inch of our land and for as long as the state of Lebanon says that the Sha'aba Farms are Lebanese, we don't care what the international community says."

Nasrallah's sentiments on the farms did not attract any particular attention in Israel. Others things the Hezbollah leader said at the end of the same month have been carved to a much greater degree into Israeli awareness. On May 26, two days after the last Israeli soldier left the soil of southern Lebanon, Hezbollah held a victory parade in the town of Bint-J'Bayel. Nasrallah was the key speaker, and his words were directed at the entire Arab world. "My dear brothers, I say this to you: with all its atomic weapons Israel, is weaker than cobwebs."

CHAPTER THREE

DENIAL

D URING THE SUMMER months of 2000, a new custom came into being in Lebanon. On weekends especially, thousands of people would flock to the fence that divided Lebanon from Israel. They didn't go merely to see Israelis up close but to throw stones at those symbols of occupation, the soldiers of the Israel Defense Forces. The fact that the occupation had recently ended with a full IDF withdrawal from southern Lebanon did nothing to reduce the men's, women's, and children's desire to hurt Israelis. Indeed, even the distinguished American Palestinian historian Professor Edward Said went to the Fatma Gate to be photographed, seated in his wheelchair, tossing a stone at an Israeli soldier.

For the IDF, these actions were embarrassing. On one hand, soldiers were being hurt. On the other, no one wanted to allow mere stone throwing to reignite the now-peaceful border. In the end, a technical solution was found: Several metal cages were built in which soldiers could stand, protected from stones. The soldiers were removed from the border eventually, in order to reduce friction with the Lebanese stone-throwers. The problem was solved for the time being, and lacking available, vulnerable targets, the Lebanese lost interest. But the way in which the IDF chose to deal with the renewed aggression was a bad sign of things to come. Clearly this was how Hezbollah saw it too.

The first crisis came on October 7, 2000, at Mount Dov in the eastern section of the border with Lebanon. After four and a half months of quiet, Hezbollah attacked a routine IDF patrol carried out by soldiers of the military engineering corps. Three soldiers, Benny Avraham, Adi Avitan, and Omar Su'ed, were driving an unarmored jeep[1] when it was hit by powerful explosive device. Valuable time was lost before it was discovered that the three soldiers of the patrol had disappeared. Israel's response was low-key: first helicopter, tank, and artillery fire; later, the Israeli Air Force (IAF) bombed a few Hezbollah objectives and a Syrian radar station in Lebanon. Chief of Staff Shaul Mofaz's proposal to attack a larger number of Syrian objectives in Lebanon was rejected by the cabinet. A small military force conducted a chase in Lebanese territory but was soon ordered back. The kidnappers were no longer in the vicinity.

Two days after the October 9, 2000 abduction, Prime Minister Ehud Barak announced, "We are reserving the right to respond at the time we see fit." The international community was even showing signs of understanding toward a potential Israeli operation in retaliation to the abduction so soon after the withdrawal from Lebanese territory, by condemning Hezbollah's attack.

An Israeli response never happened.

There were two reasons for this, one overt; one covert. The main rationale—one that Barak voiced at every opportunity—was the reluctance to open a "second northern front" at that time. The second intifada, which had broken out in the occupied territories on September 29, was drawing most of the attention of Israel's political and military echelons. Moreover, 13 Israeli Arabs were killed by police forces over a week of violent demonstrations in the recent "October riots," in which local Arabs blocked main roads in the north of the country for several hours at a time. In testifying before the Winograd Commission,[2] Ephraim Sneh explained that Israel's inactivity was due to its reluctance to broadcast to the public that its unilateral withdrawal from Lebanon had resulted in an escalation of violence on the northern border. Barak's non-reaction launched what the Winograd Commission described as "the era of containment."

Barak insisted that this was not the case. Restraint and containment, he said after the war ended, had begun after he was no longer in office. Barak is certain that the Mount Dov abduction had nothing to do with the withdrawal, which did not include that region. There had been abductions in Lebanon when the IDF were still there. Hezbollah had established its rocket system throughout the region before the unilateral withdrawal, whereas the IDF positions along the border had been built at a later stage, after the Barak government left office. He said in different interviews for the Israeli media: "In my time, there were only a few hillocks, with Hezbollah fighters sitting under sun shades with their organization's flags." Barak saw the actual abduction as a tactical-operational failure on the part of the IDF, which did not warrant a "frenzied" Israeli response. Setting the region on fire would have resulted in renewed rocket attacks in the north of Israel. Moreover, the first few days after the soldiers' abduction were filled with uncertainty regarding their fate. The prime minister feared that an irresponsible response would result in their deaths.

The policies of restraint and containment, which were sharply criticized after the outbreak of the 2006 war, will be discussed later in this book. However, there was a sizable difference between Israel's almost complete restraint in the face of Hezbollah hostility after that first provocation and its approach in the years that followed. The response to the events of October 2000 showed Hezbollah—and the Iranians, the Syrians, and the Lebanese government—that Barak's threats of fierce responses to every attack were empty. With all due respect to Israel not wanting to open a second front during that fateful week in October, the fact that—after scrupulously obeying all United Nations demands—Israel did not retaliate against the abduction and murder of three soldiers was tantamount to inviting the enemy to forge ahead, undisturbed, with its plans.

Moreover, by thoroughly internalizing this policy, field commanders actually resigned themselves to Hezbollah deployment along the border, a fact that was to play a decisive role in the 2006 abduction.

Israel's sojourn in Lebanon was never the success described by those who muse over it today. The IDF did not win its battle in southern Lebanon; it suffered heavy losses. In retrospect, the roots of the numerous mishaps discussed at such length during the last war—not sticking to the mission at hand, extreme sensitivity toward casualties, lack of social cohesion—were already evident then. There was a great deal of logic behind the decision to withdraw from Lebanon. Even the restraint policy of the years that followed can, to an extent, be justified. It is doubtful if Israel had the necessary military and civilian resources in order to launch a serious response in Lebanon. But it could have made an attempt to define the rules of the game in October 2000. By not doing so, Israel placed both sides on a slippery slope that led ultimately to the July 2006 outburst.

ARIK, KING OF SELF-RESTRAINT

From March 2001 to early January 2006, the one politician who could not, under any circumstances, allow himself the luxury of a new IDF offensive in

Lebanon held the reins of government in Israel. The very fact that Ariel Sharon was elected prime minister, beating Barak by a wide margin in February 2001, came as a big surprise. Eighteen years before, Sharon had been removed from all positions of power, by decree of the Kahan Report on the first Lebanon war. The Kahan Commission, established by the Government of Israel to investigate the massacre carried out by a Phalangist (Christian militia) unit in the Palestinian refugee camps of Sabra and Shatila in Beirut, had banned Sharon from serving as minister of defense but not as prime minister. The upheaval caused by the failure of the Camp David negotiations and the escalating violence of the second intifada led him to an unexpected electoral victory. Sharon arrived in power an experienced and veteran politician, well aware of his past failures. From time to time "the old Arik would pop out," as his aides put it, describing an old military man's instincts from his days in the Israeli special forces. Then he tended to preach on behalf of firm military reprisals, especially following particularly horrible suicide bombings by Palestinian terror organizations. But most of the time he adhered to the truths he had learned the hard way: Lebanon had been the graveyard for the ambitions of Israeli politicians, there was no point in relying blindly on the capabilities of the IDF (which had already proved very disappointing during the first Lebanon war), there is no advantage to embarking on an extensive military campaign without a broad public consensus in Israel and the world, and never, ever, must Israel undertake such an action without the (at least, unspoken) backing of the U.S. administration.

Over the years, Israel's decision not to respond to Hezbollah's seasonal provocations and to ignore its increased rocket power was joined by a series of additional considerations. The main one touched on the internal processes in Lebanon. The Syrian army's withdrawal from Lebanon in April 2004 and the establishment, albeit hesitant, of an independent democratic government in Beirut (which will be discussed later) were developments that Israel had to take into consideration, and it would have been a mistake for Israel to allow itself to be dragged into Hezbollah provocations that would have enabled Syria and the Shiites to undermine the new balance of power in Lebanon. Damascus was on the defensive; Washington had included Syria in the "axis of evil," and Jerusalem was determined not to do anything to change this. Even when Nasrallah made a public announcement of his intention to abduct more Israelis and the IDF prevented attempts at doing so, there was no significant change in policy. Sharon devoted his last cabinet meeting on January 4,

2006,[3] to the situation in Lebanon, following the thwarted kidnapping attempt the previous November in the Lebanese village of Rajar. He decided to continue with the containment policy and set a date for another meeting on the matter, which, due to his stroke, he was not able to convene.

According to his close associates, Sharon was highly aware of events in Lebanon and raised the matter of Hezbollah's rocket deployment obsessively at every meeting with foreign leaders. Yet he was also familiar with the army's assessment that it would take an extensive ground offensive to remove the threat of Katyusha rockets and many weeks of constant rocket fire could be expected in the North. Also, Sharon believed that complications in the North would have a negative influence on the army's ability to function in the Palestinian arena, which he considered to be of major importance.

WHAT HAPPENED TO THE IDF?

When war broke out in 2006, the performance of Israel's armed forces, especially those on the ground, were surprisingly disappointing, both to the public and to the army itself. The faults revealed by the abduction of Udi Goldwasser and Eldad Regev were just the beginning; things got steadily worse as more and more soldiers were sent to fight Hezbollah on Lebanese territory. The army was caught unprepared for war in the North. Even under these circumstances, however, more reasonable decisions in high quarters could have produced better results. But the faults that surfaced in the course of the war were a direct consequence of deeply rooted processes that had been eating away at the IDF's ability over the six years before the second Lebanon war.

The IDF was a full partner in the containment approach in the North. Its relative successes in the occupied territories against a Palestinian foe who was years behind the sophistication and military ability of Hezbollah prompted the IDF to conceive baseless assumptions that blended in with the new theories that had been taking hold during those years in general headquarters (GHQ). After the U.S. invasion of Iraq, the fall of Saddam Hussein, and the collapse of the "eastern front" between Iraq and Syria, the risk of full-scale war was, in any case, greatly reduced. In the event such a danger should arise, the IDF would have plenty of time to deploy and train its troops. Tank brigades were closed down because there was no apparent need for them. There seemed no real reason to provide serious training to the reserve forces, since preparation for fighting in the occupied territories required no more than a few days each time; and, of course, the budget for field training had been gradually reduced.

As usual, the IDF focused on the half-full glass. A western European military attaché who spent several years in Israel says that the Israelis "were abominably arrogant. True, the IDF and the Shin-Bet, Israel's internal security service, had some impressive successes against Palestinian terror, but their pride was inflated. The message we got was: We are world champions in this kind of warfare. You want to learn from us? By all means, but we have nothing to learn from you."

Palestinian terror had an adverse effect on Israel's economy. In order to get out of the economic crisis in 2003, Sharon's finance minister, Binyamin Netanyahu, introduced a series of far-reaching cuts. Economically, the steps were successful, but the harm they caused to Israeli society was immeasurable, as was the damage to the army's preparedness. An exceptionally large increase in the 2002 security budget (following Operation Defensive Shield) was halted, in spite of the IDF's ever-growing needs. Because it still did not appear to be delivering the goods (numbers of Palestinian terror victims dropped only toward the second half of 2003), the army was not in a position to complain. The GHQ had to decide where to cut, and it didn't have much space in which to move.

It is no easy matter to achieve efficiency in ongoing expenses without adversely affecting the service conditions of career army personnel or canceling expensive long-term projects involving the purchase of state-of-the-art weapons. The only solution was to cut back training programs, disband reserve units, and reduce weapons and ammunitions budgets. All this was rationalized by saying that the traditional threat of a united front of Iraq and Syria had lessened due to the American invasion of Iraq.[4]

In the IDF of 2006, battalion commanders—both regular and reserve—went into action without having ever commanded a battalion drill. Division commanders were not trained for the job because the division commander course had been discontinued. Infantry officers appointed to command a reserve armored corps division were given no organized retraining, since this was no longer considered of any importance. Reserve divisions were considered a way station—a kind of recommended rest period for officers who had excelled in the intifada—on their way to more important and desirable appointments. The fact that no "capability keys" to check the professional levels of the units were made among the ground forces—although doing so was routine in the IAF—made it possible for the IDF to deceive itself and cover up the real situation. Officers tend to tell their commanders what these want to hear. When Chief of Staff Dan Halutz paid a visit to Tse'elim base a few months before the war began, for example, officers boasted about the reliability and professionalism of the reserve system. In retrospect, says a senior officer, the IDF could certainly have removed troops from the occupied territories and made a point of raising the minimal level of training. "Ultimately, much of the fighting in the territories consisted of police work, but it was very easy for the army to fall in love with it. Because, with all the moral problems involved [in the territories, at least], we came out more or less victors."

NOT REALLY READY

For the officers and soldiers who years later would take part in the second Lebanon war, 2000–2006 were critical years during which they were supposed to accumulate more training and experience. For some of them, especially those in the special units and the regular infantry brigades, the second intifada did indeed pose difficult tests, demanding assignments, and experience under fire. Others, like the regular armored corps and the reserve units, were worn out by the exhausting burden of policing the occupied territories. For the young soldiers, the conflict in the territories created a misconception of what war is really like. Most of the older soldiers had had time to forget. The last time the IDF had sent troops against a real enemy had been during the first Lebanon war in 1982. Notwithstanding the impressive achievements of Operation Defensive Shield (capturing the West Bank towns in 2002), at no stage was an Israeli unit required to face down an enemy force of a size larger than an unskilled infantry squad.

PLANNING FOR WAR

The entranceway to Hezbollah's tunnel system on a steep slope near the village of Rashaf in southern Lebanon was hidden by a large rock. In order to reach the dark opening to the vast bunker, Nicholas Blanford, a correspondent for the American newspaper *Christian Science Monitor*, had to practically crawl on his hands and knees through dense vegetation and scrub oaks to the top of the hill. He squeezed through a crevice and found himself in one of the "nature reserves," as the Israelis termed them.

Once inside, Blanford turned on the flashlight tied to his head and discerned that the walls and ceiling were reinforced with steel beams and panels painted black in order to prevent a chance reflection of the sun that might reveal the secret entrance. Around a corner the walls were coated white to allow optimal light from the electric bulbs. The electrical wires that stretched along white plastic pipes fastened to the walls led to glass circuit breakers and sockets. The bunker's water supply flowed through a blue plastic pipe. Now Blanford and his two colleagues were able to stand up.

The first room that he saw was a little bathroom with a small-scale toilet, shower, sink, water boiler, and even a drainage system installed under the cement floor. The air inside was cool and pleasant compared to the broiling heat aboveground. At this stage, Blanford and his colleagues estimated that they were 30 to 50 meters underground, deep enough to withstand almost any weapon in Israel's arsenal. "The effort that went into building this facility was extraordinary," he wrote.

Like other "nature reserves," the Rashaf bunker took six years to build after the IDF withdrew from southern Lebanon. Israel and Lebanon were both aware that Hezbollah was constructing underground facilities, but only after the war in the summer of 2006 did the scope of the project become clear. "Already in 2002 UNIFIL [United Nations Interim Force In Lebanon] discerned two irregular digging operations being carried out by Hezbollah," relates Timur Goksel, a former spokesman for UNIFIL. "One was in the vicinity of the village of Al-Hiam, and the other near Ras Biada on the coast, south of Tyre. Hezbollah brought excavation equipment, and trucks removed the debris. I'm certain that the IDF also knew what was going on in these two places since Hezbollah made no effort to hide the digging, especially in Ras Biada, which is located next to the main coastal road." Goskel believes that the organization did not use these facilities during the war. "Looking back, I think that Hezbollah dug the two sites overtly on purpose in order to dupe Israel and divert our attention to Al-Hiam and Ras Biada while the real work was going on elsewhere—the entire length of the border with Israel."

GROUND PREPARATIONS

In May 2000, Prime Minister Barak proved correct in assuming that the IDF withdrawal would curtail Hezbollah's legitimacy to attack Israel. The number of violent incidents between the sides dropped significantly following the IDF pullout. However, the arming and deployment of Hezbollah toward a major clash with Israel received a vigorous push. The organization set up a vast military infrastructure with the assistance and support of Iran and Syria (both of whom were naturally interested in maintaining Hezbollah's strength). Tehran viewed the Lebanese organization as its long arm that could prevent an Israeli attack on its nuclear facilities. In Damascus, the newly instated president Bashar Assad procured (with Iranian financing) antitank missiles from Russia and transferred them to Hezbollah. While the IDF's pullback to the international border contributed to relative quiet there for six years, it also enabled Hezbollah to concentrate its efforts on strengthening and expanding its military infrastructure. Hezbollah had several explanations for this policy: Israel's continuous hold on "Lebanese land" (the Sha'aba Farms), the need to free Lebanese prisoners languishing in Israeli jails, and to help the Palestinians' intifada.

The tunnels and nature reserves were only a small part of Hezbollah's military layout. The infrastructure (including the tunnel system) in the south was intended to provide long-term defense against an IDF ground assault, while the rocket layout was planned to deter Israel from attacking the organization. Both defense mechanisms, together with the organization's weapons' stockpile, contributed to its military superiority in the domestic arena. Hezbollah's deployment in Lebanon was based on four zones:

1. The organization's "general staff" operated in Dahia in South Beirut, mainly in the Harat Harik neighborhood, an area termed the "Security Quadrant" and where Chairman Hassan Nasrallah's headquarters and offices were located. The Security Quadrant became an enclosed area. Its entranceway was protected with barriers and Hezbollah fighters who checked everyone entering and leaving.

2. The operational core was set up south of the Litani River, in an area controlled by the Nasser Brigade. Most of the missiles designed to strike Israel were concentrated in the south, but the brigade had an additional role: to be ready to counter an IDF ground assault.

3. The fighting area in the rear was assigned to the Bader Brigade in the Nabatia Heights. This area was chosen to afford Hezbollah a defensive depth and the capability of launching long-range rockets at Israel while dealing with IDF maneuvering and flanking moves.

4. The organization's training and logistical infrastructure was concentrated in the Bekaa Valley at a considerable distance from the Israeli border. Supplies from Syria and Iran reached the valley and from there were transported elsewhere.

THE SOUTH SEPARATES
FROM THE NORTH

The southern region of Lebanon, contained the "operational core" (the offensive and defensive zone) of Hezbollah organization. The offensive zone contained an enormous hoard of rockets of various ranges. (On the eve of the war, estimates varied from 14,000 to 20,000 rockets). At least 12,000 were short-range (less than 20 kilometers) Katyusha missiles, 107 and 122 millimeters in diameter—most from the former Soviet Union or Russia, others apparently from China and North Korea. The Katyushas were deployed in a 10-kilometer-wide strip north of Israel's border. Most were hidden in buildings in southern Lebanon, especially in storerooms attached to private homes. Hezbollah's general modus operandus was to rent houses and storerooms in villages populated by Shiites, who knew exactly what their property was being used for. Other Katyushas were ensconced in the nature reserves. Some of the missiles had launchers; others could simply be aimed in the direction of the target and connected to a timer, without the need for the operators' physical presence at the site. Many launchers were buried underground, raised and lowered by pneumatic lifts at launch time. These caches were usually protected from air strikes and artillery barrages. Besides Katyusha rockets, the organization possessed approximately 1,000 Russian-made rockets with a range of 42 kilometers and 1,000 Syrian- and Iranian-made 122-millimeter rockets. The latter had an intermediate range and came in a number of types: Fajar-3 rockets and Fajar-5s (with a range of 70 kilometers—both made in Iran; Syrian-made 220-millimeter rockets (with ranges of 50 and 70 kilometers); and 302-millimeter rockets (with a range of 115 kilometers). The trump cards were the Zalzel-1 and Zalzel-2 rockets—both Iranian-made, with ranges of 125 and 210 kilometers respectively. According to Israeli Intelligence estimates, Hezbollah acquired almost 7,000 short-range Katyushas even before the IDF withdrawal. The organization seems to have augmented its arsenal in this period by 100 intermediate-range Syrian rockets capable of reaching Zikhron Yaakov (30 kilometers south of

Haifa). However, the giant leap in the intermediate-range artillery occurred after the pullout. The main effort, accomplished with great secrecy, involved the distribution of the Fajr rockets among inner-core Hezbollah activists. In some cases, Iranian engineers added rooms to the homes of the activists' families. A launcher was installed and Fajr rockets were stored in these rooms. When the command was given, the activists would knock down the wall and fire the missiles from inside the house. Iran transferred the longest-range Zalzel rockets to Hezbollah two or three years before the war. These weapons required massive launchers and were kept in Beirut and the surrounding area, far from the Israeli border.

Although Nasrallah disclosed very few details, he made no effort to cover up his organization's ability to launch long-range rockets. On May 23, 2006, less than two months before the war, he announced: "We can hit anywhere in the north of Israel with thousands of rockets. . . . Today all of Israel is in our range. Ports, military bases, factories—everything is in our range. . . . We've amassed a huge amount of quality weapons."[5]

On the eve of the IDF withdrawal from Lebanon, senior Israeli Intelligence officers expressed grave concern that Hezbollah and Iran would intensify their use of Palestinian "subcontractors" to continue attacking Israeli border targets. In reality, the Palestinian organizations perpetrated a number of shooting incidents against Israel, and in one case—the attack near Kibbutz Matzuva (three kilometers south of the Lebanese border) in March 2002—Palestinian terrorists infiltrated the border and killed six Israelis. Israeli scholar Daniel Sobelman claims that Hezbollah refrained from enlisting the Palestinians mainly because of its sensitivity to the Lebanese public. According to Sobelman, all the groups in the country have an extremely negative attitude toward Palestinian organizations' activity, which is perceived as the cause of the civil war. The Palestinians were employed on an indirect axis: Hezbollah and Iranian intelligence increased their support (which eventually became actual command) of terrorist teams from the West Bank and Gaza Strip for all types of operations. At the same time, Hezbollah established "sleeper" networks in Arab countries (Jordan, Egypt, and others) that had signed peace agreements with Israel. Jordanian security forces uncovered some of these networks. Two hundred people suspected of pro-Hezbollah activity were arrested in the United States in 2006. The FBI believed that most of them had collected money for the organization from Muslim communities in the United States.

In late 2004, Iran and Hezbollah began cutting back their activity in the occupied territories, as Israel prepared to implement its plan to evacuate the Gaza Strip. On the eve of the pullout, Hezbollah ordered the terrorist teams to lower their profile and not interfere with the Israeli retreat.[6] The organization recruited agents and spies inside Israel—mostly Arab Israelis—to supply the organization with quality intelligence data, even during fighting.[7] Hezbollah's intelligence layout was divided into a number of fields: HUMINT (information from human sources), SIGINT (information collected from listening devices), and overt intelligence. "HUMINT is always preferred," says an Israeli intelligence official. "They believe in meeting their sources and looking straight into the whites of their eyes, not [getting information from] other overt sources. They honestly think that part of the Israeli population is their ally. The [Hezbollah HUMINT experts are] worthy opponents. Although it is not a political opponent, it has a 'super-professional' warfare doctrine. It succeeds in unmasking foreign agents among them who have hurt their people; in other words, it is capable of a very high level of intelligence."

In recent years, Iran and Hezbollah have tried tenaciously to gain influence, even in Israeli government centers. In December 2005, Gerias Gerias, the former head of the regional council of Fasuta, a village in the Northern part of Israel, was arrested on suspicion of having been recruited by the Iranians and instructed to join the Israeli left-wing peace party, Meretz, and run for a Knesset seat. In April 2007, the Arab Israeli parliamentarian Azmi Bashara of Balad (an Arab political party), fled the country after he was interrogated by the Shin-Bet for wide-scale contact with Hezbollah and passing on information to the organization in exchange for remuneration during the second Lebanon war. Bashara denied the charges but refused to return to Israel, and resigned from the Knesset.

Despite Hezbollah's far-reaching military activity, UN observers who were stationed in southern Lebanon during this period claimed that they never witnessed a member of the organization carrying a weapon. "Whenever we left the villages in the south we were able to identify Hezbollah members by their beards, radio equipment, and large number of motorcycles. They always wore mushroom hats and rode on 250-cc cycles suited to the terrain, but we never saw them toting weapons. They moved at night and, after Israel's pullout, the local population knew perfectly well not to pass through ravines or side roads at night because that's where the weapons were being transferred."

THE OTHER LEBANON

While Hezbollah was laying the groundwork for an Islamic republic—right under the nose of the Lebanese government—in its enclaves in the south, in the Bekaa Valley, and in Dahia—the southern Shiite neighborhood in Beirut—the political center in Beirut has completely given up on social services for the Shiite population. Even Shiites who had distanced themselves from a religious way of life became supportive of the radical religious organization. In addition to the economic factor, there was a simple explanation for this: For many Shiites, the release of Lebanese prisoners would be possible only by taking Israeli soldiers prisoner (a move that Hezbollah had carried out in October 2000 and promised to repeat). Also, the resumption of Israeli flyovers in southern Lebanon after the Mount Dov abductions infuriated parts of the population. The local population viewed Hezbollah antiaircraft fire and attacks against Israeli strongholds at the Sha'aba Farms as legitimate operations, especially as the Lebanese government stood by impotently, doing nothing to curb violations of its sovereignty.

Parallel with this, the gap between Hezbollah and other ethnic groups in Lebanon widened. This was due mainly to the accelerated pace of rapprochement with Western culture in the capital and many other areas of Lebanon. While Dahia looked like a neighborhood in downtown Tehran, other neighborhoods acquired the gloss of western European cities: bars, discotheques, coffee houses, provocatively dressed women. A resident of Beirut describes the city as "very ostentatious. The rich flaunt their wealth. Young people drive flashy sports cars, elegant nightclubs stay open till early in the morning, and drugs are ubiquitous (ecstasy is in vogue, followed by cocaine)." The world-famous Dutch disk jockey Tiësto was interviewed by the Israeli daily *Yediot Ahronot* and said that the biggest surprise in his life was performing before 10,000 partygoers in Beirut.

Many Lebanese youth, especially Christians, do not consider Hassan Nasrallah a role model (to put it mildly). The youngsters are glued to their TV sets watching *Superstar* (Lebanon's version of *American Idol*). To them, Nasrallah's pronunciations on "resistance to the Zionist enemy" sound like a voice from another planet. Hezbollah's parliamentary strength may have risen slightly after the IDF withdrawal, but the other ethnic groups view the pullout as reason enough for the Shiite organization to disarm (in accordance with the Ta'if Agreement). These groups claimed that without Israel's presence on Lebanese soil, there is no reason for the continuation of the "resistance." (The majority of the political factions do not consider the Sha'aba Farms as justification.)

Along with the growing criticism in Lebanon over Hezbollah's conduct, the organization also fell into disrepute in the international arena. George W. Bush's ascendancy to the White House in 2001 heralded the "surge" of the neoconservatives in Washington and a hostile attitude toward Hezbollah. In the wake of 9/11, the Bush administration relegated Syria and Hezbollah to membership in the "axis of evil." However, Bashar Assad's assumption of power in Damascus caused a significant change in Syrian-Hezbollah relations. While the elder Assad rarely met with Nasrallah and was reluctant to provide the organization with sophisticated weapons, Assad junior treated Chairman Nasrallah with the highest respect. Israeli intelligence discovered in 2002 that after most of the meetings between the two, Hezbollah intensified, rather than restrained, its activity against Israel. Bashar Assad became the official backer of the organization's operations in the Sha'aba Farms and seemingly allowed Nasrallah to act as he wished. Bashar transformed Hezbollah from an organization under Syria's wing into a strategic partner. Damascus regarded the shipment of advanced weapon systems to Hezbollah as a move that made the Shiite organization part of the Syrian missile layout, capable of deterring Israel from launching attacks. However, despite the rapprochement, Syria's withdrawal from Lebanon in 2005 forced Assad to cede his ranking position in the Lebanese game to Tehran.

THE BILLIONAIRE

In October 2000, Hezbollah had to face another change in the political elite, this time in Lebanon, and one that would have a dramatic impact on the organization's future: Rafiq Hariri's election to a second term as prime minister. Relations between Hezbollah and Hariri during the latter's first term had been characterized by discord and problems. Hariri was known to have extensive political links in the United States, Britain, and France. His political agenda in Lebanon and the Middle East was the exact opposite of Hezbollah's. The Lebanese prime minister favored the establishment of peaceful ties between Israel and the Arab world. (Hezbollah demanded the expulsion of Israeli Jews to their countries of origin and returning the entire area comprising Israel to the Palestinians.) Nevertheless, Hariri was careful to avoid a head-on collision with Hezbollah. He often came into conflict with

Assad as well, since he made no effort to hide his desire to see Syrian forces evacuate Lebanon and Damascus's hegemony in Beirut ended. In September 2004, the Lebanese parliament voted to extend pro-Syrian president Emile Lahoud's term in office for another three years. This decision to allow a president to serve a third term in office required changing the national constitution. Under Syrian pressure, the majority of parliament members agreed to the change. On October 20, one and a half months after the UN Security Council passed Resolution 1559 (calling for the removal of Syrian forces from Lebanon), Hariri resigned in protest over the Lebanese parliament's decision to grant Lahoud a third term.

On September 2, 2004, the UN passed Resolution 1559; its key feature consisting of four demands: withdrawal of all foreign forces from Lebanon; disarmament of all the militias; Lebanese control over all of its territory (i.e., deployment of the Lebanese army in the South); and support of presidential elections free from foreign intervention. Washington and Paris downplayed Hariri's role in advancing the resolution, but it was clear to the Syrians that the Lebanese prime minister and his colleagues were active partners in drafting the resolution. Despite the Security Council vote, the Syrians kept to their plans in Lebanon and extended President Lahoud's term. After resigning, Hariri began working more overtly as the head of the anti-Syrian camp. Events received an unexpected boost due to miscalculation on the part of Syrian intelligence when it decided to exact revenge for Hariri's involvement in Resolution 1559 and his arrangement of protests on Lebanon's Independence Day (November 2004) under the banner of "Syrians—Out."

CHRONICLE OF AN INEVITABLE DEATH

On the afternoon of February 14, 2005, Hariri's motorcade was driving through the streets of Beirut. Hariri, no longer in an official position and fearing a Syrian assassination, tended to travel in a convoy of bulletproof vehicles accompanied by a troop of bodyguards and a defense mechanism for neutralizing electronically triggered improvised explosive devices (IEDs).

At 12:55 p.m., as the procession passed the St. George Hotel in the beachside area of luxury hotels, a red Mitsubishi on the side of the road exploded with 300 kilograms of dynamite. Hariri never had a chance. The armored motorcade instantly became a heap of burning debris. The blast gouged out a 20-meter-wide hole in the street, torched at least 20 vehicles, and completely demolished the front part of the St. George. Besides Hariri, 10 other people were killed, including some of his bodyguards. Responsibility was claimed by an unknown organization. The suicide bomber, Ahmad Abu-Adas, sent a tape to the al-Jazeera network. In it he read his will and charged that Hariri had been eliminated because of his connections with the Saudi leadership. But the impression in Lebanon was that professionals had fabricated the tape. The Lebanese public was certain that Syria stood behind the assassination.

In an extraordinary gesture, French president Jacques Chirac and his wife attended Hariri's funeral in Beirut. Chirac met with Hariri's son, Sa'ad a-Din Hariri, who almost immediately became the leader of the anti-Syrian camp. The murder shocked Chirac and encouraged him to cooperate with President Bush not only in ousting the Syrians from Lebanon but also in weakening Bashar's regime. The assassination that had been intended to deter Syria's opponents proved to be a double-edged sword. Tens of thousands of Lebanese, including even Hezbollah supporters, took to the streets of Beirut and other cities, demanding the pullout of Syrian forces from Lebanon. The raucous demonstrations—referred to as the Cedar Revolution—culminated in the pro-Syrian government's resignation two weeks after the assassination, on February 28. For the first time, a government in the Arab world fell as a result of nonviolent protest.

On March 5, the president of Syria announced that "the troops would be coming home." The evacuation of 14,000 soldiers was completed within seven weeks. On March 14, a new political camp was announced: the March 14 Movement. This group was a composite of various political factions that had been opposed to Syria's presence in Lebanon (and to a certain degree to that of Hezbollah). March 14 reflected the polarity in Lebanese society and politics: The new camp was supported by the United States, France, and moderate Arab countries, while Hezbollah and its allies were backed by Syria and Iran.[8]

On April 26, after 29 years of a Syrian presence in Lebanon (which had entered as an Arab deterrent force in 1976, one year after the country plunged into civil war), the last Syrian soldier marched off Lebanese soil. All of Syria's military bases and intelligence facilities were transferred to the Lebanese government, which then became the only party actually violating Resolution 1559 since it refused to disarm the pro-Syrian organizations (including

Hezbollah). Despite the withdrawal, in April the Security Council accepted Resolution 1595, which called for the appointment of an international investigating committee on the Hariri assassination. German judge and investigator Detlev Mehlis[9] headed the committee.

Elections to the Lebanese parliament were held in late May. Hezbollah won 11 seats (and, with its allies, 14 out of 128 seats), but the victory went to March 14 and Sa'ad Hariri, who succeeded in establishing a 72-seat bloc. For the first time in 30 years, an anti-Syrian front was in control of the parliament. The Shiite front (Amal and Hezbollah) won 35 seats. The party of Christian general Aoun joined them with his 21 seats, having broken ranks with the Christian anti-Syrian leadership. The office of prime minister went to Fouad Siniora, a figure previously unknown outside Lebanon.

Although Hariri's assassination proved to be a mistake on the part of Damascus, an invisible hand (apparently Syria's) continued to liquidate Syria's enemies. Samir Kasir, a Lebanese journalist who bitterly criticized Syria's presence in his country, was killed on June 2 when he turned on the ignition of his car near his home in Beirut. On June 21, George Hawi, the former head of the Communist Party and an opponent of Syria, was murdered. On September 25, a Lebanese Broadcasting Company journalist, Mai Shediaq, was critically wounded when a bomb planted near her car exploded as she was coming out of church. On December 12, the editor of *al-Nahar*, Jubran Tweini, was killed in Beirut. In a television interview a few days earlier, the 48-year-old Tweini had accused Bashar Assad of despotism. Tweini's assassination generated widespread anger in Lebanon against Syria and Hezbollah. The day after the murder, Siniora phoned UN Secretary General Kofi Annan and requested help in forming an international tribunal to investigate Hariri's assassination and the chain of killings of Syria's opponents. Since the request was made while the cabinet was in session, the five Shiite ministers (Amal and Hezbollah representatives) considered close to Syria temporarily resigned.[10]

QUIET WORDS

Tweini's murder and the cry for an international investigation commission created an atmosphere of crisis in Lebanon. The polarity between the March 14 camp and Hezbollah increased, and, ironically, more and more questions were raised over Hezbollah's insistence on keeping its weapons, even after Syria's pullout. Given the tension between the camps, the speaker of parliament, Nabih Beri, tried to initiate a "national dialogue." Beri envisioned a conference attended by the leaders of ethnic groups and political parties for discussing various disputes. On March 2, 2006, the "dialogue" opened with an impressive fanfare in Beirut. But the meetings, which were held once every two weeks, produced nothing more tangible than promises to reconvene. At first Hezbollah refused to discuss its disarmament, but Nasrallah was unable to resist pressure from the other delegates and eventually succumbed to Beri's insistence and agreed to have the issue raised. Nasrallah opened the May 16 meeting with a long harangue on Israel's threat to Lebanon. According to the Lebanese press, he reviewed Hezbollah activities prior to and following the Israeli withdrawal (until 2006), saying: "We must distinguish between the militias and non-militia resistance whose sole aim is to countermine the enemy. . . . The Lebanese army is incapable of challenging the Israeli army, whose enormous strength is an established fact that all the Arabs combined cannot defeat. Hezbollah is willing to remain by the army's side. If anyone has a better suggestion, let's hear it."

At the next meeting, on June 8, Nasrallah again proposed that his organization defend Lebanon. Just a handful of the participants noticed something that he said almost as an aside. Israeli soldiers, he avowed, would have to be taken prisoner and used as bargaining chips for the release of three Lebanese prisoners in Israeli jails. According to Boutros Harb, a member of parliament who sat three seats away from Chairman Nasrallah: "He didn't say this in order to receive our approval. He mentioned it offhandedly, without drawing anyone's attention, as though it was written in the margin of the text."

The next national dialogue meeting was set on July 25. Again, discussion revolved around the issue of disarming Hezbollah. On July 2, Nasrallah Sfeir, the Maronite patriarch and a leader of March 14, declared that "no one will allow Nasrallah to stay armed. The organization has been in the Lebanese theater for years and has played an important part in expelling Israel from the county, but all of us must be equal before the law. When Hezbollah is left with its weapons and others aren't, this is not equality."

NASRALLAH'S OBSESSION

In the second week of July, the UN delegate in Lebanon met with Hezbollah representatives. The latter repeated Nasrallah's promise from late June that the organization would do nothing to adversely affect the tourist season. "Anyone speaking with them in that period heard the same message," a UN delegate said.

But Nasrallah was experiencing certain difficulties, mainly political, that, despite his promises of a quiet summer, may have been what drove him to embark upon a military adventure. Although he managed to set forth the agenda of the national dialogue, he failed to completely remove the demand for a discussion on the organization's disarmament. His frequently repeated promise to free the three Lebanese prisoners languishing in Israel produced expectations in sections of the Lebanese public that Hezbollah felt obliged live up to. The prisoner issue became almost an obsession with Nasrallah, and he brought it up at every opportunity. From his point of view, the prisoner swap in 2004 (in which 430 prisoners were released for the Israeli reserve officer Elhanan Tennenbaum and the bodies of three Israeli soldiers who had been abducted at Mount Dov) was a great achievement. But, ironically, stage 2 of the deal, arranged through German mediation, had placed Nasrallah in a trap. He was supposed to convey "essential and tangible" information on the fate of the missing Israeli air force navigator, Ron Arad. Whether Nasrallah really was unable to obtain such information or whether his Iranian patrons ordered him not to provide it, Nasrallah did not keep his word. In return for new information, Israel was supposed to release Samir Kuntar, a Lebanese Druze who had led a Palestinian Liberation Front organization terrorist team that murdered an Israeli policeman and three members of the Haran family in an attack in Israel's northern town of Nahariya in April 1979.

During the May 2005 election campaign to the Lebanese parliament, Nasrallah promised the Kuntar family that he would work ceaselessly to free their son. In addition to the need to break the deadlock on the Kuntar negotiations, Nasrallah also saw abduction as an opportunity to bolster his political status in Lebanon. "He believed that he would kidnap a soldier, force Israel to attack, and respond with Katyusha fire—thus proving his indispensability as the defender of Lebanon," says a former chief of Israeli intelligence. On November 21, 2005, Hezbollah tried to snatch IDF troops in the village of Rajar. The attempt failed and at least three of the organization's men were killed. Nasrallah announced at the funeral that kidnapping Israeli soldiers is the organization's natural duty and right. Immediately after the incident, a senior Western diplomat warned Hezbollah: "You're taking a difficult and dangerous path. If you make another kidnapping attempt—you risk war." A few months later, following elections in Israel, the same diplomat admonished Hezbollah a second time: "There is a new leadership in Israel. Don't test it! It might be forced to respond to your aggression in a way that is stronger than you can imagine."

CHAPTER FOUR

A NEW TRIUMVIRATE

I N THE AUTUMN of 2006, a gray, medium-size manual attracted powerful emotions of vengeance and animosity while the Israel Defense Forces went through a period of scathing self-criticism. The manual was supposed to redefine the General Headquarters' (GHQ) Doctrine. In the preface (first published in April 2006), Chief of Staff Dan Halutz defined the manual as "a basic military document" that commanders had to "internalize and implement to the letter when preparing their troops and sending them on missions." After the war, GHQ referred to the manual in entirely different tones. Major General Gadi Eisenkott penned an internal document stating that the manual was a hostile virus in the guise of an operational concept that had infiltrated the military system and made a shambles of it. Like many other expressions in the nation's postwar mea culpa, here too GHQ seemed to overreact. The IDF had not failed in Lebanon because of a doctrinal manual or a misdirected concept; it failed because of ideas that were not translated into clear moves on the ground, that were unsuited for the Lebanese battlefield, and that were written in a muddled command jargon.

The document was the last stage in a decade-long process. During this period, significant changes had taken place in the Middle East, in technological development, and in military thinking. The drafters of the new operational concept claimed that the nature of the confrontations facing the IDF had changed. The danger of conventional war against regular armies was all but past. Yet the army had to find solutions to the "first-circle" threat: attacks by terrorist and guerrilla organizations (Palestinian and Hezbollah) and the looming threat from the "third circle"—surface-to-surface missiles. And there was growing concern over nuclear weapons from more distant enemies, first and foremost Iran. The primary and immediate challenge, however, was asymmetrical warfare. This term refers to small and more or less weak organizations that employ relatively primitive technologies capable of causing serious damage to a more powerful political entity or state, thus influencing its decision making, since the weapons are directed at, in this case, Israel's soft underbelly: the civilian home front. Handling such an attack becomes even more complicated, since the opponent is a non-state using a weak state as a base for its operations.

The new operational concept was intended to transform the concept of winning and the means of setting about it. Instead of the classical concept of military victory—conquest, capturing territory, and destroying the enemy's forces—a new idea gained ground: Victory would be achieved by applying a chain of "springboards" and "effects" on the rationale of the enemy's system. The IDF's most advanced technologies—precision fire (especially from the air, but also from ground-based missiles), command and control systems, observation and intelligence-gathering devices—would make the capture of territory obsolete. Large-scale, in-depth troop maneuvering was seen as an outdated, even unnecessary combat technique. The long-term retention of territory was now perceived as an impediment, not an advantage. It was enough to employ return fire and limited ground raids, heavily supported by small, highly-trained commando forces, in order to attain the desired results. According to the manual: "The use of precision firepower and the integration of land, sea and air forces against the enemy's entire systems' layout will cause him greater problems than if piecemeal linear actions are taken." Simultaneous, multidirectional strikes would be aimed at the heart of the enemy: the perception of its leaders. Technological superiority would ensure victory and save the lives of Israeli troops that would have been lost in close contact with the enemy.

The inspiration for the new operational concept came from two success stories that seemed to reflect similar situations but in reality were almost entirely different: America's 2003 victory in Iraq and Israel's anti-guerrilla campaign in the occupied territories and in Operation Defensive Shield. In Iraq, the Americans overpowered a conventional army, a bloated, antiquated force that had "generously supplied" them with a huge number of targets and enabled them to demonstrate their technological superiority.[1] In the occupied territories, Israel successfully checked a terrorist threat stemming from highly motivated (eager for self-sacrifice and suicide attacks) but poorly trained gangs. Hezbollah, a highly trained guerrilla organization that had spent six years preparing for a major clash with Israel, was different from both cases.

FROM CONCEPT TO PLAN

Haltingly and furtively, the IDF began to draft an operative plan for the Lebanese theater. From 2000 to 2002, Major General Eyal Ben-Reuven and the generals of the Northern Command, Gabi Ashkenazi and later Benny Gantz, began planning in detail a possible operation in Lebanon. Chief of Staff Mofaz approved the move but requested that it be undertaken in a compartmentalized fashion, with a minimum number of people privy to the plans. Mofaz feared a public outcry if IDF plans for another incursion into Lebanon were leaked. While Ben-Reuven spotted a hole in the military activity in the north, he had no desire to provoke a new war. Nevertheless, he believed that the IDF had to be prepared, even in the theater from which it had exited ignominiously in May 2000. By late 2002, the Northern Command came up with a new plan—Defense of the Land—which involved several days of air strikes on Hezbollah targets and Syrian forces in Lebanon, followed by the engagement of a number of divisions in ground action. Two divisions would deploy at a relatively short distance north of the border, while forces from another elite paratroop unit—the Fire Division—would be helicoptered to the Litani River in a vertical flanking move. Hezbollah fighters would be trapped in a ring. But not all the areas would be captured; instead, the IDF would gain "control" of them. Rather than seizing and mopping up village after village, where the enemy could easily disappear through the houses, the IDF would concentrate on the rocket launch sites. It would seize key, dominating positions and, with close air support, destroy the launchers. According to the succeeding chief of staff, Lieutenant General Ya'alon, the plan's next stage would require six weeks, during which IDF forces would raid specific targets belonging to Hezbollah while the air strike continued, thereby gradually reducing the number of Katyusha rockets that could be fired into Israel. At the end of this period, the IDF would redeploy on or close to the international border.

With the withdrawal of Syrian forces in April 2005, the original rationale of Defense of the Land was eliminated. Without Syria's presence in Lebanon, the close ties between Damascus and Beirut were sapped. Israel, although it viewed Syria's exit in a positive light, lost a vital fulcrum for pressuring Hezbollah. During this period the IDF was deeply involved in preparing the disengagement plan from the Gaza Strip and Ya'alon was on his way out; Ariel Sharon and his Defense Minister Mofaz had decided not to extend his tenure as chief of staff. Ya'alon ordered Gantz to head a team to examine the implications of Continental Shift—Syria's departure from Lebanon. During the next two months the general staff, under Gantz and his successor, Udi Adam, drafted Elevated Waters—an alternative to Defense of the Land; its principles were similar, except for the pressure on Syria. The basic approach had not changed: Katyusha shelling could not be stopped by return fire alone. Ground action would be necessary, following an Israeli air strike, and would include the regular army and the reserves, while maintaining political pressure on Hezbollah and the Lebanese government.

ISRAELI SCRIPT, LEBANESE DIRECTION

In May 2006, Halutz approved the basic rationale of Elevated Waters. In June the plan was examined for the first time in a command exercise that proceeded according to a scenario very similar to what would actually happen just one month later: a kidnapping in the Gaza Strip followed by the abduction of soldiers in the north and several weeks of Katyusha attacks and escalated fighting. A senior officer in the Northern Command described the chain of events: "It was as though we were the scriptwriters and Nasrallah the director." The IDF had no time to assess the lessons of the exercise, but from the outset it became clear that the IAF would be hard-pressed to deal with the short-range Katyusha threat (IAF commander Major General Eliezer Shkedi estimated the rate of hits against short-range Katyusha launchers to be about 3 percent), and their elimination would require ground action. A sharp disagreement flared up in the course of the exercise between Halutz and Brigadier General Eyal Eisenberg, the commander of the Fire Division, over whether the hourglass that was running out as the end of the fighting approached was a political or civilian one. Eisenberg claimed that the main flaw was the inability of the civilian population in the north to weather a missile barrage. Halutz claimed that the international community would determine the length of the campaign. "Look at Sderot," he said. "The city's been bombarded from Gaza for six years and nothing's happened." Eisenberg pointed out that the Qassam rocket was less lethal than the Katyusha and that the IDF mission had to be directed against the launchers. "Our clients are the state's citizens. From their point of view, success means removing the

Katyusha threat from the home front. A line has to be found that puts the maximum number of citizens at a safe distance from the line of fire. The towns along the northern border have relatively good bomb shelters, so that a war of attrition can be waged against Hezbollah. The most critical problem is how to quickly remove the residents of Haifa and Acre from the Katyushas' range," Eisenberg said.

There was not enough time for Elevated Waters to undergo a lengthy approval process. Thus, on the eve of the July 2006 war, the only operational plan on the table was Defense of the Land, and its primary sting had been extracted.[2]

OUT OF SIGHT, OUT OF MIND

In early 2006, the IDF's operations branch prepared a presentation describing mission priorities for daily security matters. The Lebanese border was seventh on the list, sharing its place of honor with the Jordanian Arava (Israel's long and quiet southern border in the east), a region where no rocket layout had been built that posed a threat to a number of Israelis. In comparison with more urgent fronts and in light of the positive processes taking place in Lebanon (from Israel's point of view), the chief of staff appeared to pay less attention to the northern theater. The fading concern found expression in cutbacks—not just in quantity but also in quality—in resources, intelligence gathering, and manpower. Field commanders' senses sharpen proportionally to the degree that their personal advancement is affected. Until the withdrawal from Lebanon, it was understood that the most promising commanders, especially in the infantry and Special Forces, would be promoted to brigade commanders in Lebanon. In less than two years after the outbreak of the intifada, the focus shifted to the occupied territories. Service in the West Bank and Gaza Strip became mandatory for career advancement. Thus, in the spring of 2006, a "dream team" of brigade commanders was serving on the West Bank—six officers who headed every list of top-notch commanders. The situation on the Lebanese border was less auspicious, even for those at the level of staff officers. In general, the best commanders were assigned to the occupied territories, not to Lebanon.

In no place were the shortcomings in the Israeli approach more glaring than along the border. Along the border, in the 91st Division's sector, various processes converged: the containment approach, the application of the new concept, and cutbacks in resources and manpower. Everything played into Hezbollah's hands and paved the way for its next operation—a border attack with the objective, Israeli intelligence estimated, of abducting IDF soldiers. When Udi Adam replaced Benny Gantz as head of the Northern Command in October 2005, the latter said that the Northern Command had been carrying out its assignments with the current order of battle, "but we feel that we're scraping the bottom of the barrel." Gantz explained the rules to his successor: Even when Hezbollah initiates a provocation, it has to be ended as quickly as possible lest the violence spread to other sectors along the border. The IDF was forbidden to cross the border even where the international boundary line spilled over a "few inches" to the north. (The fence that was built in 2000 did not meticulously overlap the international border and left unprotected a small number of Israeli enclaves to its north.)

In daily security operations, this approach was implemented by the IDF's limited, low-profile presence along the border. The army closed its strongholds there, transferred other strongholds to the rear, and limited the number of patrols close to the border, especially in areas considered prime targets for Hezbollah attacks. Paradoxically, these security measures were not binding for Israeli citizens. Parts of the road near the frontier were off-limits to the military, but civilians continued traveling along them. When the state of alert was at its height, the IDF's presence on the border was reduced to a minimum: The entry and exit of strongholds was drastically limited, as if the IDF was still deployed in Lebanon rather than in sovereign Israeli territory. The rationale was "zero targets" and preventing Hezbollah from kidnapping soldiers. Adam interpreted the containment policy on the border as "ceding Israeli sovereignty on the northern frontier while giving Hezbollah a free hand on the border line, as long as it doesn't open fire or infiltrate into our territory." Adam regarded this approach as a major mistake since it enabled Hezbollah to build its power and prepare the immediate border area in such a way that "would make it impossible for the IDF to prevent it from attacking first and gaining a victory."

When Adam spoke with Halutz about this, the chief of staff replied that there was no reason to change the policy since it had proven itself and brought quiet in the Galilee for over five years. Like Adam and Gantz, the brigade commanders also felt increasingly uncomfortable with the uncompromising passivism imposed on the Northern Command. "We acted as though we signed a peace agreement with Lebanon, when in reality there was nothing," one lamented. "Any military officer will tell you that defending a line never stopped an attack. We didn't even post a lookout in Lebanon. We put no pressure on Hezbollah and this is why we found it so problematic to collect information on them. [The enemy] leaves gaps when it's under pressure and this causes it to make mistakes. Nothing was interfering with Hezbollah. The fence in Lebanon was a barrier for us, not for them."

ENTER: HALUTZ

Beginning in May 2006, Israel found itself with an extraordinary new triumvirate in the political-security leadership that was facing the growing threat in the north. The trio's stage entry in this period was purely accidental, but it was rooted in the steps that Ariel Sharon had taken in his relatively long term as Israel's popular prime minister and in the upheaval left by his sudden departure following his second collapse. Lieutenant General Dan Halutz, undoubtedly the most political chief of staff since the era of Mapai (Israel's legendary, all-embracing Labor Party in the 1950s and 60s), was one of Sharon's most high-profile insiders and his most outstanding appointment. Prime Minister Ehud Olmert became Sharon's successor. The defense minister, Amir Peretz, the head of the Labor Party, emerged as Olmert's political ally. In this role, Peretz hastened the exit of a number of senior figures from Labor to Kadima (the party recently formed by Sharon and Olmert).

Halutz was the first—and in many ways the most decisive—side of the triangle. At 57, he became Israel's eighteenth chief of staff, six months before Olmert stepped into office and one year before Peretz was sworn in as defense minister. Overall responsibility for the war fell on the government, but the chief of staff, with his domineering personality, self-confidence, and (given his air force background) inability and inexperience in managing a ground war, was also a contributing factor. In February 2005, Sharon, in his typical roughshod manner, strove to get rid of Ya'alon, mainly because of his opposition to Israel's unilateral disengagement from Gaza and his jeremiads that Palestinian terror would mount from that direction. Sharon made no effort to conceal the fact that Halutz was a regular visitor at his farm and that the two spoke by phone frequently, while sidestepping Mofaz and Ya'alon. Sharon's son, Omri Sharon, a member of the Knesset, contributed to the felicitous relationship between the two men. Omri had known Halutz since the time he served under him as a reserve officer in Shaldag (the air force's commando unit). Halutz's political views were considered an additional advantage.[3] In every media interview, Halutz espoused a hawkish line, and a skeptical view of Arab intentions—an outlook that mirrored Sharon's approach.

The chief of staff and Halutz's successor in the air force, Eliezer Shkedi, supported the idea of air hegemony: aircraft (and even more—unmanned aerial vehicles [UAVs]) as the solution to every problem. Since these weapons were operated by remote control, they saved the lives of IDF troops. After the Gaza Strip disengagement, the air force had been presented as the ideal answer to Qassam rockets (before the limitations of aircraft were realized). At the same time, Halutz energetically embarked on a massive organizational reform. He left almost no stone unturned in the GHQ's structure, adopting many ideas from his handling of the air force. But with all the time being invested in the pullout from the Gaza Strip and in organizational upgrading, there was no time to plan for war. Around the time of Halutz's appointment, Sharon was asked whether he was convinced that the air force commander was suited for the job. The prime minister replied positively. At any rate, he believed that he and defense minister Mofaz would remain on the scene to restrain the chief of staff if matters started getting out of control. This, of course, did not happen. When Halutz's moment of truth arrived, Sharon and Mofaz were gone—and dealing with that moment was infinitely more difficult than implementing the disengagement plan.

THE SUCCESSOR AND THE BACKROOM DEAL

In 2000, Ehud Olmert probably never dreamed that it would be his fate to replace Ariel Sharon as head of government. But the complicated chain of political events, along with the pact he signed with Sharon, eventually swept him into office.

Olmert ran against Sharon in the Likud primaries in 1999 and lost. In the especially tense race, Olmert railed against his rival. But three years later, when Sharon needed an ally to block Binyamin Netanyahu, who was trying to recapture the party, the two Likudniks reached an understanding. Olmert backed Sharon in this struggle and pitted himself directly against Netanyahu. Still, Sharon did not see Olmert as his successor; it is doubtful whether the question of succession even entered his mind. Sharon, then in his 70s, was fond of saying that longevity was a well-known trait in his family and was proud of an aunt who lived to be 100. "I have no intention of leaving my job for quite some time," he assured listeners at every opportunity. After the Likud victory over Labor in the 2003 elections, Olmert's appointment as his deputy happened almost by chance. When Olmert was miffed over the relatively minor government post being extended to him, Sharon offered him the role of deputy prime minister as a consolation prize. Less than a year later, Olmert was the first member of government to launch a trial balloon, in a conversation with an Israeli journalist, regarding unilateral disengagement from the Gaza Strip; this came a few weeks before Sharon's announcement. When rebellious MKs from the Likud party made life hell for Sharon, Olmert urged his boss to quit the party and found a new one. And when Sharon finally decided to dissolve the government and establish the Kadima Party in late 2005, he deliberated between Olmert and Tzipi Livni for the number-two spot. The choice fell to Olmert, who was perceived as the more senior and experienced minister. In January 2006, Sharon collapsed. The fact that he sank into a coma dictated the nature of the transfer of government. The legal situation was defined as Sharon's "temporary suspension from duties," and the deputy prime minister automatically stepped into the prime minister's office. Had Sharon suddenly died, the government would have elected a replacement—and it is far from certain that Olmert would have received more votes than Livni. Public shock over Sharon's collapse worked to Olmert's advantage. The media backed him almost immediately, and he seemed to adapt quickly to the rigors of the new role. Olmert, who was famous for his merciless polemic style, behaved in an exemplary manner. He calmly handled the crisis over the arrest of the Palestinian suspects (among them the murderers of the extreme-right-wing minister Rechavam Zeevi) during the raid on Jericho Prison, where they were held by the Palestinian Authority, and expressed the correct amount of sentimentality toward Sharon in his public appearances. As a temporary replacement, Olmert was extremely careful not to have his picture taken in the prime minister's seat in his office or in the Knesset lest he appear overly hasty to accede to Sharon's primacy. The press praised his conduct as "zero errors." Even his mediocre showing in the March 2006 elections (29 seats for Kadima, 19 for Labor, and 12 for Likud) failed to dampen his upbeat mood.

After the elections, Olmert quickly began replacing his predecessor's advisors who had assisted him in the transfer of government and the victory at the polls. Dov Weissglas, a Sharon insider and close friend of Condoleezza Rice, lost his influence. Sharon's original coterie was almost completely recalled, except for government secretary Israel Maimon and Udi Shani, who stayed on as the prime minister's unofficial advisor. The power figure in Olmert's office was attorney Yoram Turbovitz, his chief of staff (a new role that Olmert created modeled after the White House position). For Olmert, Turbovitz symbolized a figure that the media could quickly idolize. He was the epitome of a civil servant, with a doctorate in law from Harvard University, and he was a fast-track millionaire in the private sector to boot.

At the age of 60, having spent over half his life in the forefront of the political stage, Olmert appeared seasoned for the role of his career. But two weak points in his character and behavior loomed over this ideal picture, though they received only limited attention in this period of grace. Both of these foibles would eventually cast a dark shadow across his role as prime minister: unproven charges of personal corruption and a lack of experience in security matters. Ironically, given the allegations, as a young parliamentarian, Olmert began his political career as a fighter of corruption, a young lawyer who waged a public campaign against organized crime and kickbacks to soccer referees. But a cloud of suspicion hung over him regarding other aspects of his career: his blatant hedonism and his close ties with tycoons in Israel and the United States. More than once he had even come under criminal investigation.

In early March 2006, a few weeks before the elections, Olmert met with Ehud Barak in the prime minister's residence in Jerusalem. Olmert told his guest that after he won the elections, he intended to offer Amir Peretz, the head of Labor, the defense portfolio. Two other senior positions were already taken: Tzipi Livni had been promised the Foreign Ministry and Avraham Hirshson, a longtime political ally of Olmert's, the Finance Ministry. The possibility of a Labor leader being appointed finance minister troubled big business, among Olmert's main supporters. And Barak had reservations. "At some point, a few months after your government is sworn in," he said to Olmert, "a major security crisis will break out and you'll look to the right and see Livni and look to the left and see Hirshson and then you'll look in front of you and see Amir Peretz. In other words, you'll be completely on your own." "I can always go over Peretz's head and speak with the chief of staff," Olmert answered. Barak disagreed, saying that things never work that way.

A SUCCESS STORY

Today when Olmert's people are asked at what point the prime minister realized that he screwed up by offering Peretz the defense portfolio, they say it was about one hour after the appointment. Although Peretz himself was capable of very creative commentary regarding the interim Winograd Report and tended to focus on the handful of credits it accorded him, he admitted to this mistake only indirectly: During the Labor primaries in April 2007 he declared that even if he won the primaries, he would ask for the Finance Ministry.

Peretz, who came to Israel from Morocco as a young child, was 54 years old when he became defense minister. In the army, he had served as an ordinance officer in a paratroop brigade and was seriously wounded in an accident in Sinai in 1974. At the age of 31 he was elected mayor of Sderot (a development town a few miles northeast of the Gaza Strip) and in 1988 he entered the Knesset as a Labor delegate. In 1995 he was appointed chairman of the General Labor Federation (Histadrut), a role that he held for nearly a decade. He returned to the Labor Party, along with two-thirds of the mandates of the "One Nation" (Am Ahad) Party that he founded in 2004. Shimon Peres was responsible for his return, believing that this would thwart Ehud Barak's renewed attempt at taking over the party. Peres ignored the warnings of several senior Labor members regarding Peretz. One of their main admonitions was that during Peretz's reign in the Histadrut, he had stood out not only as a successful trade union leader but also as a firebrand who diverted the union's mechanisms to his own party's needs. Indeed, Peretz eventually beat Peres in the Labor primaries (Peres later bolted to Kadima at Sharon's urging) and quickly gained control of the party. Peretz's campaign against Olmert focused on an alternative to regular government and a new social agenda for the country. During his years in the Knesset, Peretz had rarely been involved in security/national matters and hardly mentioned these issues in the election campaign, but when he did he took a moderately dovish stance. After the 2006 elections, he intended to ask for the finance portfolio but the offer of the Defense Ministry was just too enticing. He realized that admitting that he was unsuitable for the job and relinquishing it to another senior party member (such as Ami Ayalon or Ephraim Sneh) would spell political suicide. His advisors suggested that a successful term in the Defense Ministry would shorten his path to the Prime Minister's Office. "Our basic assumption," a close associate revealed, "was that any politician would benefit from assuming the role of defense minister. Only Peretz with his 'luck' had to go and ruin everything."

One of the charges against Peretz's appointment as defense minister was his lack of a serious military background. Peretz supporters countered by saying that the Defense Ministry had more need of a "civilian" who did not see things solely from the generals' point of view and who did not see himself as the army's representative in government. There had been "civilian" defense ministers in the past who excelled at their job; Moshe Arens was the most outstanding example. The problem was that Peretz, not having a full understanding of the army's capabilities and limitations, seemed to have failed to introduce a skeptical view of the army during his tenure. This deficiency seems to have slammed the Defense Ministry's door against the people with a civilian background for a long time to come. Israel's failure in the second Lebanon war produced a long list of factors that we will discuss in detail, but, if we had to point to one factor, the sine qua non for the war's dismal outcome, decision making in the government and in GHQ would take first place. Leaderships always err, especially when under pressure. In wartime, the pressure on a democracy's leadership is ten times greater because of the constant need to respect public opinion (and keep an eye on tomorrow's voters). But the Olmert-Peretz-Halutz triumvirate not only committed many mistakes but also obstinately pursued them until the war's end, against all evidence brought to it in real time. The Israeli leadership during the war of 2006 manifested a rare combination of inexperience, lack of understanding, self-destructive internal rivalry, and overweening pride. The preceding triumvirate—Sharon, Mofaz, and Ya'alon—must share much of the responsibility for creating the conditions that led to the fiasco, but it seems that even if only one figure in the 2006 trio had been switched before the war, the result may have been different.

A man who still has a senior role in the security system says that if he could have imagined that this would be the trio leading Israel to war, he would have given its odds as "something like the chances of winning the national lottery. But in this case we won the booby prize. The loss was entirely ours."

A POLICY CHANGE?

On November 22, 2005, Ariel Sharon convened one of his last meetings on the Lebanese issue. On the agenda was the possibility of an escalated Israeli response to Hezbollah's provocations, after the previous day's failed attempt to kidnap Israeli soldiers in the border village of Rajar. Halutz proposed attacking Lebanon's civilian infrastructure the next time. The prime minister's concluding words were unequivocal: "As for operations on the Lebanese border, this has been the policy for the last five years at least. I said that whatever doesn't have to be done over there—shouldn't be done."

When Olmert succeeded Sharon in January 2006, the chief of staff considered him a potential partner for change in the Lebanon policy. Olmert held several meetings with the leaders of the security establishment, the most significant of which was held on March 5. With the exception of the need to maintain a state of high alert on the border in order to prevent another abduction attempt, the question of what the nature of Israel's response should be was broached again. Olmert made a few vacuous statements. "We must be prepared with patterns of response that are suited to the type of provocation that exists." His impression of an updated Intelligence survey was that Hezbollah had reached an advantageous position since there was no certainty that Israel's reaction would stop it from continuing to operate. Israelis held another discussion in May. Olmert drafted the lines of the preferred end situation in case of deterioration in the North: The Lebanese army moves into the South and Hezbollah withdraws and is disarmed. "Anything that can lead to the removal of the Hezbollah threat . . . interests us very much."

Olmert built his defense line on the basis of these insipid phrases. The prime minister wanted to rebuff the criticism that he set out to war in a slapdash manner before having intelligently weighed the pros and cons. He claimed that he had been dealing with the Lebanese situation continuously since the day he entered office and had, in effect, prepared the army for the possible escalation that culminated in the war in the North. In May 2006, following a border incident near Kibbutz Manara, Halutz stated that the next incident that Hezbollah initiated would have to be used as a springboard "for a new arrangement along the border." He compared the IDF to a soccer goalie who has been instructed "to hold the line without moving in the five-yard zone . . . and wait to receive a goal."

Halutz's and Olmert's words remained preliminary ideas, not crystallized operational plans.

THE WRITING ON THE WALL

On July 11, the prime minister sat in on the GHQ forum. Olmert, Peretz, Halutz, and the generals met on the fourteenth floor of the Kiriya-HQ building in central Tel Aviv. The defense budget had been a key issue in the

March election campaign. The parties competed in promulgating a "social" line, and heavier budget cuts seemed virtually inevitable. The deputy chief of staff, Moshe Kaplinsky, selected certain surveys for the prime minister and defense minister to hear in order to convince them that another cutback would be dangerous. The head of the planning branch, General Yitzhak (Khaki) Harel, presented a detailed report on the implications of the budget cuts for the IDF. "I'll be retiring next month," he told Olmert. "I want to speak from the heart. The IDF is a hollow army. In order to fulfill its missions, it needs more money." Major General Adam warned: "We're on the verge of another event on the Lebanese border. . . . It's a stagnant swamp there. If we don't breathe new air into the dialogue, if we don't progress on the Shaba'a Farms issue and the Lebanese prisoners, this story will blow up in our faces."

Major General Yishai Beer, president of the military court of appeals and an expert on tax law, asked Kaplinsky for the right to speak. Beer seemed almost like a guest from another planet. More than once he was portrayed as the GHQ's "bête noir" who had no qualms about pointing to shortcomings, contrasting sharply with the rather bland GHQ that Halutz surrounded himself with.

Beer cut no slack, not even for the prime minister. He told Olmert about the Fifth Brigade, a reserve infantry unit, 13 of whose soldiers were killed in a bloody fight in the Jenin refugee camp during Operation Defensive Shield. More than four years had passed since then, Beer said, and the brigade's combat proficiency had not improved by much. The land army's capability, he added, was like a check with no backing funds—at some point there will be a phone call from the bank. Beer's criticism did not stop at the reserve level. "The IDF is a mediocre army," the general told the prime minister bluntly. "Here and there are islands of excellence, but they're surrounded by a sea of mediocrity."

Olmert did not respond directly to Beer's statements. He rejected the generals' arguments against budget cuts. "I have enough problems with the financial situation of old people in Tel Aviv," he told them. "You'll have to make do with whatever there is." But the warnings of Generals Beer and Harel should have penetrated Olmert's consciousness over the following days. During the war, he probably recalled their words when he was besieged with depressing reports of IDF blunders and the number of soldiers killed by Hezbollah.

Major General (Res.) Giora Eiland, head of the National Security Council and Planning Branch of the IDF in the years preceding the war, says in retrospect that there was a "black hole" that was not taken into account before running off to war. "For four years we put the army at grave risk that, in retrospect, may have been unreasonable. We dismantled units, cut back training schedules and reduced the replenishment of ammunition. We thought that the regional and budgetary realities necessitated this and that we'd have enough time to take the necessary steps to fill in the gaps if the situation worsened. But Israel surprised itself with the decision to go to war. The ministers didn't even know how to ask the IDF what its real state of affairs was; and the army made no effort to divulge."

CHAPTER FIVE

GOING TO WAR

A T 10:15 A.M. on Wednesday, July 12, 2006, Hezbollah television station Al-Manar reported a successful "kidnapping of two Israeli soldiers operation in Area 2. . . . We've kept our promise to free our prisoners." In interviews on Arab satellite TV stations, Hezbollah spokesmen stated that the organization did its natural duty to free Lebanese prisoners and was interested in a completing a new comprehensive prisoner exchange. The residents in South Beirut's Shiite quarter, Dahia, waved pictures of Hassan Nasrallah, tossed out candy, and lit up the sky with a fireworks display. The euphoria also infected Hezbollah leadership. The Lebanese prime minister, Fouad Siniora, called for an urgent talk with Hussein Halil, Chairman Nasrallah's closest advisor. "What have you done?" Siniora fumed. According to the *Washington Post*, Halil answered coolly, "Everything will quiet down in 24 to 48 hours." But Siniora remained pessimistic. The Israel Defense Forces ravaged Gaza after Gilad Shalit was captured in June 2006, he said. Still, Halil kept his poise. "Lebanon isn't Gaza," he shot back.

Representatives of the International Red Cross in Beirut spoke with Hezbollah after the announcement of the abduction was issued. The Red Cross wanted one of their doctors to examine the two Israelis. The request was flatly rejected. "Give us some more time until things calm down" was the reply. But Hezbollah severed contact with the Red Cross the next day, apparently fearing Israeli surveillance. UN representative in Lebanon Geir Pedersen also contacted Hezbollah. "Why did you break your promise about keeping the summer quiet?" he asked. Hezbollah representatives conjured up a twisted reply: "We didn't give our word not to carry out a kidnapping. We promised there'd be quiet. We're not looking for a confrontation. We only acted according to the general rules of the game between us and Israel." Pedersen was extremely upset and flabbergasted by the answer. "Do you know what you've just done? You've started a war. We warned you. You've made a stupid mistake and the cost will be exorbitant." Pedersen conveyed to the UN offices in Jerusalem that Hezbollah was not interested in escalating the situation. But when the UN staff in Jerusalem tried to meet with senior Israeli officials that day, they encountered the same answer that other Western diplomats had received: "Sorry. We're busy."

A THUNDERING RESPONSE

Ehud Olmert first heard of the incident, the casualties, and the likelihood of abduction from his military secretary, General Gadi Shamni. Around 10:00 a.m., while Olmert was speaking in his Jerusalem office with the parents of abducted soldier Gilad Shalit, who was being held in Gaza, he was handed a message describing the situation in the north. The prime minister showed it to Shalit's parents. "They [IDF] better be careful, Hezbollah will be waiting for them," he called after Shamni as the officer left the room. Olmert then held a private session with his closest advisors. Two urgent issues topped the agenda: a powerful Israeli response and Olmert's timetable for the rest of the day. Like their boss, the advisors felt that a sharp response had to be made and the scheduled meeting with the prime minister of Japan, Junichiro Koizumi (whose visit to Israel had been postponed a number of times), had to take place. At 12:50 that afternoon Olmert held a joint press conference with his Japanese guest. Koizumi asked that Israel respond with restraint to Hezbollah's latest provocation and weigh the consequences. Olmert, however, took an entirely different approach: "The events of this morning cannot be considered a terrorist strike; they are the acts of a sovereign state that has attacked Israel without cause. The Lebanese government, which Hezbollah is part of, is trying to upset regional stability. . . . We will not give in to blackmail or negotiate with terrorists on any aspect of the lives of IDF soldiers." Olmert also stated that the government would convene that evening to discuss the situation and, he warned, the Israeli response would be "thundering."

Like Ariel Sharon in the Palestinian theater, Olmert wanted to react quickly, on the assumption that the Hezbollah attack offered him a "window of opportunity" to receive international support for a tough Israeli response. When Sharon was prime minister, senior IDF officers on more than one occasion tried to curb his anger and postpone impulsive decisions. This time, however, the chief of staff was no less bullish than the prime minister. Olmert's advisors claim that no one broached the question of whether to respond. "It was clear to all of us that we had to respond," they say. "The nature of the response was rooted in the decisions that had been made in March 2006, when a basket of targets had been approved. In previous discussions, all the security agencies had recommended a major military operation in the event of another kidnapping attempt. We understood that in our neighborhood if you don't react after being hit, next time you'll get whacked even harder. On July 12, nobody suggested that Israel wait before acting."

LEBANON IN HOT WATER

Amir Peretz heard about the abduction shortly before the news reached Olmert. Peretz was in his office with senior security officials assessing the situation in Gaza. The head of the Operations Branch, General Gadi Eisenkott, provided initial details of the incident. He said that the radio contact with the operational force was lost in a number of vehicles, and he had decided to declare "Hannibal"—the code name for a kidnapping. In the meantime, reports came in that the ambushed patrol included two Humvees. The meeting ended when senior officers left for the general headquarters to follow developments in the North. "This is the most important event right now," the defense minister said. "Otherwise, we'll go into a tailspin." Later Peretz approved the immediate implementation of two options: attacking all of Hezbollah's strongholds along the border and air strikes deep in Lebanon along possible escape routes heading north. In the pit with senior officers, the chief of staff held his first discussion. Eisenkott proposed "simmering down and thinking matters over before acting [and] limiting the air strikes to a few hours." Let's wait a few days and organize the operation, he suggested. But Eisenkott was alone in this approach. As at the government meeting that was held a few hours later, several of the senior officers seemed to be competing to see who could come up with the most far-reaching proposals and gutsy declarations, while the chief of staff orchestrated the proceedings. Dan Halutz insisted that the incident had to be seen "as a watershed in the Israeli-Lebanese dialogue" and that targets linked to the Lebanese government had to be hit hard. But, he cautioned, Israel had to avoid dragging Syria into the fray. Like Olmert in the press conference with the Japanese prime minister, the chief of staff also stressed that the Lebanese government was responsible for the incident. "They are to blame," he asserted. The chief of the Planning Branch, General Yitzak (Khaki) Harel, proposed targeting Beirut. Lebanon, he told Halutz, is at the high point of the tourist season. This is where we have to hit them. "Shut down the airport in Beirut and signal to the Siniora government that its days are numbered." At the end of the meeting, even before Halutz held a scheduled session with the defense minister, IDF spokeswoman Brigadier General Miri Regev briefed reporters that the chief of staff had stated that Israel "had to put Lebanon back 20 years." Within minutes, his words were broadcast on Israeli television stations (some of which announced that they were setting up 24-hour news broadcasts because of events in the North) and Internet news sites. If Peretz would not understand in a person-to-person conversation the desired direction, then the media would relay it.

At 12:45 p.m., Peretz, Halutz, and their aides met for talks in the defense minister's office on the fourteenth floor of the Kirya (military GHQ) building in Tel Aviv. The chief of staff was bellicose. "We have to bang on the table as loudly and roughly as possible," he told the defense minister, even if Hezbollah's response would be missile-fire against Israel. He advocated "extremely aggressive activity along the line [border], employing bulldozers and flattening the area, creating new rules in the game." Peretz, a civilian, was somewhat more skeptical. Later that day, Halutz came up with the idea of attacking the civilian infrastructure in Lebanon as Israel's main response to the kidnapping and asked for approval to bomb Beirut's civilian airport and the country's power stations. "We have to put out all the lights in Lebanon. We can shut off their electricity for a year, damage at a cost of billions." Peretz wavered. Wouldn't this result in rockets falling on Haifa and Hadera? he asked. And if we decide on such an aggressive step, wouldn't it be better to deal with the Fajrs first—Hezbollah's long-range missiles—instead of the airport? Halutz favored a quick response. It was important to take advantage of the coming night, he said. Israel had a limited margin of time, two or three days at most, before the international community intervened. He suggested that the return of the abducted soldiers should not be declared as an operational goal. He felt that it was an unrealistic objective. "I'd demand that the Lebanese government return them," Halutz advised Peretz. Where are the soldiers now? Peretz asked. In the best of circumstances, they're in Beirut, Halutz replied, but they also could be in Syria or Iran. Halutz was convinced that the abductees had been transferred across the bridges to the North before they were bombed by the Israeli planes an hour earlier.

The discussion that was held in the defense minister's office at three in the afternoon was of singular importance. In the public debate after the war—the Winograd Commission's interim report, for example—there has been a pronounced tendency to discredit Amir Peretz's part in the events due to his inexperience in defense matters and because he was often manipulated by the generals. But during this crucial discussion, Peretz did in fact play a significant role. It was he who pressed for the harshest possible operation (from the "basket of steps" that the IDF proposed): attacking the Fajr layout, despite warnings that a large number of Lebanese civilians were likely to be injured. Even today, Peretz is proud of this decision and the fact that he made it, despite the admonishments of senior members in the defense establishment regarding the inevitable damage to the Israeli home front and the rear's lack of preparedness. He was not alone in his desire for a harsh response: The chief of staff and generals, and, later that day, the prime minister and government ministers advocated a similar path. But at this critical point, Peretz was the deciding figure.

General Amos Yadlin, head of Israeli Military Intelligence, opened the discussion with an intelligence review. The abduction, he said, was a windfall for Hezbollah. The organization's next trump card was its medium-range rockets. Peretz asked if a preemptive operation was possible. Yadlin and Meir Dagan, the head of the Mossad, answered that the rockets could be destroyed in a preventive air strike. Halutz spoke up: "We suggest attacking tonight up to 50 percent of Lebanon's electric infrastructure and the airport." "What about the missiles?" Peretz asked. "As of now," Eisenkott said, "we suggest not attacking. This will bring fire deep into Israel." Peretz demanded to know whether an attack on Beirut airport would result in the same thing. Less, answered Eisenkott. "If we hit the infrastructure, Hezbollah will be in a dilemma whether to respond." I want to look at this from an Israeli civilian's point of view, Peretz insisted. If a missile falls on Haifa tomorrow, what difference does it make to him why it fell? Halutz: "I want to attack Hezbollah and the Lebanese government. Both of them." The chief of staff stuck to his position in this point: The attack against the Fajrs had to be left to the next stage. Halutz added that he strongly opposed attacking targets inside Syria. Dagan also had reservations. Israel, he claimed, responds reflexively, as it always has. Dagan recommended striking terrorist targets in Syria and forgoing the attack against the Lebanese infrastructure. Let's not unite the Lebanese [against us], he recommended. "Tell me, Yadlin," Peretz asked, "if I was a Christian in Beirut, sitting in the dark, how would I react?" The intelligence head: "You'd be angry at Hezbollah." Peretz disagreed: "Do you know what I'd say? I'd say that Hezbollah was right—those Jews are crazy."

An air strike against the Fajrs, the chief of staff said, citing estimates by the air force's research branch, could result in the death of 100 to 400 civilians—"collateral damage" of "innocent bystanders" in their houses. What do you mean by "innocent bystanders"? asked Shin Bet head Yuval Diskin. These people go to sleep with rockets in their bedrooms. Halutz reminded them that they were speaking of families and children. Hitting them at this point would undermine the international community's support for Israel's moves. Peretz listed the options: Attack only Hezbollah; attack Hezbollah and targets in Syria; attack Hezbollah and the Lebanese infrastructure. The question of the IDF soldier in the South (Shalit), he stated, had receded in urgency. Then he rebuked the officers: The destruction of the Israeli tank in Lebanon had been a disaster waiting to happen. Patrols must be at a higher level of alert. Now "we find ourselves in the aftermath of an event that has put the IDF and the state of Israel into a position that none of us is prepared for." In all the scenarios that we've gone over here, Peretz added, they unleash rockets on Haifa or Hadera and Israel would retaliate with everything they had: "Again we appear as the party waiting for a situation to happen so we can respond to it. We have to stop threatening and start doing things." The defense minister recommended knocking out the Fajrs immediately.

He also approved of bombing the airport but not the power stations. The airfield, he pointed out, could be repaired quickly. Knocking out the electric grid would unify the Lebanese people and turn them against the Israelis. As for the "innocent bystanders," said Peretz, "I don't know what the numbers are, but after the first strike every family will run for their lives, leaving only the missiles behind." He considered the IDF's concern over this to be exaggerated. They were not at the stage where they could play with the "collateral damage," he declared. The operation's objective, he concluded, was to make Hezbollah regret the day it initiated the war, to feel battered and persecuted. Furthermore, Israel would do everything in its power to limit the organization's ability to launch missiles and expand its area of operations.

Even Halutz, who favored attacking at once in the belief that the international community would stop Israel in a few days, admitted at the meeting that the IDF was unable to take out the short-range Katyushas. Major General (Res.) Amos Gilad, head of the Defense Ministry's Political Branch, prophesied: "You're going to have to prepare for a long war without enough shelters in the Galilee. This is a public secret. People will leave [the area] and you'll probably emerge as the losers on this matter. Eventually we'll have to gear up for a ground operation which is bound to be unpopular." There is no trace of Gilad's dire warnings in the summaries of subsequent meetings that day, all headed by Olmert in the prime minister's Kirya bureau. The die had been cast. Peretz concurred—and the heads of the security branches went along with him.

A CALL FROM WASHINGTON

A brief phone call to Washington in the afternoon hours put the final cap on GHQ's original plan and gave the green light to Peretz's proposal. The prime minister spoke with U.S. Secretary of State Condoleezza Rice. The tone was friendly. The Bush administration understood Israel's need to respond in light of the second kidnapping within three weeks. But Rice carefully brought up two American no-gos regarding the Israeli operation: Siniora must not be hurt and the civilian infrastructure must not be bombed. The Americans saw the Lebanese prime minister as a relatively weak but promising leader. He was on a list of "good guys" working against the axis of evil, especially because of his commitment to ousting the Syrians from his country. Olmert accepted both demands in their entirety. As he saw it, the Americans were not asking him to do the impossible. He too feared that damaging the Lebanese infrastructure would lessen the international community's patience with the Israeli response. Olmert explained to his advisors that if Israel crippled the Lebanese infrastructure, the inhabitants of South Lebanon would most likely be driven to embrace Hezbollah, ethnic rifts would intensify, and Hezbollah would emerge as the national defender. He also worried about the effects a massive air strike against power stations would have on the hospitals, the incubators in the premature infant wards, and Lebanon's water supply.

Halutz knew nothing about Olmert's conversation with Washington, but the prime minister had essentially pulled the rug out from under the rationale behind the IDF's plan. In the following weeks, all the chief of staff's requests for approving a strike against the power stations were rejected. In reality, however, the government did allow a strike against civilian targets more than once. During the war, the air force destroyed most of the bridges in southern and central Lebanon, knocked out cellular phone antennas, attacked the Hezbollah television station Al-Manar several times (without once managing to shut down its broadcasts), blasted oil reserves and gasoline stations, and cratered the takeoff and landing lanes of Beirut International Airport. The Bush Administration considered Israel's determination to attack the infrastructure as a huge mistake that reflected Jerusalem's total lack of understanding of Lebanon's domestic reality. Washington failed to see the connection that Halutz and the army made between bombing oil reserves located in Beirut and the war against Hezbollah in South Lebanon. The international community regarded the Israeli bombings as wanton destruction. But senior IDF officers were still not satisfied. They viewed the American veto dictated to them via Olmert as a paralyzing injunction that interfered with their war plan. Until the last days of the campaign, Halutz repeatedly raised the issue of bombing the infrastructure to Olmert and Peretz.

NASRALLAH'S ADVICE

Not only did Hezbollah misjudge the Israeli response, it also underestimated the implications of the abduction of Israeli soldiers in the Lebanese political arena. Nasrallah's defense—that he acted in order to free Lebanese prisoners—failed to defuse the bitter internal criticism against him. At the end of the cabinet meeting that Siniora held in Beirut on the afternoon of July 12, the minister of information, Razi al-Aridi, announced, "The government of Lebanon knew nothing about this morning's incident and is not responsible for it." A list of prominent politicians in Lebanon from the anti-Syrian March 14 camp openly castigated Hezbollah and mentioned its direct link to Damascus and Tehran. Amin Gemayel, the country's former president, stated: "Hezbollah was responsible for dragging all of Lebanon into a military struggle far larger than it could handle. It is inconceivable that Hezbollah has decided on its own that little Lebanon will lead the Arab struggle against Israel, especially given the fact that the Syrians and other Arab states have chosen to maintain absolute silence in their sectors. Why doesn't Syria open a second front against Israel on the Golan Heights? Why is Lebanon, of all countries, [the one to be involved in a shoot-out with Israel]?"

State Department spokesman Shawn McCormick said that the United States was concerned that Lebanese civilians would pay the price for the abduction: "We know that Syria and Iran are trying to jack up tension in the region through the Palestinians and Lebanese."

At 5:00 p.m., Nasrallah held a press conference before scores of journalists gathered in a hall in Beirut. Hezbollah representatives displayed no sign of fear that Israel wanted to eliminate their leader. It was a slick show put on by a politician who had still not digested the fact that he was facing all-out war. "The captured soldiers are in a safe place far from here. The only way of returning them is through indirect negotiations for a prisoner exchange," he said, adding that the operation had been five months in the planning. "We surprised no one. We've been saying for a year that we'd kidnap Israeli soldiers. . . . From the beginning of the year we've placed the capture of soldiers at the top of our priorities in order to bring about the release of Palestinian and Lebanese prisoners." Next he took up the subject of Lebanese prisoners in Israeli jails and told them that they were on their way to freedom. Only two Lebanese prisoners were being held by Israel, Samir Kuntar and Nissim Nasser, but Hezbollah swore that Israel was secretly keeping another Lebanese prisoner, Yihiye Sakaf.[1]

Nasrallah said something else that caused quite a stir in Israel: He would not reject the use of multiple channels in the negotiations for the release of the two soldiers, held by his organization, and for Gilad Shalit, held by Hamas. Israeli security officials interpreted this as Hezbollah's attempt to gain control of the Palestinian track and lead the occupied territories to a more radical line. Then Nasrallah turned to Olmert, Peretz, and Halutz, mocking them for their inexperience. "Olmert is a new prime minister, and the defense minister and chief of staff are also new to their roles. Therefore I want to urge you before you convene a government meeting this evening to seek advice from former prime ministers and ministers about their experiences in Lebanon. When someone is new in office, it's easy to pull the wool over his eyes. Don't let this happen to you. Ask questions, check things through, be certain before you make a decision. . . . You know Hezbollah. The prisoners will be returned and we are prepared for a period of quiet, but we are also ready for confrontation. If [you] want confrontation, get ready for some surprises," he threatened.

In hindsight, Nasrallah's goading words sound like a warning that Israel's leaders should have paid closer attention to. But they also illustrate a missed opportunity on the part of Hezbollah's leadership. Ironically, the person who boasted that he knew how to read the Israelis like the palm of his hand did not dream that their response to the kidnapping would be so devastating. According to Professor Eyal Susser of Tel Aviv University, Nasrallah saw the abduction as a logical move. "He gambled. Israel was the side that changed the game rules. Nasrallah would have been happy to relinquish the pleasure, but he went to war with his head held high."

A Western diplomat posted to Beirut in this period claims that Nasrallah did not foresee war. "Not even in his worst nightmare. Hezbollah's leaders envisioned a medium-intensity confrontation: heavy shelling for a week immediately followed by negotiations. They believed that the abduction would strengthen their position in Lebanon's political arena. If Israel released the Lebanese prisoners, Hezbollah's prestige would swell and the discourse in Lebanon—on disarming the organization—would be forgotten." Another Western diplomat holds that Nasrallah's mistake was understandable: "I know of no state other than Israel that would go to war because of two kidnapped soldiers."[2]

FOUR STEPS FORWARD

The government meeting opened in Tel Aviv shortly after eight that evening. Yadlin, the head of Military Intelligence, reported that "Hezbollah has thousands of rockets of various types and is ready to use them if it felt that the event would not be contained. The rockets can reach the northern Galilee and some can hit even farther. Haifa is definitely within range." Tourism Minister Yitzhak Herzog said that "if there's a possibility of a [missile] response, the home front has to be prepared, the public must be told the truth. The entire Home Front Command and Civil Defense layouts have to be mobilized."

The ministers understood what the heads of the security agencies were saying: A Katyusha attack in the North was to be expected in response to Israeli retaliation. But it was not clear if Israel would advance to another stage in the fighting, and hardly anyone asked what that next stage would be. Looking back, Foreign Minister Tzipi Livni says that she believed at the time that the campaign would be over the next day. Peretz testified to Winograd that he thought a move was being discussed that would continue from ten days to two weeks. According to Olmert's advisors, the prime minister assumed that Lebanon would be pounded from the air for a few days, during which time Israel would weather Katyusha fire until Hezbollah sued for a cease-fire. Of all the ministers taking part in the meeting, only Shimon Peres had the presence of mind to ask, as Barak had advised him in a phone conversation a few hours earlier, what would happen after the Israeli strike. "We have to think two steps ahead," he said. Halutz shot back in a circuitous, smart-aleck way: "I also think four steps ahead, but each step looks to me four times as complicated." With no direct answer forthcoming, Peres kept quiet thereafter. Livni expressed her doubts regarding the operation's goals and recommended concentrating on the demand for Lebanon to implement Security Council Resolution 1559. Her proposal: "A strike short and quick, without harming civilians and no ground operations. . . . And tomorrow morning we'll see if it has to continue." Unable to restrain himself, Halutz replied: "We won't prevent another kidnapping through our inaction."

One of the senior ministers acknowledges that the chief of staff and the IDF failed to present any tangible plan to the government that evening. "All the army did was to give the ministers pep talks. They went on about determination and maintenance of the objective. They [the army] did everything but raise their hands and shout 'hip hip hooray' in unison. The Israeli government decided not to go to war, but to launch an operation that would inform Nasrallah loud and clear—that the time of abductions was over." Minister without Portfolio Eitan Cabel, who resigned from the government after the war, says, "In retrospect, I didn't receive all the necessary information in the first government meeting or the opportunity to get answers. Innocently enough I thought that since we were going to war, each minister would receive a 'war portfolio'—something that would provide us with a perspective." According to Cabel, who still serves in a reserve combat unit, "Prior to each operation in the reserves, no matter how simple it is, the level of preparations is higher than what took place in the government that evening. In every operation we ask what the objective is, where the entry point and retreat routes are, where we're going, who we can expect to encounter. Nobody in the government meeting said: 'These are the objectives, this is the timetable.' We weren't given the necessary information. All we were told was 'Gentlemen we have to end the meeting quickly and approve the plans.' But this was war, not an ordinary operation. The meeting should have lasted ten hours and the political and security levels should have merged, like in a briefing before an operation. The military system should have answered some basic questions: What do you want to achieve and how do you plan to achieve it? Months later, when I learned of the recommendations that Meir Dagan and Amos Gilad had presented—not to embark immediately on an operation—I wanted to wring somebody's neck. These views were not presented to us. Had they been, the government might not have voted unanimously for the operation."

As the meeting came to an end, the ministers voted unanimously for "Israel to move against Hezbollah in a manner that its actions required. . . . Israel would respond aggressively and forcefully against the perpetrators of the [abduction] and the parties responsible for it. There are times when a state must preserve its most vital interests: the security of its civilians and soldiers."

After the meeting, a special forum, delegated by the government to make operative decisions, convened. "The Seven"—the prime minister and six senior ministers: Peretz, Livni, Peres, Mofaz, Eli Yishai, and Avi Dichter— approved Operation Specific Weight for an attack on the Fajr layout. Olmert and his staff felt that the cabinet was too unwieldy (almost 30 people participated, with many ministers and their various advisors) and leaks of classified information were liable to occur, whereas a moderate-size forum might compensate for Peretz's lack of experience. The military men briefly showed the ministers some maps and a list of targets. Attorney General Meni Mazuz was asked about strikes against homes where rockets had been hidden, with the full knowledge that civilians would be killed. Mazuz decided that international law allowed harming civilians when they knowingly dwell in the presence of missiles ("a family with a pet rocket in the living room," as Peretz put it). The foreign minister wanted to know how much time the army needed to complete the task. Halutz answered: "It'll be over tonight. A few hours. Maybe tomorrow morning." In other words tonight and it's finished? Livni asked, trying to get a final answer. The officers replied affirmatively. In addition to approving the attack against the rockets, the government also sanctioned a limited bombing of the infrastructure—the Beirut airport tarmac and the Beirut–Damascus highway—putatively in order to block the kidnappers' escape routes beyond the country's borders. The IDF representatives left the meeting immediately and hurried over to the chief of staff's office, where Halutz had assembled a coterie of senior officers for last-minute instructions. At this point, the air force squadrons received the green light.

GOING TO WAR

On the night of July 12, the Israeli government made the decision to go to war. This was the real meaning of a powerful response to the abduction, although it was apparently not sufficiently clear to the majority of participants who attended the meeting. The chief of staff believed that the battering would last two or three days. Some senior ministers thought it would take even less time. It is doubtful whether Israel ever went to war in so slapdash a fashion. Part of the blame must be placed on the IDF, which failed to convey the probable results of the government's approval to bomb the Fajr rocket emplacements. But it is hard to exonerate the ministers, who exhibited only mild interest in what was happening, and Olmert, who orchestrated the meetings. Naturally there are extenuating circumstances: After Shalit's abduction and the crisis in Gaza, Israel could not allow itself to be subject to so humiliating an attack, this time from the North. Ethically, Israel was fully justified, with universal public support and understanding in the international arena to implement a strong action. The charge that the decision to retaliate was a mistake seems questionable. To a certain degree, Olmert's July 2006 decision to approve an army operation appears sounder than Barak's October 2000 decision to refrain from responding after the Mount Dov kidnapping. Would a powerful Israeli response then have averted a major military operation six years later?

In retrospect, the ministers seem to have approved the move without seriously discussing its implications. The next day, when the air force completed its mission of knocking out the Fajrs, the ministers felt the momentum should continue without letup. Only later did they realize that the IDF had no plans for defeating Hezbollah or countering short-range Katyusha fire. In conversations with ministers who participated in the meeting, it was shocking to hear of the disinterest some displayed toward the details of the war. A few gnashed their teeth. Others sounded nonchalant, as if "it's not our problem but Olmert's and Peretz's." Voting to go to war is one of the most important decisions a government can make. It is a transformational decision, the results of which will bring certain death to many soldiers and civilians on both sides. It demands a meticulous examination in every direction on the crucial questions: What is the aim of the campaign? How can it be attained? What will happen if the operation goes awry? Almost none of the ministers raised these questions at the government meeting. When Peres gingerly asked about the operation's objectives, Halutz brushed him aside. The prime minister pressed other ministers who wanted to contribute their input to hurry up and finish talking in order to allow "the Seven" to discuss operative plans.

Nor should the inexperience of Olmert and Peretz absolve them of responsibility. For decades, Olmert served in high-level offices as a member of Knesset and minister. He had enough time to gain experience in security affairs. As for why he appointed Peretz to the office of defense minister, only Olmert himself knows the reason. On the evening of July 12, most of the ministers who voted for the IDF's proposal to attack the Fajrs were unaware that it was not the army's original recommendation. The IDF turned to the less preferable option on Peretz's instructions, and only after Olmert refused to the idea of bombing Lebanon's infrastructure.

Chief of Staff Halutz, who was aware that most of the senior figures lacked experience, especially on Lebanon, was keen to strike immediately. He didn't mull over a detailed analysis of the power centers in Lebanon. He exuded self-confidence—and the ministers followed him. They did not ask him about the reservists' level of readiness, the level of preparedness on the home front, the chances that a local engagement with Hezbollah might escalate into a major confrontation with Syria. They had no idea that in earlier consultations that day, some generals, such as Eisenkott and Gantz, had recommended mobilizing the reserves. Even in the later stages of the war, the government ministers were not privy to the IDF's internal debates.

The Winograd Commission's interim report, published in April 2007, is probably the most vituperative verdict ever passed on an Israeli prime minister. Ehud Olmert was scourged, and justifiably so, for the curt and slipshod manner in which the July 12 decisions were reached. The prime minister was too hasty. He entered the war impulsively, with the government trailing behind him. But the commission, which took the moral high road, overlooked the very practical considerations that Olmert undoubtedly had to take into account. There was a double challenge here, for Olmert's leadership and for the army's abilities: the second kidnapping on another front in less than three weeks, while the IDF was bogged down in a futile campaign in Gaza in response to Shalit's abduction. Israel had been attacked twice in two different theaters, both of which it had withdrawn from unilaterally in the hope of ending the military conflict. Israel's deterrence in the region had suffered a major blow, and Nasrallah added insult to injury the next day when he lacerated the new leadership for its inexperience. Olmert realized that, from the security and political points of view, he had no alternative but to order a swift and devastating response. And his decisions, the next day and thereafter, won almost universal public support in Israel.

After the publication of the prime minister's testimony to the Winograd Commission, Nachum Barnea, political analyst for *Yediot Ahronot* (Israel's largest daily) wrote that Olmert was mesmerized by a concept. The government meeting had proceeded according to the book, but Olmert had not budged one jot from his position. Chief of staff Yoram Turbovitz told the commission that Olmert believed he had to respond with force, knowing that such a step would increase the risk of a missile attack on the home front. Nevertheless, his fear of not responding was much greater. The prime minister apparently reached a conclusion on the morning of the first day that not responding would have worse consequences; the other conferences that day only served as a rubber stamp to the approach he had already decided on while the IDF completed its preparations for taking out the Fajrs.

The Olmert government's muddled handling of the crisis was not only the result of the leadership skills of the state's captain. The Winograd Commission devotes a large part of the report to the serious structural omissions in Israel's political leadership. Dr. Chuck Freilich, who was the deputy national security advisor at the time, wrote in an article that the decisions of Israeli leaders are motivated by their concern for political survival. Improvisation, disorganized planning, and responses to fleeting events characterize decision making. The prime minister has no staff; ministers are appointed according to their political weight, not their managerial skills; and the government decides according to a prewritten formula, without studying alternatives. The fact that the army is the most organized body gives it greater weight in decision making.

The government, asserts Giora Eiland, former head of the National Security Council, should have deliberated that evening over three alternatives that no one took the trouble to present:

1. A retaliatory air strike lasting one or two days against the strategic infrastructure and long-range launchers (although neither target would return the kidnapped soldiers, they would restore Israeli deterrence vis-à-vis another round of fighting);
2. large-scale ground operations, mobilizing three divisions, training them, and gaining control of territory south of the Litani; and
3. making the strategic decision for a full-scale campaign in Lebanon but, in recognition of the army's need for improvement, waiting for the next Hezbollah provocation and launching an offensive at the time best suited for Israel.

But, during the meeting of July 12, Eiland admits that things went differently. "Intelligence told how bad the Arabs are. The ministers asked the army what it intended to do. The officers answered: We'll attack and see what happens. And that's how it was."

"I REALIZED I WAS INVOLVED"

Close to midnight on July 12, Olmert's media advisor, Asi Shariv, phoned a number of political journalists to deliver a briefing. Where are we going? the journalists asked. This is going to be war, answered Shariv. This analysis was closer to the truth than that of many of the ministers who had just voted for the operation. The next day the headlines on all the major newspapers screamed: "WAR!"

At the time that his son Udi was being abducted, Shlomo Goldwasser was on a business trip in Namibia. Packing for the flight to Durban, he saw the first report of the incident on CNN. He called his daughter-in-law, Karnit, who told him tearfully that Udi was not answering his cell phone. "At that moment," Shlomo recalled, "I realized that I was involved in this thing. This was not a mystical feeling. I saw that two soldiers had been abducted at Zar'it and I knew that Udi was going out on patrols. When I eventually found out the he was one of the abducted soldiers and not dead, I breathed a sigh of relief."

CHAPTER SIX

THE SHIP LEAVES PORT

O PERATION SPECIFIC WEIGHT—the attack on Hezbollah's Fajr missile layout—was Israel's most impressive military action in the second Lebanon war and the crowning point of a six-year operational and intelligence effort. In 34 minutes, in the early hours of July 13, Israeli planes destroyed 59 stationary rocket launchers concealed in the homes of Hezbollah activists and Shiite families in southern Lebanon.[1] It was a devastating blow for Hezbollah. The surprise was complete. The organization never expected the Israel Defense Forces to carry out so massive an air strike, apparently believing that the whereabouts of its Iranian-made rockets remained a safely guarded secret. A huge number of intermediate-range rockets (estimates vary from one-half to two-thirds) were knocked out before they could be fired. Hezbollah's ability to strike deep into Israel—between Afula and Hadera (approximately 90 kilometers from the border)—was significantly impaired. Just as problematic for Nasrallah was the fact that a project as secret as the Fajr stashes was proven transparent, completely visible to Israeli eyes. Credit goes to the Shin Bet, Mossad, and Military Intelligence. All of the Israeli hits in this operation were bull's-eyes. The amount of collateral damage was much lower than the air force's estimates: about 20 Lebanese citizens were killed. After the war, the remnants of only one Iranian rocket, apparently a Fajr-3, fired from Lebanon, were found in Israel (in Haifa). On another occasion, when the air force attacked long-range Zilzal rocket launchers in the Beirut area, one rocket was fired but exploded on the ground just after takeoff. Military analyst Uzi Rubin, who presents these data, poses two possible explanations:

1. The Iranian rocket layout was completely wiped out (which does not square with IDF assessments); or

2. Tehran ordered Hezbollah not to fire Iranian-made rockets at Israeli cities since the sight of the ensuing carnage, in the middle of the international debate on sanctions against Iran's nuclear program, would probably have a counter-effect on Iran's efforts to block sanctions. As an alternative, Hezbollah launched Syrian-made rockets.

At the Thursday, July 13 general headquarters assessment, the head of Military Intelligence's research division, Brigadier General Yossi Beidetz, defined Operation Specific Weight as a singular achievement for Israel. Hezbollah, he said, had been caught off guard. The organization was now "in the stage of internalizing its miscalculation." Nevertheless, he warned, "if we continue hitting Beirut, I would venture that Hezbollah will fire in the direction of Haifa. It is still capable of this." Israel's political and military leaders received news of the attack's success with great satisfaction. Prime Minister Ehud Olmert later said that the removal of the rockets had been "an impressive and perhaps unprecedented achievement." His aides and advisors went so far as to compare it to another, more famous preemptive strike: the destruction of still-grounded Arab air forces on the first day of the Six-Day War. In the coming days, Israeli jets struck at a large number of Zilzal launchers deployed in the Beirut area. The IDF's dazzling success in knocking out the launchers and rockets intoxicated the leadership. Olmert and Defense Minister Amir Peretz seemed to consider the air strike incontestable proof of their boldness and savvy. Their decision to raise the ante had produced the bombing success. The IDF and especially the Israeli Air Force had again demonstrated that they could be counted on. According to the conventional wisdom emanating from the leaders' offices, in a few days Hezbollah would come begging for a cease-fire. And if this was the prognosis, then all the more reason to continue ravaging the terrorist organization.

Just as the chiefs of the Intelligence agencies had predicted, Hezbollah reacted to the air strike with heavy Katyusha barrages beginning in the morning of July 13. The inhabitants of the Israeli border settlements were prepared and had been in bomb shelters and security rooms for the previous 24 hours. But the missile salvos that landed farther south came without any prior warning from the Home Front Command, shocking the population. That day Hezbollah shot off nearly 125 Katyushas. Two Israeli citizens, a woman in Nahariya and a man in Safed, were killed; 69 people, including 2 soldiers, were wounded. Safed, a city that had not experienced Katyusha fire since the end of the first Lebanon war, came under heavy shelling. One of the first attacks occurred in mid-afternoon while Amir Peretz was visiting the Northern Command's headquarters, close to the city. The minister's bodyguards hurried him into the command pit until the danger abated and his helicopter flight was postponed. The reporters who dashed to the sites where the Katyushas had fallen immediately recognized that the missiles were not the Qassam rockets they were familiar with from Sderot. Unlike the Palestinians' Qassams, every Katyusha hit caused immense damage and often fatalities. Next to Safed, on Mount Meron, a large forest fire raged out of control. That month many such wildfires caused by the rockets would gut other woodlands in the Galilee. Every few minutes the alarm went off in the city. Dazed citizens caught outdoors sought shelter under the plastic awnings of stores like tourists in a midsummer rainstorm.

THE EXIT PLAN

The IAF's round-the-clock bombing on Thursday surprised Foreign Minister Tzipi Livni. From meetings with the government and the Seven on the previous night, she believed that the operation would probably be over by that afternoon at the latest. At noon, while Israeli jets were pounding Lebanon, Livni met with U.S. representatives to the Middle East, David Welch and Elliot Abrams. The foreign minister told the two Americans that Israel had to respond to the abduction. "Tell me, my friends, do you think a situation can be created in which the Lebanese army deploys in the south and Siniora is given the key?" The Americans kept silent. Another proposal that was broached during the conversation was the deployment of NATO (North Atlantic Treaty Organization) forces in South Lebanon. That evening, Livni spoke with Olmert by phone. In her testimony before the Winograd Commission she stressed that she told Olmert that since the military objectives had been completed, the time had come to find a political way out. According to Livni's statements, she believed that "on Thursday noon we were in the best position we could have been. . . . Therefore at this point I didn't want any deterioration and said let's begin [the exit. . .]. The prime minister told me not to worry and to calm down." There is no record of this conversation except for what Livni later wrote in her notebook. Olmert's staff denies that the prime minister ever heard such things from Livni that day. Livni relied on the supporting evidence of her media advisor, who did not actually hear the full conversation (he heard Livni's side) but only stated that it took place. Livni's conversations in the following days testify to her tireless efforts to reach a speedy end to the military operations. The big question is: To what degree did she make an effort to express her position to Olmert?

In the Foreign Office, at least, Livni continued her efforts to reach an agreement. The idea of an exit plan first emerged in Israel in the evening of July 13. The core feature of the plan—an international presence in South Lebanon—came up in a chance conversation between Livni's policy advisor, Tal Becker, and the director of the foreign ministry, Aharon Abramovitch, who was responsible for "the convergence file" in the West Bank (another issue in which the involvement of international forces was being weighed). Becker was asked if he thought the crisis in Lebanon could be solved with the help of Western countries. Despite his youth (he was 33), Becker was regarded as one of the shrewdest diplomatic and legal brains in the Foreign Ministry. Due to his previous role as legal advisor to the Israeli delegation to the United Nations and his service in the military as an attorney, Becker was familiar with the issue of international involvement. That night, Livni instructed him to prepare the first draft of an exit plan for discussion in the ministry. On Friday morning, Becker and Abramovitch presented the plan's basic principles to Livni and other senior Foreign Ministry officials.

The document stated:

The war will end after a Security Council decision that alters the situation in Lebanon and leads to the implementation of Resolution 1559 and removal of Hezbollah from the south. The Security Council resolution will have to include the following principles:

1. No armed militias in the south.
2. A change in UNIFIL's (United Nations Interim Force in Lebanon) mandate allowing it to act according to Article 7 of the United Nations Charter—opening fire so it can perform its missions.
3. The Lebanese army will immediately deploy in the south and be supported by UNIFIL (or some other international force stationed in the south).
4. Demilitarization of the area between the Litani River and Israeli border.
5. Hezbollah will be disarmed in accordance with an arranged plan and supervisory mechanism.

6. Israel and Lebanon will set up a security-political coordination mechanism.
7. The international community will grant assistance to Lebanon in accordance with the progress made in implementing Resolution 1559 (Hezbollah's disarmament).
8. The United Nations will enforce an arms embargo on the non-government militias in Lebanon.
9. A cease-fire will go into effect.
10. The secretary-general of the United Nations will submit a report on the implementation of the resolution.[2]

Israel wanted additional conditions: condemnation of Hezbollah's surprise attack; acknowledgment of the Iranian and Syrian connection to the abduction; a call to release the captive soldiers and respect Lebanon's sovereignty; and categorizing Hezbollah as an armed militia and specifically stating that Hezbollah is a terrorist organization with links to Syria and Iran.

In the meeting with Livni, the disadvantages of such a resolution were also discussed: The IDF's freedom to operate might be hamstrung. Doubts were voiced regarding the ability of the Lebanese army and UNIFIL to stop Hezbollah's gradual return to the South. According to the exit plan, France and the United States would jointly initiate the resolution, together with the support of the UN Secretary-General. (There was no mention of Israel's involvement.) Most of the principles in the document, which was formulated two days after the war erupted, appeared in another version—Security Council Resolution 1701—that was passed four weeks and 100 deaths later.

The Foreign Ministry was not alone. On July 16, Israel's National Security Council presented the prime minister with a document stating that the military operation had attained its objective and the time had come to end the war as quickly as possible. In the war's first week, Ehud Barak (ex-Prime Minister) and Dan Meridor (ex-minister), neither of whom served in any official capacity during the war, held phone conversations with a number of political analysts and expressed grave doubts over the direction that Olmert and Peretz had taken. Meridor warned that the decision to continue the bombing would lead to a catastrophe. He mentioned the security concept in the report that a committee he chaired had presented to the government a few months before: Israel lacks an answer to steep-trajectory weapons. Barak, too, spoke with Olmert and suggested trying to end the hostilities as early as possible. He argued that without additional training, the IDF was unready to tackle the Katyushas and its failure to do so would seriously erode Israel's deterrent strength. Yet neither man had significant influence on the government's decision making, nor did either go public with his recommendations. Livni, too, could not have known that the number-two figure in GHQ held the same views as hers. While Chief of Staff Dan Halutz was reassessing the situation and, after observing that the fighting was not about to end, advised "taking a deep breath and looking a few days, if not weeks, ahead,"[3] his deputy, Major General Moshe Kaplinsky, took a completely different tone. Between Friday and Monday (July 14–17), Kaplinsky held a number of private talks with Halutz, in which he urged his boss to look for an exit strategy. "If the air attacks go on and we don't receive permission to mobilize the reserves, we'll have to sit down with the political echelons and ask them how to get out of this. The air force has just about used up all of its known targets. This will result in our inflicting heavy civilian losses in Lebanon, as happened in the Kfar Qana massacre in 1996." In one of the HQ meetings, Kaplinsky said that now was time for "Olmert to phone Condie [Condoleezza Rice] and see how we can reach a deal with Siniora and end this story." Halutz felt that it was too early to discuss this. "Forget about the end mechanisms for now, we are two weeks away," he said. Only on Monday, after another private talk with his deputy, did he agree to appoint a military team headed by Kaplinsky (and including Brigadier General Beidetz and the chief of the Strategic Branch, Brigadier General Udi Dekel) to deal with a possible end to the fighting. The first time Olmert saw Kaplinsky's ideas was on July 23, the same day he was handed Livni's first document.

Months later, a former chief of staff, Amnon Lipkin-Shahak, said that Halutz's charisma and domineering personality, combined with most ministers' lack of pertinent information, created a lethal concoction. "We didn't speak with the government in terms of a victory," General Eisenkott recalled after the war. "Victory was of no relevance in this story. What was important was the disproportionate smashing of Hezbollah and implementation of Resolution 1559. We realized that we couldn't return the abducted men by military means." But this wisdom, even if obvious to the high-ranking officers, was not expressed to the ministers, who were enthralled by the general euphoria of a mighty Israel exacting revenge on its enemies. Speaking to high school pupils in Nahariya in April 2007, Eisenkott said, "The operation had been planned to take four to six days, but things got out of control.

Instructions were issued for a limited operation against limited targets, but we were unable to limit the duration of the fighting."

MEANWHILE, BACK IN LEBANON

I'm so tired and there's so much to report on from Beirut. The streets are empty, except for some strange Philippine maid walking a dog, some clean-up men and a few taxi drivers looking for customers. The shelves in the supermarkets are completely nude, people having stored up on all basic goods. A long line of cars at the gas station. It turns out there's a six-hour wait at the Syrian border. People pay $450 to leave the country by taxi. The electricity will probably be shut off soon. Over fifty Lebanese were killed today and the people of Beirut are deeply concerned about the loss of income from Saudi tourism. . . . Israeli planes fly overhead. I only saw the anti-aircraft fire and heard what sounded like thunder. Here they come again. The electricity just went off. Dogs are barking like crazy. The planes seem to return every twenty minutes or so for another bombing run. Now it seems like every five minutes.

—Emily, a Lebanese blogger, reporting from Beirut,
Thursday morning, July 13, 2006[4]

The bombing of Beirut's airport runways on the night of July 12 paralyzed air traffic to and from Lebanon. Many tourists, mostly from Gulf countries, were stranded in Lebanon after the IAF fired on the Beirut–Damascus road. On Friday, July 14, nearly 17,000 people entered Syria via the al-Masna crossing after managing to reach it on foot. But that evening the crossing was bombed by the IAF. The United States and European countries set about extricating tens of thousands of their nationals, many of whom also held Lebanese citizenship. These people had emigrated to the West and were now in Lebanon on summer vacation. Two days after the war broke out, Lebanon's minister of tourism, Joe Sarkis, said that the tourist industry would lose billions of dollars.

The number of Lebanese casualties—the vast majority of whom were civilians—climbed higher and higher. In the first days of the fighting, 45 people were killed; by the end of the fifth day, the number had risen to 153. Arab television broadcast pictures of the carnage from areas that had been bombed from the air. Early Thursday morning the parents and eight children of the Akash family were killed in a private house near the city of Nabatea in the south. The father was a Shiite imam (Muslim religious leader) and the house was hit during an IAF strike against Fajr rockets. Israeli aircraft blew up a bus filled with refugees fleeing to Tyre from the southern village of Marwahin. Twenty-one people were killed, and the pictures of the lacerated bodies were telecast worldwide.

But even the photographs of civilian casualties—the result of Israel's air offensive—failed to swerve public opinion in Lebanon or the Arab world toward support of Hezbollah. In fact, the opposite was true. The scope of criticism in Lebanon of Hezbollah, at least in the first 48 hours of the war, was unprecedented. In a television interview, Druze leader Walid Junbalatt claimed that the time had come for Hezbollah to say loud and clear if its decisions were made by the Lebanese people or if it was carrying out Syrian and Iranian instructions that Lebanon paid the price for. "What's happening now in Lebanon is, among other things, Tehran's answer to the international community on the Iranian nuclear issue," he charged.[5] Hezbollah and Syria viewed these statements as an attempt to encourage Israel to continue its attack on the organization, charges that turned out to be true: Members of the March 14 movement were against a cease-fire. A Western diplomat, who spoke with several people in the anti-Syrian camp in Lebanon in the first days of the war, says that most of them looked favorably on Israel's action. "Siniora's people went even further. They were downright happy to see Israel attacking Hezbollah. Top leaders in the March 14 camp asked the United States to see to it that Israel did not end the war after only a few days. This was an open secret in Beirut. Like the Israelis, the Lebanese believed that the IDF would dramatically weaken Hezbollah. Lebanon's leaders thought the Israeli offensive would exhaust Hezbollah and make it hard for it to retain its arsenal. It was a case of merging Lebanon's seething anger at the organization for starting the war and the heartfelt hope that Israel would help rid them of this pestilence." The diplomat also claimed that Israel was aware of Lebanese expectations. According to one Israeli official, "All of the March 14 people wanted to see the liquidation of Hezbollah. They understood that only an Israeli military operation would lead to the organization's disarmament." In this light, Dan Halutz disappointed not only Olmert and Peretz but also Fouad Siniora and Sa'ad a-Din Hariri.

BOMBING DAHIA

In Israel, "the Seven" met for a second time on Friday afternoon. The prime minister asked his senior ministers to approve another critical stage in the campaign: bombing Dahia in southern Beirut (especially two buildings, one of which housed Hezbollah's headquarters and the other, Nasrallah's private residence). Ten minutes before the meeting, Olmert had a short talk with his transport minister, Shaul Mofaz. Given Peretz's lack of experience and unfamiliarity with military operations, Olmert preferred to ask Mofaz, a former chief of staff, for his opinion. But during the war, relations between the two men soured because of the unsatisfactory results in the fighting and Olmert's unwillingness to accept Mofaz's advice. The prime minister showed Mofaz the IDF's plan to attack Dahia. Are there still any civilians around? Mofaz wanted to know. Olmert answered that according to Military Intelligence, all the civilians had abandoned the quarter after Israel's 24-hour warnings that it intended to attack. "If so," Mofaz replied, "there's no problem." Olmert left the table and called the chief of staff, who (unknown to Mofaz) was sitting in the next room: "We attack tonight, make the necessary preparations. The Seven will give its approval at the next meeting." Thus it is clear that Olmert entered the discussion (with the Seven) having already decided on the strike. At this point he had little patience for other opinions.

The foreign minister had the same impression of Olmert's attentiveness to other views. "I arrived at the meeting feeling that they listen to me less and less," Livni testified before the Winograd Commission. "When I began speaking, the prime minister started talking with the chief of staff or someone. I held my tongue and he said, 'Go ahead.' I said, "'Thanks, I haven't finished, I want you to hear me out.' Then the prime minister said, 'I'm listening to every word you say, to every vibration.'" The ministers came away with the sense that, like Olmert, the IDF officers were impatient to end the discussion and get to the bombing. The ministers were told that the planes' engines were revving up on the runway. Still, two ministers remained opposed to the attack. Livni wanted to know what a strike on the Shiite quarter would gain and if the Israeli home front was sufficiently prepared for Hezbollah's expected response. General Eisenkott answered, "Everything is ready." Livni insisted, "The operation will not end by military means. Hezbollah will not willingly get up and leave. Goals must be set. The operation won't bring the soldiers back. The solution can only be a political one." Avi Dichter took another line of reasoning. "Since Hezbollah is already under pressure, blasting away at Dahia is liable to harm innocent civilians, which would play into Hezbollah's hands and cause the international community to withdraw its support of Israel. The bombings should remain concentrated in South Lebanon. On the other hand, if the refugees from the south arrive in Beirut only to find that the capital is also destroyed, Lebanese solidarity will be strengthened." Olmert again urged the ministers to be brief. The Sabbath was about to begin, and Eli Yishai (of the religious Shas party) was itching to leave. Dichter refused to cut short what he was saying in order to observe the Sabbath. Yishai was insulted. "This matter is too serious," Dichter asserted. "I want to present my points." Like Livni, he too felt that Olmert saw his arguments as a waste of time. A high-ranking officer butted in: "An attack on Dahia will shorten the campaign." Dichter immediately took issue with him, saying, "There's no indication of this. Prove it! It's an attack on real estate—and real estate by its nature will remain where it is after [the attack]." But the minister of internal security realized that no one was listening. Everybody wanted to wind up the meeting and go home for the Sabbath, he said later.

Four members of the forum voted in favor of bombing Dahia (Shimon Peres, who was not present, telephoned his support). Two ministers, Dichter and Livni, were opposed. The military benefits of the bombing were marginal. Nasrallah, ensconced in a bunker beneath his residence, was protected by enough layers of cement to avoid injury. But Dahia was a symbol, and Israel's ministers and officers wanted a move that would deliver a painful surgical blow to Hezbollah's strength and honor. Although this was not specifically stated at the meeting, some participants realized that an attack on Dahia presaged all-out war against Hezbollah. The idea of "bang and it's over" increasingly receded.

Dichter received an update on the air strike on his way home to Ashkelon. When he reached his house, he turned on the TV and began to surf the networks. Israel's three major channels were televising a press conference with Dan Halutz. Only then did Dichter suspect why he was asked to hurry up and finish what he was saying. Olmert and Halutz may not have been worried about the approaching Sabbath after all. The chief of staff's press conference was scheduled for eight in the evening, prime time—and perhaps the two leaders wanted to present the results. The minister of internal security felt cheated. "As I saw it," Dichter noted after the war, "the attack on Dahia was a fatal mistake that only complicated the campaign."

HANIT IN FLAMES

The attack on Dahia did not come as a surprise to Lebanon. The previous morning—Friday—the Israeli media reported that the IAF was planning to bomb the neighborhood. Tens of thousands of residents fled to Beirut's northern neighborhoods. A little after 2 p.m., al-Manar broadcast a special bulletin—a Hezbollah threat: "We will bomb Haifa if the southern neighborhood of Beirut is attacked. . . . This will be a new situation in the region and Israel alone will be responsible for it." Simultaneously a similar message was conveyed to Jerusalem through diplomatic channels: "Without an immediate cease-fire Israel can expect surprises." The air pounding of Dahia began in the early evening of July 14. Israeli planes leveled the multistory buildings where Hezbollah headquarters were located, causing enormous damage. The area was transformed into a sea of rubble. Among the main targets was al-Manar's building, which was totally destroyed this time. But the station continued transmitting from a secret location where it was linked to three Arab satellites. A Western diplomat in contact with Hezbollah members recalls that this was the first time since the war started that he detected anxiety in their voices.

But Hassan Nasrallah was far from caving in to pressure. At 8:45 p.m., in the middle of Halutz's press conference, Nasrallah appeared on al-Manar. In a telephone speech that was also broadcast live on Israeli television, Nasrallah asked the people of Beirut to look to the west, to the Mediterranean across from the city's shores. "The vessel that bombed Beirut will now be demolished," he promised. A few minutes earlier, a C-802 missile—the Iranian version of a shore-to-ship missile originally developed in China—slammed into the Israeli missile boat *Hanit*, one of the Israeli navy's most advanced vessels. Four sailors were killed but the boat remained afloat. According to some claims, the missile was fired with the help of Iranian Revolutionary Guards—an elite Iranian military unit.

N., an Arab journalist living in Beirut during the war, remembers that hundreds of people went to the coast that evening. "This was the turning point in Lebanese public opinion. We saw flames on the sea and realized like everyone else that he [Nasrallah] had spoken the truth, not like other Arab leaders who tended to vaunt capabilities that they didn't have. Nasrallah kept his word. The targeting of the Israeli missile boat strengthened popular support of Hezbollah. In the following days you sensed Lebanese solidarity: Sunnis hosted Shiite refugees; even Christians in wealthy neighborhoods treated Shiites cordially. Suddenly there was a feeling of national pride in Hezbollah, which had stood up to Israel and bloodied her. The criticism was aimed at Hariri junior and his band of followers."

A few hours after the Dahia air strike, Nasrallah came on al-Manar again and declared, "This is total war that Israel is waging, revenge for the past. You will very soon discover how much your new government is stupid and inexperienced." Addressing Israel's citizens, he said, "You say you believe me. Then listen closely. Our patience is worn out. You wanted war? Alright then, we've been preparing for such a war. Believe me, the response will reach much further than Haifa. The equation 'Beirut-Haifa' is no longer valid. It is you who have violated it and you who will pay the price. You wanted a change in the game rules—you will get it."

Despite these threats, Israel continued attacking Dahia's "security quadrant" throughout Saturday and Sunday. Scores of other targets were also hit, some close to the Syrian border. At the same time, the air force dispersed leaflets calling on the inhabitants of South Lebanon to leave their homes. Hundreds of thousands fled. Still, dozens of civilians were killed in the air strikes.

THE ARAB QUARTET

Despite the improvement in Lebanese public opinion toward him, Nasrallah still had problems to contend with, first and foremost because of the large Arab states. Saudi Arabia's announcement on the night of July 12, after the abduction, came as an unwelcome surprise to Hezbollah's leadership. The fact that the Royal House of Saud and Rafiq Hariri had been among its closest friends supporting the March 14 camp was a well-known fact. But the wording of the Saudi announcement exceeded the usual rules of the game in the Arab world. "There's a difference between legitimate opposition and reckless adventurism perpetrated by elements in the state working without the government's knowledge. . . . The time has come for these elements and they alone, to bear responsibility for their actions, since it is their adventurism which is liable to bring ruination down on all the Arab sates." A Hezbollah spokesman, Hussein Rachel, admitted to al-Jazeera that his organization had been stunned by the Saudi condemnation. "Hezbollah is currently studying the Saudi position and will respond later," muttered the confused spokesman.

On noon Friday, King Abdullah of Jordan arrived in Cairo for an unplanned meeting with President Hosni Mubarak. At its conclusion, the two leaders issued a joint statement that, along with the standard criticism of Israel's aggression in Lebanon, again left little margin for misinterpretation: "We condemn the irresponsible escalatory acts that have the potential of leading the region into a dangerous situation." On Saturday, during an Arab League summit meeting in Cairo attended by foreign ministers, the rift in the Arab world finally came out in the open. The Saudi foreign minister, Saud al-Feisal, termed Hezbollah's acts as "unexpected, dishonorable and irresponsible. They will put the region back years and are utterly unacceptable." Egyptian foreign minister Ahmed Aboul Gheit and his Jordanian counterpart, Abdullah al-Khatib, concurred with the Saudis' rebuke. Kuwait and the United Arab Emirates also criticized the "dangerous adventure." The only diplomat who went out of his way to defend Hezbollah was Syrian foreign minister Walid Muallem. He shouted at his Saudi colleague: "How can we come here to discuss the burning situation in Lebanon when condemnations are being voiced against the resistance? Syria will agree to nothing that Israel can exploit for its own purposes."[6] The debate ended without a decision, but, according to Hassan Izz al-Din, a senior member of the organization in South Lebanon, Hezbollah now realized that "an Arab and international plot was afoot, along with forces in Lebanon, that was designed to liquidate us."

The Arab Quartet—Saudi Arabia, Egypt, Jordan, and the Gulf emirates—that formed that Saturday in Cairo was more concerned with Iran's intentions than Hezbollah's. The latter's recent provocations merely highlighted in bold relief the fracture lines that already defined the Arab and Muslim world, especially against the background of the savage war being waged between the Shiites and Sunnis in Iraq and the ongoing tension between Iran and the moderate Sunni countries of the crescent, first and foremost Saudi Arabia. The moderate countries feared that Tehran and its radical president, Mahmoud Ahmadinejad, wanted to return to the failed idea of the 1980s—the exportation of the Islamic Revolution—first by completing the revolution in Lebanon and then by increasingly fomenting extremist Islamic groups in the moderate Muslim countries to revolt against the government.

From the Quartet's point of view, Hezbollah had presented Israel with an opportunity to block Iran's rise before it was armed with nuclear weapons. But the Arab Quartet was not satisfied with declarations. In the following days, Saudi Arabia and Jordan denied access across their airspace to Iranian planes on the way to Syria with weapons designated for Hezbollah. Saudi religious sages pronounced that "Hezbollah is not the 'Party of God' [the meaning of the organization's name in Arabic], but the 'Party of Satan.'" A senior Israeli source says that a Saudi delegation visiting Washington in this period was asked by its State Department hosts if the Bush administration should put pressure on Israel to end the fighting. After consultation with Egypt, the Saudis explained that there was no reason to hurry. Even Israel received messages in a similar spirit. Arab ambassadors to the United Nations from the moderate Arab states begged the Israeli delegation to "break Hezbollah's spine." A high-level Israeli official smiled sheepishly and tried to outline the situation in a more diplomatic way. The Arab Diplomats cut him short: "Finish with them now and get it over with as quickly as possible." In conversations after the war, Arab diplomats described Hezbollah and its links to Iran and Syria in crude and acrimonious terms. "But," they said, "Israel had to limit its activity in Lebanon to raids or assassinations. Once the operation turns into the pulverization of South Lebanon, you've hurt your friendship with Egypt, Jordan, and Saudi Arabia which are against Hezbollah."

TARGET: DAMASCUS

In Washington, the Saudis' criticism of Hezbollah, Iran, and Syria was interpreted as a great change. Senior figures in the administration, especially the hawks—Vice President Dick Cheney's staff and the National Security Council—viewed the war as an opportunity to dispose of Bashar Assad's regime in Damascus. This direction had already been brought up on the day after the abduction when President George W. Bush stated, "Syria is responsible for what's happening and must be dealt with." Bush also noted that Syria was aiding Hamas and Hezbollah. "Israel has the right to defend itself, but the Lebanese government does not have to be weakened."

In the first days of the fighting, the gaps between Washington's and Jerusalem's perception of the war were glaring. As the IDF was bombing Hezbollah and to a limited degree the Lebanese infrastructure, the Bush administration was hunting for Assad's head. On several occasions, the Americans told the Israeli ambassador in Washington, Dani Ayalon, and the Israeli military attaché, Major General Dan Harel, that the problem was Syria. "'Why aren't you thinking about Syria? The trail leads to Syria.' This mantra was repeated in several talks," recalls a senior Israeli official. "Every time Israel issued a mollifying statement to the effect that it had no intention of attacking Syria, Washington was in an uproar. 'Bashar will think you're scared of him,'" they said. Secretary of State Condoleezza Rice saw the events in an entirely different light. In a briefing to journalists, she claimed that the war offered an opportunity to remove Syria from the axis of evil. Two senior State Department officials, Nick Burns and David Welch, also came out against the neoconservative position, asserting that the United States had to provide a calming influence in the Middle East and not stir up wars.[7] "Eventually Rice buckled under to the dictates of Cheney and Bush that there was no talking with Syria," says an American news analyst. On Sunday afternoon, July 16, Rice announced, "This is not the time for a cease-fire. This is not the way to solve the problem." Her staff made it clear to Israel that as long as the IDF refrained from hurting Fouad Siniora and reduced the death toll among Lebanese civilians, the United States would provide full backing for the continuation of the military operation.

A former highly-placed official in the U.S. Defense Department says that the administration still regarded Iraq as the main problem. "The war in Lebanon gave Washington an easy opportunity to stick it to the Iranians who had brazenly intervened in Iraq and Syria and were assisting the terrorist cells operating against the American army. Everyone hoped that Israel would do their work for them. Congress was unanimously in support of Israel, and the White House informed Israel that it had nothing to worry about if Syria attacked. On the other hand, the administration viewed Siniora as a symbol of the efforts in the democratization of the Middle East and the struggle against the axis of evil. From Washington's point of view, the problems began after a few days when no one had a clear picture of where Israel was heading."

The French were less forthcoming than the Americans. "Although nobody in France would be sorry to see Hezbollah crushed," says a French diplomat, "our concern regarding the future of the Siniora government grew with every day that passed. The Lebanese prime minister spoke with Paris dozens of times and conveyed a message to Jerusalem through us: 'You're destroying us and strengthening Hezbollah.' But the Israelis persisted stubbornly." Two days after the kidnapping, in a Bastille Day speech, the president of France, Jacques Chirac, declared, "There will be no military solution to this conflict. . . . The Israeli response is disproportionate." He called for an end to hostile actions by both sides and the release of the soldiers. According to an American diplomat, the French played a double game: "They had to appear as the official backer of Lebanon, but they also listened to the demands of the March 14th camp that Israel continue pounding Hezbollah."

PINNACLE OF SUPPORT

On July 16, the G-8 Conference—the summit meeting of the leaders of the world's eight most powerful industrial states—came to a close in Saint Petersburg in Russia. The concluding statement (whose wording President Chirac accepted even though two days earlier he had condemned Israel) was the most significant declaration of support that Israel received since the onset of the fighting four days earlier. The statement cast full responsibility on Hamas and Hezbollah for the region's crisis: "We must not allow extremist elements and their supporters to sow chaos in the Middle East and incite larger clashes." The G-8 leaders called on Israel to avoid injuring civilians and infrastructure that would undermine the stability of the Lebanese government. The announcement also demanded the implementation of Security Council Resolution 1559 and called on the Security Council to draft a plan for its full implementation. The leaders also called on the Lebanese army to deploy in the south of the country and proposed examining the idea of stationing an international force in the region. Israel and Lebanon were asked to open up a political dialogue. Israel welcomed the concluding statement, which incorporated every one of its demands.[8]

That morning, the Israeli Foreign Ministry began discussing the possible deployment of a foreign military force in Lebanon. Israel's Channel 2 reported the proposal and caused a considerable political firestorm that evening. The Prime Minister's Office was furious over the disclosure and rejected the idea. Two days later, Olmert issued an official response: A multinational force in Lebanon "is a good headline but our experience has shown that there's nothing behind it. Right now there's a multinational force in Lebanon (UNIFIL) and look what they're doing." The Prime Minister's Office made it clear that Israel agreed to the Lebanese army's deployment in the south but would oppose the presence of any other force. Some in the Foreign Ministry are still convinced that Olmert opposed the idea because it did not emanate from his office first, but there is no evidence to support that view. The rare international support, as expressed in the G-8 announcement, boosted the confidence of Olmert and Peretz and cemented their conviction that the attack on Lebanon had to continue. The debate over the exit plan being drafted by the Foreign Ministry was put on hold for a week until Rice's arrival in the region and the start of her shuttle diplomacy. By then, the names of two Lebanese villages in the south, Maroun a-Ras and Bint-J'Bayel, were familiar in every Israeli household.

ISRAEL'S CHURCHILL

Ariel Sharon had never been good at making speeches. In his last years as prime minister, it was obvious that he found public speaking an increasingly difficult task. He would fix his stare on the written text, get through the words with a jowly heaviness, and miss the places he was supposed to stop for emphasis. As an orator, at least, his successor, Ehud Olmert, may be considered a great improvement. Two months before the war, when Olmert appeared in Washington before both houses of Congress, he made a powerful impression with his fluency, sagacity, and cogent reasoning. In the Knesset on July 17, he was ready for the speech of his life. Five days after the outbreak of war, the Israeli parliament convened for a special session. The atmosphere was overtly patriotic. Even the opposition leader, Binyamin Netanyahu, lent his full support to the government's policy toward Hezbollah. "Fight them, bash them, smash them," he told the ministers. Netanyahu had his own message for the Lebanese: "Don't mess with us. Nobody fires missiles at us."

The prime minister's speech was later described as "Churchillian." "There are moments in the life of a nation," Olmert said, "when it is compelled to look directly into the face of reality and say 'no more!'" He described the fighting as a two-front campaign, Lebanon and the Gaza Strip. Israel, he continued, "will not be held hostage—not by terror gangs or by a terrorist authority or by any sovereign state. . . . We will search every compound, target every terrorist who assists in attacking the citizens of Israel and destroy every terrorist infrastructure, everywhere. We will persist until Hezbollah and Hamas comply with those basic and decent things required of them by every civilized person." Olmert said that the pictures of the three abductees were hanging on the wall in his office and embedded in the wall of his heart. "I do not forget them for one minute. They were there on our behalf and for our state. We will do everything and make every effort to bring them home, we will do this, but not in a pattern that will encourage more kidnappings." He listed the conditions for ending the fighting: return of the kidnapped soldiers, an unconditional cease-fire, deployment of the Lebanese army in the entire south of the country, and the ouster of Hezbollah from the south according to Resolution 1559.

The media went wild. A leader is born, the press boomed the next day. Scores of articles were published over the following days, praising Olmert for his coolness under fire, his determination and common sense. Even Israel's citizens were impressed. Surveys taken that week revealed that 78 percent of the public was pleased with the prime minister's conduct, 72 percent with the defense minister's performance, and 87 percent with the IDF, despite the abduction and attack on the missile boat. Amir Peretz, however, was somewhat uneasy—not only because of the army's performance, but because the prime minister alone appeared to be reaping all the credit for the successful military operation. On Monday, reporters who spoke with members of the Knesset (MKs) close to Peretz heard that the minister had asked their advice on how to spotlight his part in the campaign and not concede the whole "show" to Olmert.

Ironically, what was perceived at the time as the height of Israeli resolve now, with the wisdom of hindsight and the advantageous position of knowing how the plot ends, seems like the nadir. The Winograd Commission asked Olmert why he presented the return of the abductees as a condition for ending the fighting. Didn't he realize that the threshold of expectation was too high? His answer: "Some things are said because they have to be said." He acknowledged that he had to consider the mood of the public sitting in the bomb shelters and instill a ray of hope for the soldiers' return. "I didn't take into account that one day I'd have to face a commission of inquiry and explain exactly what I meant on July 17." Olmert's statement regarding conditions for a cease-fire was received with a degree of surprise in Beirut, too. A Western diplomat who was in close contact with Hezbollah during the war testified that "until around July 17 the organization was prepared to make serious concessions in order to end the conflict. They suffered a heavy beating in Israel's opening round. But the chance was lost because of Olmert's public diplomacy. Hezbollah are not fools. They understood that the two stipulations that Olmert presented (the return of the kidnapped soldiers and the death blow to Hezbollah) were too high a threshold for ending the war. The Lebanese realized that Olmert didn't know how to play cards. Any amateur could see that. The moment he set unattainable stipulations, Hezbollah only had to dig in, stiffen its position, hang on till the end of the war, and then present itself as the victor. You Israelis knew so much about Hezbollah, how could you have made the mistake in thinking that the adversary facing you resembled the Palestinians? Your prime minister played into Hezbollah's hands with his official declarations—and he appeared to believe in them."

Even if we accept the prime minister's position that the devastating response to the July 12 kidnapping was necessary, perhaps unavoidable, on July 16 and 17, Israel seemed to have had an opportunity for a strategic exit from the campaign. According to eyewitnesses in Beirut, Hezbollah incurred heavy losses, especially in its intermediate- and long-range missile layouts. The IAF attacked most of its prescribed targets and had a limited ability to continue to cause real damage to Hezbollah (Olmert rejected Halutz's recommendation to bomb the civilian infrastructure.) International support for Israel seems to have been at its highest since the Six-Day War. Even the moderate Arab states and elements in the Lebanese government expressed their deep understanding of Israel's steps. In his July 15 speech, Siniora presented a reasonable framework for concluding the fighting, and for the first time he agreed to deploy his army in the south. Senior officials in the Israeli Foreign Ministry as well as the deputy chief of staff and number of high-ranking officers felt that this was the right time to reach a cease-fire. But the Prime Minister's Office was not ready yet. With the media extolling him and his popularity touching the stratosphere, what politician would halt such a phenomenal campaign?

During this period, Olmert, like the IDF, expressed his hope that the attack would nudge Lebanon into a political process that would enfeeble Hezbollah and strengthen the Siniora government. But, as events in the Palestinian arena had shown, Israel was incapable of having a serious influence on Lebanese politics. Professor Ephraim Inbar of Bar-Ilan University believes that Israel suffered from a cognitive failure. "We learned this the hard way in 1982. The strength of local political and cultural forces in the Middle East exceeds any external intervention." According to Inbar, this also holds true for the U.S. presence in Iraq. The creation of a more congenial political environment for Israel is an unrealistic goal. Israel, he argues, must focus its energy on obstructing its enemies' political goals or on foiling their ability to employ their power against it.

CHAPTER SEVEN

THE SOLDIERS CAN WAIT

O N JULY 23, when a dazzling, super-swift Israeli victory was no longer on the horizon, a debate took place in the office of the defense minister on a desirable end to the war. Conditions for an Israeli cease-fire included the demand that "responsibility for the abducted Israeli soldiers and negotiations for their release be entrusted to the Lebanese government; or, as a compromise, [responsibility will be placed in the] hands of [Shiite] government secretary, Nabih Beri."

Today, the demand sounds somewhat fanciful—and that is why it was not included in Security Council Resolution 1701, which brought about the end of the war. However, examination of events during the first few days of the war reveals that not only was Israel offered a cease-fire agreement (between July 16 and 18), but the agreement would most probably have included transferring the two abducted soldiers to the authority of the Lebanese government. United Nations diplomats involved in indirect communications between Israel and Hezbollah claimed that the Shiite organization did not rule out, at that stage, the possibility of handing over Udi Goldwasser and Eldad Regev to Fouad Siniora. Senior Israeli Intelligence officers admit that the possibility was brought to the negotiating table at the time and Hezbollah could have agreed to it. But when the UN emissaries tried to push it forward, they claim that they were told by Jerusalem that the abducted soldiers no longer topped the agenda.

TALKS ON THE NILE

The UN Special Delegation to Israel and Lebanon arrived in the region on Saturday, July 15. Their first stop was Egypt, where they stayed at the Nile

Hilton in Cairo. Less than 48 hours earlier, UN Secretary-General Kofi Annan had called together several of the organization's senior staff and told them of his decision to send them to the Middle East, in an attempt to bring about a cease-fire. The veteran diplomats—the "three wise men," as they were called in the UN corridors in New York—were familiar with the region from previous postings. They were also aware of Israel's long-standing derisive attitude toward the United Nations. Although 50 years had passed since Israel's first prime minister, David Ben-Gurion, had coined the term "Um-Shmum" (which meant in Hebrew slang—the UN is worthless), little had changed with regard to Israel's view of the international organization. Indian diplomat Vijay Nambiar, political advisor to Annan, headed the delegation. Other members included Annan's special emissary for implementing Resolution 1559, the Norwegian Terje Larsen, and UN Permanent Under-Secretary for the Middle East, Alvaro de Soto of Peru.

While diplomats consulted with their aides in one of the halls of the Arab League, next door to the Cairo hotel, the League held a meeting of Arab foreign ministers. The UN delegation tried to formulate a proposal that could be presented to Israel and Lebanon with the objective of ending the hostilities. "These were three men with rather large egos," relates one of the people present at the meeting, "and it was no easy task to reach a commonly agreed-upon formula." The foreign ministers of Egypt, Jordan, and Saudi Arabia entered and left the room in turn. According to a member of the UN delegation, "Each of them released an explosive flow of curses against Hezbollah, which caused [his fellow delegates] to blush."

On landing in Beirut, the UN delegation made straight for the first stop on their whistle-stop tour of persuasion, the bureau of the prime minister of Lebanon. At the entrance to the elegantly restored Ottoman building that housed Siniora's bureau, they were met by two of the prime minister's closest confidantes, his cousin and political advisor, Rolla Nur a-Din, and Mohammad Shata, the man who later composed the seven-point document—Siniora's proposal for a ceasefire. Shata, a former employee of the World Bank and a long-time diplomat in Washington, knew the members of the delegation well and led them into Siniora's office. The delegation noted that Siniora appeared tired but confident that he could take advantage of the situation in order to lead Lebanon to a better future once the war was over. Siniora voiced sharp criticism of Hezbollah. The delegation raised the possibility of Israel's willingness to hand the Sha'aba Farms over to the UN for safekeeping. According to one of the diplomats, "The Lebanese stressed Siniora's political vulnerability, but agreed in principle to having the Israeli soldiers transferred to their care. But they added that the final decision was not theirs to make, but was subject to Hassan Nasrallah's consideration." From Siniora's office, they went to meet parliamentary chairman Beri, who, although he headed the Amal movement and was an enemy of Hezbollah in the Shiite community, acted as mediator for Nasrallah. "Beri had no choices," says a Lebanese journalist. "If he hadn't accepted the job of mediator, he would have become irrelevant in the war."

To the surprise of the UN delegates, Beri did not dismiss the proposal to transfer the two abducted Israeli soldiers to Siniora but did say that he would first have to check out the possibility with Hezbollah.[1] At the same time, the delegation received further notice that their initiative might prove fruitful. After meetings with senior Hezbollah officials, the UN's emissary in Lebanon, Geir Pedersen, reported that the organization would be willing to accept the deal, including the transfer of the Israeli soldiers to the Lebanese government. Pedersen also spoke with Lebanese minister of defense, Elias el-Mor, with whom he had previously discussed the possibility of deploying the Lebanese army in southern Lebanon. Siniora's relationship with el-Mor, son-in-law of pro-Syrian president Emile Lahoud, was tense, but he promised Pedersen that, despite the friction, he would raise the issue with Siniora.

The following day, after an almost sleepless night (the combination of jet lag and Israeli Air Force bombing was too much for their already-frayed nerves), the UN officials returned to Siniora's office and to that of the government secretary. According to a member of the delegation, "We received advance approval from the head of the Lebanese government agreeing to our proposal, and it was concluded that we should not demand from Israel a binding formula regarding Sha'aba, but we shall ask for action to be taken toward a solution." The meeting with Beri was more complex. The chairman of the government had already spoken to Hezbollah, and it was obvious that he had chosen a cautious approach. "He avoided affirmative or negative responses to the proposed transfer of the soldiers to Siniora," explained a UN official. "Beri was not prepared to commit until we heard from Israel regarding its position on the agreement. We agreed to return to Beirut immediately after our visit to Jerusalem, in order to continue talks, if, of course, Jerusalem were to agree in principle to the deal."

On the way to Israel, the delegates were quite optimistic. "We have managed to arrive at an agreement acceptable to Siniora, which has not been rejected by Hezbollah, and there was a fairly good chance of it being accepted by Israel." The delegation met with Israel's Foreign Minister Tzipi Livni early on Tuesday, July 18, and presented her with the details of the agreement. "Livni almost jumped out of her seat as soon as she heard the word Sha'aba," said one of the diplomats. "She said that if it will be written in the history books that Hezbollah attacked Israel, kidnapped soldiers, and was given the Sha'aba Farms in return, all of Israel's deterrence will have gone down the drain. Livni refused even to discuss the matter, claiming that any further negotiations on the agreement would focus on the farms." Whereas Livni was at least willing to discuss a cease-fire, in the prime minister's bureau the UN delegation was met with arrogance and a flat rejection of any political solution that would lead to the end of hostilities, even one that included transferring the soldiers to Siniora.

Because of Prime Minister Olmert's refusal to meet with the UN delegation, the "three wise men" were supposed to meet only with his chief of staff, Yoram Turbovitz, and political advisor Shalom Turgeman (Western diplomats called the two "TNT"). Shortly after the delegates arrived at Turbovitz's office, the prime minister paid them a surprise visit. "Turgeman left the room. Turbovitz remained and repeated, word for word, what had been said earlier. It was amazing to watch him quote with absolute accuracy the conversation that had taken place before the prime minister's entry. And then Olmert said, 'I don't like the idea. We can't accept the idea of Shaba'a. We can't allow ourselves to be in a position whereby after the UN had said we have completely evacuated Lebanese territory, you come to us with a demand to withdraw further. We have no quarrel with Siniora, nor have we a problem with him. On the whole we think he's 'good news.' The abducted soldiers would obviously be treated well by him. But we don't want [a situation whereby] Siniora holds the soldiers and we see him as a target."

After Olmert's official explanation came some commentary. "Everyone who spoke to us in Jerusalem pointed out that there was no chance of Israel halting the campaign," said the diplomat. "Senior officials stressed that the release of the abducted soldiers was no longer the main objective of the operation, but the destruction of Hezbollah." Another senior member of the delegation agreed, saying that "unlike Lebanon, [the Israelis] wouldn't hear of cooperating with us on the agreement. It was made clear to us on several occasions that the matter at hand was not the release of the soldiers but a change of the political arena. Olmert pointed out that he had no intention of conducting negotiations on any subject connected with the war, and this is what the other Israeli representatives we met said. They were certain of their victory. The fate of the abducted soldiers was no longer on the agenda."

Olmert's associates recall things differently. "At the meeting in Turbovitz's office, the UN delegation said they would transfer the soldiers to the Lebanese government, after which a cease-fire would be agreed upon. They were asked: 'Would you be able to promise that Hezbollah will hand over the soldiers?' and replied, 'That's the part of the equation that is still missing.' We asked them to go and check this point. We announced as soon as we began this war that our main objective was the release of our soldiers and we would do everything to achieve that objective. But we knew that by agreeing to hand over the soldiers to Siniora Hezbollah would be admitting defeat. At that point, Nasrallah had not yet reached a position where his fear for his organization was that great and we felt he wouldn't agree to such an arrangement." But members of the UN delegation who participated in talks in Jerusalem insist that the Israeli government had a real opportunity to reach an agreement. According to them, the most reliable proof of Israel's intransigent attitude to the possible deal was provided at the end of the delegation's visit. "We were supposed to return to Beirut immediately after our visit to Jerusalem. But when we realized that Olmert . . . was rejecting out of hand all negotiations on an immediate political arrangement to bring about a cease-fire, we canceled our journey." Senior members of Israeli Intelligence verify the UN delegation's version. "In every intelligence estimate between July 16 and 18 we pointed out that Hezbollah was ready for a cease-fire. The question was, under what conditions? Nasrallah had been surprised by Israel's reaction and his spider's web myth was blown apart. The national dialog in Lebanon had stopped; he felt his life was in danger. The Shiite neighborhood in Beirut was under heavy fire. He was in strategic shock, but his operative campaign continued to function. Under peak pressure, Nasrallah even agreed to transfer the kidnapped soldiers to Siniora, but there was no available mechanism to organize this." According to a former senior intelligence officer: "After a week [of fighting], an Archimedean point had been created: Olmert's 'Churchill' speech, Israel's destruction of the Iranian-made Zilzal rocket, the G-8 support for Israel, moderate Sunni Muslim understanding of Israel's position, Hezbollah was prepared to declare a cease-fire and hand the kidnapped soldiers over to Siniora, the Shiite organization was on its knees, its entire strategic layout, from the Fajr-3 rockets and up, had been destroyed. The whole 'after Haifa' story had disappeared. Nasrallah woke up one morning and found himself left with only his short-range missiles—and he was afraid that Israel knew all about these, too. He was wrong on this, but in any case, he was keen, at that stage, on reaching an agreement." According to a member of the UN delegation, the arrogance of the Israeli political echelons at that time was the main reason for the failure of a possible arrangement. "We saw that Hezbollah were interested in a cease-fire. But the approach we encountered in Jerusalem was 'forget it. We're going to win.' They even managed to persuade the delegation of this. In the end, the proposal at that stage was the same as the one in Resolution 1701, but at that time you could have had the soldiers transferred to Siniora. It was a unique opportunity to end the war, under conditions more favorable to Israel."

When Olmert was talking about getting back the kidnapped soldiers by force as being one of the objectives of the war, an objective so unfeasible as to be obvious to anyone with eyes in his head, an agreement to bring about their release might have been possible. There appears to have been a chance of at least receiving information on the two soldiers' condition; now, over a year later, Israel has no idea as to whether they are alive or not. Additionally, Olmert was saying one thing and Defense Minister Amir Peretz another, their associates were leaking information about plans to smash Hezbollah—and all the while the feeling in general headquarters was that this objective, too, was impossible to achieve. Maybe the prime minister's people were right, that Hezbollah would, in the end, have refused to hand over Goldwasser and Regev to Siniora. Nevertheless, it seems that Jerusalem did not give any serious consideration to the chance to transfer the soldiers to more reliable hands. The emphasis was on elaborate plans for destroying Hezbollah—and other heroic campaigns to follow the success of the "night of the Fajrs." From the officials' point of view, the abducted soldiers could wait.

UPDATES FROM BEIRUT

Our apartment building is now inhabited by dozens of refugees. I don't know where they are from. The list of neighborhoods and villages that have been razed to the ground gets longer all the time and my memory is blurred. They don't respond to my polite smiles and my "a-salam aleikum" greetings. I don't blame them. They sleep on mattresses spread across the floors of the unfurnished apartments in the building. They appear displaced. Over five days, the Israeli bombers can change the entire demographic character of the town.

—Emily, Monday, July 17, 12:07 a.m.

A few days after the outbreak of war, dozens of Beirut inhabitants who jogged every morning in the city's Saniye Park discovered that it had new tenants. About 250 refugees, mostly Shiite, had taken shelter there. The newcomers—mostly refugees from the bombed-out Shiite neighborhood—looked around with interest at the elegant buildings surrounding the park, which housed Beirut's wealthy Christian population. The Christians helped their new neighbors by providing food, clothes, and diapers, but the solidarity between the two communities was limited. Less than 20 people attended the rally organized by Hezbollah's Christian supporters in east Beirut on the fifth day of the war.

The refugees in the park were but a drop in the ocean of civilians suffering from the IAF attacks. During the second week of war, the Lebanese authorities reported that around half a million people had left their homes because of the heavy Israeli bombing. The number of dead on the Lebanese side on July 18 stood at 240, most of them civilians. In the South, the situation was even worse than in the Shiite neighborhoods of Beirut. After heavy bombing from the air, some villages looked as if they had been struck by an earthquake. In many, the Israel Defense Forces distributed flyers calling on the inhabitants to leave their homes immediately to avoid being hurt. On July 17, nine members of one family were killed in the village of Eitarun, when their home was blown up. Among the dead were seven children. The remaining inhabitants suffered a shortage of water, gasoline, bread, and other basic commodities. As always, there were those who found ways to make money out of the situation. Taxi drivers—although they did risk their lives doing so—charged exorbitant prices to drive people from the South to Beirut.

Despite public support for Hezbollah, which grew as a result of the growing circle of casualties, the anti-Syrian camp continued with its aggressive line against the Shiite organization. From his position on the extreme right, Walid Junbalatt even spoke in favor of Israel's position that there was no point to a cease-fire if it did not include a new political order. "We want a cease-fire, but at not at all costs," he said on July 19. "The condition for this must be that the Lebanese state will be the one responsible for decisions on matters of war and peace and it is Lebanon that will be responsible for defending the south. In the event of a cease-fire being declared just for the sake of it, the country will be unable to continue governing itself, since war could break out again at any moment, under any excuse [on the side of Hezbollah]."

ESCAPE FROM LEBANON

The international understanding for Israel's sharp reprisal, which peaked at the G-8 summit on July 16, gradually eroded as the bombing of Lebanon continued. During the first few days of war, the foreign and defense ministries of several European countries as well as their counterparts in Washington, assumed that, by defeating Hezbollah, the IDF would help the West remove a big nuisance from the map of the Middle East. European ambassadors in Arab states, especially the Persian Gulf, reported similar sentiments to their governments back home. The Gulf states were terrified of Iran—and Hezbollah was considered to be a tool in Tehran's hands. But while Israel was convinced that the industrial superpowers were providing a virtual carte blanche to do in Beirut more or less as it wished, in Europe patience for the IDF bombings was running out. Many countries in the West found it hard to justify them with daily reports and footage of Beirut being destroyed by Israeli bombs. By the end of July, the United States was almost alone in its view that this was one more front in the global war on Islamic terror. The Europeans talked mainly about proportion and were unable to equate the dozens of Israelis killed by Hezbollah Katyusha rockets with the hundreds of Lebanese citizens killed by the IDF. A European diplomat stationed in Israel during the war says that army officers in his country were perplexed as to what Israel was trying to achieve. "Even the political objectives were incomprehensible. . . . Our impression was that a strategy had been created here, in which Lebanon gets bombed, with no final date and with no potential situation that will bring about an end [to the bombing]. So we said: you're overdoing it. Start roping yourselves in. . . . You are destroying the rebuilding of Lebanon that has already been in progress for 18 months. The message was passed on to Shalom Turgeman several times."[2]

CHAPTER EIGHT

BINT J'BAYEL, FIRST ROUND

SINCE ISRAEL REFRAINED from discussing an early way out of the conflict, it was easy enough to assume—especially with the quantity of Katyusha rockets Hezbollah rained on the North—that it would speed up its military operations. What actually happened was the exact opposite. Three weeks would pass between Prime Minister Olmert's speech in the Knesset and the Israel Defense Forces' first attempt at an extensive operation in southern Lebanon, an operation that began too late to achieve any kind of practical outcome. The option of an extensive ground offensive, with all its complicated repercussions, had been placed before the political leaders and the chief of staff at the start of the crisis by Mossad head Dagan. Several generals suggested calling up reserves, the most obvious step to take when planning such an operation. But Olmert and Defense Minister Peretz accepted Halutz's suggestion of gradually increasing air attacks while utilizing ground forces for limited assignments; the idea was that Hezbollah's spirit would be broken by the massive bombing. This did not happen; indeed, more Katyushas continued to fall on northern Israel. Although it had not been the army's preferred option from the start, the decision to attack the Fajr missiles received almost universal support. General headquarters realized quite early on what the operation would entail: escalated and continuous bombing of northern Galilee. However, no one at that time except Dagan seriously suggested a ground offensive in Lebanon, which would have been the natural reaction. As one of the commanders who fought in Lebanon would say months later, "Our main problem was that everyone in the army knew what had to be done and no one wanted to do it, especially since we knew that it would cost us a lot of casualties. In the end, we did it in spite of ourselves. But the conclusion was already known from the first abduction of our soldiers in October 2000." Faced with the threat of Katyusha rockets, Israel should have found a swift political solution or embarked on a ground offensive. It did neither. In the meantime, the politicians and generals were trapped in their own declarations. The success of the "night of the Fajrs" had raised false hopes: of turning Lebanon back 20 years (Halutz had promised this the day before the attack); of destroying Hezbollah and installing the name of Israel's defense minister firmly in the mind of its leader, Nasrallah (Peretz's promise the day after the attack); and of the return of the kidnapped Israeli soldiers as soon as the war was over (Olmert, on July 17).

Although some GHQ officers thought differently during the first weeks of war, their opinions were barely heard by the politicians. The reasons for this are unknown—whether Halutz had clearly forbidden them from expressing themselves, their access to Olmert had been blocked, or they were not voicing their positions loudly or vehemently enough. When Major General Eyal Ben-Reuven (deputy head of Northern Command) was asked after the war if he should not have insisted on a personal audience with Olmert, he replied that probably he should have, but "the chances were that he [Olmert] would have made straight for the chief of staff who would have reassured him that everything was moving ahead according to plan." One of the great mysteries of the war was what appears to have happened to Chief of Staff Halutz, by all accounts a wise man with finely honed instincts. "What the hell was Halutz thinking, when he drove to the Kirya [GHQ in Tel Aviv] every morning and heard that the Katyushas were still falling?" asked a veteran officer on the general staff, who considered himself a friend of the chief of staff. "OK, on the fifth day of war, but what about the twelfth or thirteenth? Did he simply assume that things would work out, without the need to send in ground forces?"

THE NORTHERN COMMAND HAS
RUN OUT OF OBJECTIVES

After one week of warfare and against the better judgment of other members of GHQ, the chief of staff made do with a minimal call-up of several hundred reserve officers and soldiers. By doing this, he probably hoped to limit damage to the economy; he also had a strong belief in the ability of air force.

In hindsight, Halutz admitted to the Winograd Commission and in media interviews that postponing a call-up of reserves had been a mistake.

From transcripts of discussions during the war, Halutz's GHQ emerges as hesitant and confused.[1] Many reports from the discussions that reached these authors showed that the meetings were fraught with contradicting opinions. The difficulties involved in pushing forth the campaign resulted in frequent changes in the army's position regarding "What should we do from here?" In various debates, sometimes only days apart, Halutz appeared to vacillate. At least some of the generals, who refrained from saying what was on their minds in the face of Halutz's noticeable heavy-handedness, zigzagged their way after him. Their statements only served to further confuse Defense Minister Amir Peretz, who in any case had entered the war totally ignorant of the army's abilities, plans, and objectives. Actually, even with all the information now available about the second Lebanon war, it is often hard to create a clear and accurate picture of the events. But by studying Halutz's statements during the first two weeks of war, it is possible to conclude that the chief of staff underestimated the threat from short-range Katyusha rockets, did not believe in the need for a ground offensive that would reduce the threat, had no faith in the ground forces, and chose to adhere to the kind of war he was most familiar with—air attacks—preferably incorporating the plan (which Olmert stubbornly refused to approve) to destroy Lebanon's infrastructure.

At meetings with his generals, Halutz was quite candid and continued to voice his misgivings and hesitations about a ground offensive. "We must create the threat and the motivation to carry out a ground offensive, but I don't think it should happen at the end of this week," he told them on July 12. In the same breath, although he was discussing the possibility of calling up reserves—who only reached the government more than a week later—he explained, "[Our regular army] knows how to deal with these things." Ultimately, July 13's "night of the Fajrs," coupled with the following day's bombing of the Shiite Dahia quarter in Beirut, convinced Halutz that justice was on his side. "All that's left now are the ruins of Beirut," he told the generals on the fifteenth. "And now we'll focus all the Israel defense forces on hunting down Katyushas. If the weather's good tomorrow, our entire [defense] system is coming down on southern Lebanon. That's all, friends. I plan to escalate [things] as a worldview, not out of weakness." "A ground offensive," he said at another GHQ discussion on July 16, is "the place where we stand a chance of leaving IDF soldiers dead in southern Lebanon. . . . If this happens, it really doesn't matter what we [say;] it's not part of the mandate we were given by the government, the Israeli public [is not in our sphere of our interest]. We'll leave behind a hundred [dead] soldiers." In Israel, he said in another discussion, "the nation doesn't like [our] entering Lebanon, the media doesn't like it, the world doesn't like it." Nonetheless, "I am not against plans for a ground offensive. We have a plan. . . . It's being worked on right now." In effect, as later transpired, preparation was low-key and included none of the steps necessary for turning it into a real alternative, such as a major troop call-up and quick troop training. On July 17, Halutz told the Foreign Affairs and Security Committee, "This [capturing southern Lebanon] is the very last alternative. . . . Before it happens, a large number of very complex things have to happen [to make me] recommend such a direction." A further development on July 16—the day Halutz promised to "place a shadow over southern Lebanon"—greatly reduced the chances of the chief of staff's forecast succeeding. The Northern Command's targets for attack had run out. Over the previous four days, the Israeli Air Force and artillery batteries had battered all 83 objectives on the Command's list.

On being appointed Head of the Northern Command in October 2005, Udi Adam instructed the command's Military Intelligence to single out 200 targets for attack. The list had not been completed by the time war broke out, and in the absence of objectives for attack, MI and the IAF began operating along a speeded-up patchwork system, creating new objectives as the war proceeded. Successes were most impressive in cases where the IAF exposed rocket emplacements. The IAF boasted that they immediately attacked and destroyed every medium-range launcher identified. But some of the other objectives to come under attack were dummies, created out of nothing. These were points that were singled out according to various analytic methods and were of dubious strategic value. With no approval for a larger offensive, the Northern Command acted in a similar way on the ground. Artillery batteries rained thousands of rockets on Lebanese soil, mostly with no significant objectives for attack. With no targets and directives from the political leaders to continue fighting, the obvious step was to at least make preparations for a large ground offensive. But preparations weren't started. The next 11 days of fighting, between July 17 and 27 were, in many ways, a continuation of a policy that provided no results and brought no change.

BOGIE IS AMAZED

At the outbreak of war, Halutz's predecessor, Moshe (Bogie) Ya'alon, was in the United States, involved in research on behalf of the Washington Institute for Near East Policy. On July 13, he was summoned to a meeting with Vice President Richard Cheney's advisors. Ya'alon, who informed Olmert of his intention to attend the meeting, saw in the war in Lebanon a rare opportunity for Israel and the United States. To him, the previous two years in the Middle East were bad for the interests of the two countries. The Americans had moved from attacks on Afghanistan and Iraq to intense involvement, especially in Iraq; in Israel, the fighting spirit of being in charge of the West Bank had been replaced by packing up and leaving the Gaza Strip. Hezbollah, Ya'alon believed, provided an opportunity for both countries to cause significant damage to Iranian interests. The direction, said the former chief of staff to Cheney's people, has to move toward a quick cease-fire. At the same time, we must draft a Security Council resolution that will strengthen the moderates in Lebanon and promote an internal confrontation on disarming Hezbollah after it had committed an abduction that contradicted Lebanese interests. Ya'alon saw no reason for an IDF ground offensive. On July 19, he was summoned to another meeting with Cheney's assistants. He expected to be informed of progress in negotiations for a cease-fire, which he already felt was being delayed for no good reason. However, he was flabbergasted by what he heard. "You do know that [Israel] has asked for a further two months to crack down on Hezbollah?" he was asked. A shocked Ya'alon returned to his office and made urgent phone calls to two of his former subordinates, IDF military attaché in Washington, Dan Harel, and Olmert's military secretary, General Gadi Shamni. "Why do you need two months?" he asked. "What [do you think] to achieve? What are you planning on doing? You haven't even called up the reserves and without a major ground offensive, we have no solutions to the Katyushas. On the one hand, you're going to lose the understanding of the moderate Lebanese—because you'll continue to hurt them—and the sympathy of the moderate Sunni Arab states. On the other hand, the Katyushas will continue to fall and weaken Israel's home front."

PROBLEMS IN THE NORTHERN COMMAND

The feeling that something was going badly wrong in the Northern Command was already obvious in GHQ during the first week of war. As was later written in a report by Gen. Udi Shani regarding the army's functioning during the war, the Northern Command was "insulted, confused and in shock" following the abduction of the two soldiers. But its function was largely influenced by the personalities of two major players in that war, Major General Udi Adam and the commander of the 91st Division, Brigadier Gal Hirsch, their relationship with each other, and, not least, the tense relations between the men and their superiors in Tel Aviv.

Relations between Adam and Hirsch had been tense even before the war. The major general found it hard to cope with the division commander's hyperactivity and was convinced that he was whipping things up unnecessarily. Always thorough, Hirsch was sure that he was ahead of the Northern Command, both in preparing to thwart a possible abduction and in planning for the war that would inevitably follow it. The tension between the two men only got worse following the kidnapping of Udi Goldwasser and Miri Regev and the tank being bombed in pursuit of the kidnappers. Adam, who apparently had not been aware that the tank had entered Lebanese territory (the decision was within the authority of the division commander) was furious. The incident increased his fear of casualties and contributed to his exaggerated caution in the weeks to come, an approach that suited periods of routine security measures but not a period requiring the employment of ground forces in a grand operation to reduce the threat to home front security.

Mutual appreciation is an outstanding trait among senior army officers, but the commotion surrounding the head of NC and the division commander immediately after the abduction broke all previous IDF records for ugliness. While Adam and Hirsch were embroiled in the conflict with Hezbollah, some of their colleagues were busy systematically sticking a wrench in the works of the already faltering mechanism. Hirsch in particular had a way of drawing the antagonism of his colleagues. A few days after the abduction, a story was already making the rounds in the army that two retired generals were overseeing the war because it was obvious that Adam and Hirsch were going to be dismissed as soon as it ended.

On July 16, the deputy chief of staff, Moshe Kaplinsky, made a tour of the North and returned to the Kirya with some very harsh impressions. First, Kaplinsky had visited Colonel Chen Livni, the brigade commander in whose section the abduction had taken place; he concluded that Livni was a under immense pressure. Livni, who had barely had a moment's sleep since the abduction, was exhausted and incapable of stringing two sentences together.

Kaplinsky says he took him to a side room. "You are in a war. Pull yourself together," he told the officer. From there, Kaplinsky went on to the division GHQ, where the situation could not have been worse. Hirsch appeared depressed and unfocused, complaining about lack of common language with Adam. At his next stop, the Northern Command, Kaplinsky found Adam angry and disturbed. The man appeared to be struggling to come to terms with the tank bombing four days before. Today, both Hirsch and Adam insist that Kaplinsky's impressions were overly pessimistic. Hirsch suspects that Kaplinsky's tour may have been prearranged to orchestrate his dismissal. In the division, the atmosphere was not good, he admits, but Livni was neither exhausted nor struggling. On the contrary, in Hirch's eyes, it was Kaplinsky who appeared somewhat agitated: capricious, moody, and wavering between fury and sympathy.

Relations between Adam and the chief of staff were not much better. Two days after the outbreak of war, the latter's adjutant, Colonel Ronny Numa, said to Halutz, "You and Udi Adam aren't speaking the same language." The next morning, July 15, Halutz took Numa's advice and flew to the Northern Command HQ, where he had a 40-minute private meeting with Adam. He later met with a number of division commanders. Halutz subsequently expressed his dissatisfaction with Adam's work in the Northern Command. Halutz's request, therefore, to "straighten" Hezbollah's line of fighting positions close to the border was met with what he believed was a dragging of heels. Also, Halutz was convinced that instead of pushing his people forward, Adam was placing unnecessary restrictions on the war. Kaplinsky's visits to the North suggested that there may have been some truth in Halutz's beliefs. On one trip, he found a convoy of bulldozers parked by an IDF outpost near the border. Livni's second in command was unable to explain to Kaplinsky why the dozers had not been sent to destroy Hezbollah outposts.

PIANO ASSAULT

An important debate was held in GHQ on July 15. Not only was Adam not invited to participate, but he learned of the debate only when the war was over. The participants left with a clear understanding that the campaign was going to be mainly from the air. Ground maneuvers were, in fact, to be frozen, while IAF attacks would pressure inhabitants of southern Lebanese villages into leaving the area; this, in turn, would make it possible to reduce the number of Katyusha rockets. "If we were to storm . . . 20 or 30 villages and cause [the inhabitants] to run away, you reduce the number of Katyushas altogether," said the chief of staff. At that debate, Halutz rejected a proposal to prepare for a vertical flanking plan: flying in units from a crack reserve division by helicopter, under the command of Colonel Eyal Eisenberg, and dropping them in the Litani region, from which point they would move south to surround and cut off Hezbollah troops. "I'm telling you that on Israel's deterrence level this can be done without [calling up] reserves . . . do you know the kind of deterrence there is here?" Nor did Halutz like the idea of the troops moving from north to south. When Kaplinsky pointed out that it was much easier for the IDF to operate deep in Lebanese territory, behind Hezbollah defense posts and nature reserves, Halutz replied that he was aware of this fact but that having a special force suffering casualties in the field would "not be easy on the public."

Adam told the Winograd Commission that "Halutz decided on his own, without me being present, without asking my opinion about canceling everything that had been learned, studied, planned and practiced in 'Defense of the Country' and 'Elevated Waters.'[2] Instead he drafted a completely new plan of action, based on what he considered to be the success of the air campaign and the [amount of] counter fire at the time. A combination of attacking short range missiles from the air and enough pressure to cause the inhabitants to escape to the north, using only the regular army, not resorting to reserves, small and short raids, limited in time and scope." The idea, which took shape between July 15 and 18, was for limited ground activity and a series of raids (swift entry and exit) rather than occupation (a lengthier, more prolonged sojourn). Halutz, again in the absence of Adam and without his knowledge, convened an additional debate on July 18. Benny Gantz presented the alternative idea of moving "to a 'piano assault,' whereby you focus on a specific area, report on it and then do it. A different place each time. Then you go home . . . you don't settle in Lebanon . . . and when you come back you bring the lads so they can sing songs at night with singers. Nothing happened. You say: I've got time. I have no intention of placing anything long-term here." Gantz, it appears, was still hoping for a "luxury war"—minimum casualties, with no need of occupying land.

Halutz, who by now must have been furious with the Northern Command for its failures, summed up, "I absolutely accept this approach. Operations that are regimental-plus, no more. . . . I am already saying that we must speak with [Northern] Command today—and he has to place a plan on the table. If this is not done by the Command, I shall take it [out of their hands] and place it under the responsibility of GHQ. At this point in time, I am not approving a major ground offensive. Moreover: at this time, it is a waste of time to even plan a ground operation. Period."[3]

The only officer "at this time" (as Halutz put it) outside of the circle of those in the know was the very man responsible for carrying out ground offensives, Udi Adam. Throughout the first two weeks, Adam and his deputy, Ben-Reuven, continued diligently to prepare for the possibility of a major offensive, Elevated Waters, with the assumption that the necessary plans (including regular army reinforcements and a call-up of reserves) would be approved. In this was the OC showing an exceptional measure of denial and insensitivity to events surrounding him? Not entirely. On Halutz's orders, Adam was kept out of most of the more important discussions, and in those to which he was invited, Adam participated via videoconference mode. Throughout the discussions, someone in GHQ had left his microphone on mute. Adam, who thus was prevented from active participation in discussions and usually found it hard to hear what was being said in Tel Aviv, gradually reduced his input at those meetings. The penny, so it seemed, finally dropped on July 21. On that day, Halutz went up for a further meeting with the division commanders and told them unequivocally that he saw no chance for a major ground incentive. ("No way" was the exact expression he used, in a previous meeting.) But even then it would take another four days before the head of NC confronted his chief of staff.

The raids began even earlier. The first Israeli forces, from the Shaldag, Egoz, and Yamam units, had already been in action across the border on July 14 and had taken control of the northern part of the divided village of Rajar. A more systematic process began on July 17 to erase Hezbollah's line of fighting positions. The following day, with Hirsch's zealous encouragement, the process was extended to a number of simultaneous raids a kilometer or two north of the border.[4] In a number of discussions, Halutz presented the objectives of the campaign: to force Hezbollah to pay, with "emphasis on taking terrorists alive." On July 21 he said, "the main objective is to create an awareness of Hezbollah's weakening by, among other things, capturing/killing members of the organization and making the public aware of it." The chief of staff was still busy worrying about public perception. What about stopping the Katyushas? Although by that time almost 1,000 Katyushas had fallen on the home front, destroying them was still not being presented as an important objective.

Adam was not overly enthusiastic about the raids, which he saw as "Gal's [Hirsch] tricks, sharpening the force until blood was drawn." Those days, he felt, would have been better spent in mustering force and concentrating on a blow so large that Hezbollah would be unable to absorb it. Instead, the troops were worn out by a long series of small campaigns whose objectives seemed dubious. The Northern Command also had difficulties obtaining suitable reinforcements. Since the chief of staff did not press, the government was in no hurry to recruit large numbers of reserves, and the regular forces were mustered only gradually. The IDF had not completely abandoned the idea of attacking the Gaza Strip. Some of the Golani units, for example, arrived in the north only two weeks after the abduction of the two soldiers. The report drafted by Major General Udi Shani determined that the IDF "entered the period of the second campaign, between July 17 and 27, by chance rather than intent. Ground operations intensified, but their efficacy in harming symbols and reducing the launching of Katyusha rockets was constantly plummeting."

HEZBOLLAH PULLED TOGETHER FIRST

From the second week of the war, the method used by the IDF—more out of circumstance and improvisation than from educated choice—ultimately played straight into the hands of Hezbollah. Even though the organization included classic high-profile, easily recognizable military elements (such as bunkers and headquarters), much of its activity followed a low-profile guerrilla format. On the whole, Hezbollah did not seek face-to-face encounters with the IDF.

From the moment that Israel chose to continue the fight (and Olmert handed out impossible-to-achieve objectives for the war), all Hezbollah had to do was survive, to stand its ground, and to prove that it could fire a reasonable number of Katyusha rockets right up to the last day of the conflict. When the IDF achieved surprise with its secret special unit raids behind Hezbollah lines, there was a much greater chance of seriously harming the enemy. But in face-offs, the organization's main objective was to delay the Israelis and to cause losses and embarrassment. On several occasions during the course of the war, senior Israeli officers were encouraged when Hezbollah fled the battlefield. But flight is an integral part of guerrilla warfare. Guerrillas seek their enemy's weak points—and hit them. They have no obligation to attack an opponent in a location or under conditions convenient to the enemy, where a regular army would enjoy the advantages of technology, large manpower forces, and professional skills. In such a case, a guerrilla organization disentangles itself and goes off to locate the next weak point. Therefore, although the courage of the Israeli soldiers is commendable, it made no change in the big picture because of the way in which the troops were put to use.

Although Hezbollah was surprised by the fact that the abduction led to a war, it had been prepared for exactly the kind of battle that ensued. Despite its claims, the organization did not defeat the IDF, but its steadfastness was enough to boost its image and public status. This newfound popularity was expressed in a growing sense of victory in Lebanon and in the Arab street, which disregarded many results of achievements in the field. Bearing in mind the effects of this war on terrorist and guerrilla organizations in Afghanistan and Iraq, European experts believe that the capabilities demonstrated by Hezbollah in its war against the IDF are an ominous sign. In principle, Hezbollah did not deal on a tactical level; it had no interest in holding territory (certainly not occupying it), preferring to bomb the civilian population of northern Israel and kill IDF soldiers, to spread panic and lower the morale in the country. Hezbollah hardly ever fought to defend a settlement, road, or bridge, because territory was of no concern to the organization. Hassan Suliman, a Hezbollah member who was later taken prisoner by the IDF, had been sent by his commanders to the village of Eyta a-Sha'ab to prepare for Israeli raids. He was equipped with three antitank rockets and instructed to fire on any armed Israeli vehicle approaching the village. Suliman set up his position on the balcony of an abandoned house and waited for the Israelis to arrive. "I found the balcony to be the most comfortable place. I brought a wooden table that I used as a launching pad. The entire region was uninhabited and I could move freely among the houses, which we knew belonged to the families of Hezbollah supporters." In a similar position in a nearby house, another Hezbollah activist, Muhammad Srur, also waited. Srur, a native of the village, had received a phone call a few days earlier from his commander, ordering him to equip himself with an AT-4 Spigot antitank missile and wait on the outskirts of the village. "I took everything I needed with me on . . . motorbike. Another activist rode pillion. . . . We carried the rocket in a large cloth. The Israeli army used to bomb all the motorbikes, so [we] covered ourselves [with] a large white flag, while we were carrying the rocket.

I arrived at the outskirts of Eyta a-Sha'ab, threw the motorbike aside under a tree, concealed it and hid myself from the RPVs. My friends and I stayed in two neighboring houses. In one . . . we stored additional antitank missiles. We slept in the other house, on the top floor. We left the missile on the ground floor. Our assignment was to fire at every Israeli Merkava tank to enter Lebanon from Zar'it." Srur, who was also taken prisoner, recalled how the villagers had told the Hezbollah fighters they could use any food and water left in the houses. In southern Lebanon, Hezbollah deployed its Nasser battalion in a similar fashion. The forces were ordered to prepare themselves: The demolitions specialists laid bombs and mines along the main roads and in houses in the villages. Antitank personnel deployed in detached houses and were ordered to fire on tanks and any houses entered by Israeli infantry forces. Hezbollah called up its infantry and antitank units immediately after kidnapping the Israeli soldiers. Houses in suitable locations in the villages were turned into observation and command posts. Others were used for storing ammunition. Mosques served as entry and exit points for attacks on Israel.

The only challenge to face these forces was survival. On July 21, Nasrallah told al-Jazeera: "Victory in this case does not mean that I go in and conquer northern Palestine and liberate Nahariya, Haifa and Tiberias. . . . The victory we are talking about is whether [our] resistance will survive. . . . So long as a lone rocket is launched against the Zionist enemy, so long as a lone fighter is still firing his weapon, this is proof that resistance continues to exist." Hezbollah teams in the villages, he said, aim to make the IDF bleed, to inflict as many casualties as possible and to slow down the Israeli army's northward advance. "We are not an army in the classic sense, we do not present a classic line of defense. We are conducting a guerrilla war, a system that is familiar to everyone. So that the important thing in ground warfare is the number of casualties [we] inflict on the Israeli enemy. I am telling you: It makes no difference how deep the Israeli invasion of Lebanon, it will not achieve its desired objective—an end of the bombing of settlements in occupied northern Palestine," he added in an interview the same day to Al-Manar.

Hezbollah fighters in the villages had a relatively free rein to make decisions, which allowed them considerable flexibility. Because they were independent, it also saved them the problem of supplies. Hezbollah personnel had enough water, food, and supplies to last weeks of war if necessary. Nevertheless, according to researcher Andrew Exum, "The decentralized way in which Hezbollah arrayed its forces prevented its units from supporting one another in the way that the IDF's small units were able to do," both because their high command did not intervene and because of the semi-isolation that IDF activity caused between them. The units moved with relative freedom inside the villages but found it difficult to move from village to village. They were thus forced to fight a more or less static defense. Heavy air attacks by the Israeli Air Force made it impossible for units to retreat or move forward to support other units. "But what is 'withdrawal' for a unit to the village from which it fights?" asks former UN official Timur Goksel. "For a guy fighting in Eyta a-Sha'ab, 'withdrawal' means going home, putting your AK-47 under the bed and changing your clothes.' "

MAROUN A-RAS

Was the battle at Maroun a-Ras part of a considered, well-planned campaign, whose objective was to take control of areas close to the Israel-Lebanon border, or the first of many blunders that got the IDF caught up in a bloody battle in the neighboring village of Bint J'Bayel one week later? Like much in the war that is connected to Gal Hirsch, the answer to this question is highly contentious. A thorough examination, also based on transcripts of conversations in Hirsch's possession, shows that the division commander was not improvising. Nonetheless, short-circuits in communications among the division, the regional command, and GHQ surprised the senior officers in the Kirya and prevented the war from proceeding as planned by Operations Branch. And the fact that within 48 hours, seven soldiers from two of the IDF's select fighting units had been killed on Lebanese soil increased fears of further heavy losses. One week into the war, the IDF was still acting as if its assignments were routine security in the West Bank or the Gaza Strip, not only in its attitude but also in its obvious shock at the casualty numbers. Maroun a-Ras and Bint J'Bayel have been so carved into Israeli awareness as to have inspired both the prime minister and the chief of staff to mention them to the Winograd Commission as examples of major blunders in the war. In Olmert's eyes—and in those of most Israelis—the fact that dozens of Hezbollah were killed in these battles is of absolutely no consequence.

Maroun a-Ras is a Shiite village, located on a hill about a kilometer and a half north of the Israeli border. Bint J'Bayel stands about four kilometers to the northwest. From Maroun a-Ras and from the nearby Shaked range of hills, on which a small IDF outpost stood during the years of Israeli occupation in southern Lebanon, Hezbollah attacked northern Israeli settlements with artillery fire, recoilless guns, and Katyusha rockets. Moshav Avivim, one of these northern villages, well versed in suffering and economic problems, was almost completely deserted by the morning of July 19, many of its inhabitants having left for central Israel.

Hirsch recalls having ordered the capture of hilly territories overlooking the areas north of the border. At 7:34 a.m., Udi Adam telephoned his approval of Hirsch's program: a series of attacks on villages and Hezbollah positions close to the border. Shaked, a hill on which one of Hezbollah's positions was located, was included in the first group of objectives. The second stage, which was planned for the following day, included the villages of Maruahin and Maroun a-Ras. Before dawn, an 18-man fighting force from the Maglan unit crossed the border in the direction of Shaked. On the border, as reinforcement, there waited an additional 76-man force and four Merkava tanks. When the approval was issued that morning, Hirsch ordered the Maglan force to advance toward the hill. The division had general information that dugouts had been identified on Shaked. No one had full information on the "nature reserves" built only a few meters from the border. While Hirsch was carrying out what he saw as the first step in a series, GHQ believed that an observation force was being formed to locate Katyusha launching positions, with express instructions to avoid confrontation with nature reserves. At 11:40, the Israeli soldiers recognized that they were at the center of a nature reserve. In the undergrowth, they discovered the opening to a bunker with a metal door behind it. They started throwing hand grenades into openings and air vents. At 2:00 p.m., shrapnel from ricocheting grenades injured two soldiers. Nearby Hezbollah identified a tank force that came in to rescue the casualties and attacked them with mortars. Four other soldiers were wounded. At the same time, a round of fire came from inside the bunker and grenades were hurled out. Two members of the Maglan force were killed. The officer in command had trouble functioning, probably from the shock, and some of the soldiers froze. Major (Res.) Amit Ze'evi, a former company commander in a paratroop regiment, took over, slapping some soldiers to shake them back into action. Under his command, the force killed five Hezbollah fighters. In the meantime, Maglan commander Colonel Eliezer arrived with reinforcements and joined Ze'evi.

Of all the soldiers who participated in the battle for Shaked up to Eliezer's arrival, Ze'evi was the only one with experience in fighting in Lebanon before the 2000 withdrawal. He had no illusions as he exited the nature reserve. "We've lost the sense of the land in Lebanon," he said to a friend the following day. "Fighting there has become much more complicated. They have studied us and have only become more bitter adversaries. In the meantime, we have forgotten how to fight in the underbrush." Later he phoned home to his father, Major General Ahron Ze'evi (Farkash), who was on retirement leave from the IDF. The younger man described in great detail all that he had seen: a well-appointed, air-conditioned bunker, with internal telephone lines connecting all points to the nearby village and firing positions. Ze'evi the elder was concerned. As former chief of intelligence, he recalled that his department had prepared detailed files on some nature reserves, but his son had gone out equipped with only the most rudimentary information. A week had passed since war had erupted, and no essential information had reached the special units. The question of distributing intelligence on the nature reserves had been discussed several times by Military Intelligence in the years prior to the war. After the 2003 arrest of a commanding officer of the Northern Command's tracker unit, suspected of aiding Hezbollah, Ze'evi had feared the Command was still exposed. In order to prevent the Lebanese from knowing that some IDF secrets had been uncovered, it was decided to keep detailed information on the nature reserves with MI and Northern Command Intelligence rather than distribute it among the units. A mock-up of a Hezbollah bunker system was constructed in the northern training facility at Elyakim and used by units preparing for fighting in Lebanon. Specific information on the reserves was kept in crates, with instructions to pass it on to the troops in case of war. But the information did not reach the units in time. When the younger Ze'evi stumbled on the nature reserve in Shaked, he possessed none of the intelligence collected and preserved by his father's officers. He was not alone. Some days later, paratroop commander Colonel Hagai Mordechai was asked what had most surprised him during the first battles in Lebanon. "The [nature] reserves," he replied. "We were led to understand that these consisted of a few scout tents with sleeping bags and tinned food." And this is in spite of the fact that the paratroopers had undergone relatively extensive training in fighting on Lebanese terrain.

Two totally different interpretations exist of events of the day following the battle for Shaked. Kaplinsky and Gadi Eisenkott, head of operations, see them as avoidable blunders, a result of Hirsch acting against the chief of staff's expectations. The outcome, according to them, was an unnecessary ground initiative, before the Northern Command had had the chance to muster the necessary troops. According to the division commander, the battalion continued its attack as planned and approved by Adam before the collision in Shaked.

The attack on Maroun a-Ras began at first light. Under the command of Colonel Nimrod Aloni, the paratroop reconnaissance battalion entered the village, took control of several houses, and started firing at Hezbollah forces. As this was going on, Hirsch received reinforcements from the Northern Command in the form of Golani's Egoz unit. He sent the Egoz commander, Colonel Mordechai Kahana, to provide urgent backup to the regional regimental commander, Livni, who was in charge of the operation in the village. Kahana began planning immediately. At the same time, one of his company commanders, Major Benjie Hillman, received a phone call from a member of the committee investigating the abductions. Hillman, who had commanded the last force to have positioned an ambush at Phase Line 105 a few days before the abduction, was required to answer some questions. Hillman had no time to respond; "We'll talk when I get back," he promised.

When Kahana reached Livni, the latter explained that he was in urgent need of Egoz unit. He ordered Egoz to capture an area on the outskirts of Maroun a-Ras and win the battle. Kahana later claimed that Livni had told him "Nimrod is in trouble," and to make his way straight up to the village, in daylight, to help the paratroopers. "I asked him, in daylight?" Kahana said in an interview with Israeli newspaper *Yediot Ahronot* two weeks later. "He replied, as quickly as possible. There's no choice. They have to be rescued. I told him it was dangerous in daylight. Once, twice I offered my professional opinion, but we have commanding officers . . . even if you don't agree professionally, in the end you do what you're told." Livni, in contrast, denies having told Kahana that Nimrod was in trouble.

In the initial battle, Hillman and four of his men were killed. Fighting in Maroun a-Ras continued over the next two days. The Israelis killed a large number of Hezbollah fighters without suffering any further casualties. In the course of battle, a paratrooper picked up a field radio from a dead Hezbollah fighter. The radio allowed the paratroopers to follow Hezbollah's movements and prepare to block their counterattack. Hezbollah employed dozens of people, within a coordinated framework, in the battle. "These were not the small sections we were familiar with," says a paratroop officer. "Before suffering casualties and leaving behind bodies, these didn't retreat from the field."

As far as Hirsch was concerned, the battle at Maroun a-Ras was a success. Tactical mistakes were made, but Hezbollah was beaten, suffered losses, and retreated.[5] As usual, his commanding officers did not see things in quite the same way. Major General Adam paid a visit to Colonel Livni's forward command post a short time after five Egoz soldiers were killed. Adam was sure that Livni, who had not slept and was exhausted, was not in control of matters in the field. He summoned Hirsch for a tense conversation. "Sort things out. Don't allow them to kill [our] soldiers [for no reason]," said Adam, and ordered Hirsch to transfer command of the remainder of the Maroun a-Ras campaign from Livni to paratroop commander Mordechai. Hirsch was furious. "It's a war," he said to Adam. "There are going to be hundreds of dead and wounded. You'd better get used to it.'"

A week after the battle at Maroun a-Ras, Colonel Tamir Yadai, commander of the Golani Brigade, was the first high-ranking officer on active service to openly criticize the management of the war. He was deeply affected by the death of Hillman, who had long served under him. Interviewed by *Ma'ariv* reporter Omri Assenheim, Yadai referred to the hasty dispatch of Egoz to the village in daylight, the soldiers exposed to Hezbollah fire, and the many casualties. "I am on emotional override right now and it's better I shouldn't talk," said Yadai. But as is usual in such cases, talk is what he did. "But I hope that the reason for which we were sent is a good enough one. I don't like these 'half-pregnancies' as a worldview. It is imperative that people [in the ranks] should know what is expected of them, what the outcome is of what they are doing. All that mini-war at the beginning. Either you go to war, or you don't." Things that until then had been whispered in war rooms were suddenly being said outright. The criticism referred not just to Hirsch and Livni, but to the policies handed down from above: the slow and hesitant start to a ground offensive, without fully thinking out its objectives. They were conducting a semi-war in Lebanon, said the officers north of the border that week—and Hezbollah was naming its price. If they didn't devote the necessary number of troops and the required determination, they would achieve nothing.

The GHQ also was critical of the way the battle at Maroun a-Ras was handled. The fighting there, complained the generals, had achieved nothing and dragged Israel into Lebanon before it was ready. That weekend, the chief of staff announced that he was transferring authority for operations across the border from the Northern Command to the Operations Branch. While Egoz was counting its dead in Maroun a-Ras, the unit's first commander, Brigadier General Erez Zuckerman, worried, was running around restlessly in Avivim, watching the battle. Zuckerman felt unable to offer any help. "Something amazing happened there," he said later. "An entire army stands along the border, while at the front a single courageous colonel is lying on the range, with no real cover all around. The great IDF do not exist. The losses of Maglan and Egoz are referred to as the losses of the whole army, because they are the only units that were there, inside. It affected the awareness of us all. From Maroun a-Ras there began a slippery slope, straight down to Bint J'Bayel."[6]

COMPLEXITY OF LOSS

The losses at Maroun a-Ras, coupled with the never-ending Katyusha fire, sped up two intertwined processes: growing disappointment among Israel's politicians, public, and media with the IDF's conduct in the war, and an almost paralyzing fear of further losses. Their close familiarity with the IDF caused Ariel Sharon and Shaul Mofaz to be cautious and skeptical of the army's real capabilities. Sharon's advisors enjoyed recalling an incident in which the prime minister rejected a military operation in the Gaza Strip because he was the only one to notice that the bridgehead over which the officers had planned to move a convoy of armored personnel carriers had already been destroyed by the IAF. Olmert and Peretz did not have the benefit of such experience. (Both often repeated the excuse, "I am not a general.") Any doubts they may have had during the early stages of the war as to the army's performance were dispelled by the chief of staff's obvious self-confidence. However, the painful discrepancy between their expectations and the actual results aroused profound disappointment in them both. The prime minister's people say that the continuous flow of bad news, Hezbollah's successful attack on the missile boat, and the battles in Maroun a-Ras and Bint J'Bayel gradually undermined his faith in the ability of the defense forces. But Olmert knew that he must not criticize the army while the country was at war. No politician had ever done something like that and survived in office for long. Even in his testimony before the Winograd

Commission in late January 2007, the prime minister declared his love for the generals.

Israel's losses became the main topic of conversation among politicians and the public at large. Peretz, too, was concerned. At a situation assessment on July 20 (the day of the Egoz battle), he pointed out that "the number of casualties is high in relation to the number of troops in the field. We must not take these numbers for granted. The public requires a suitable explanation." Even Shaul Mofaz made a point of saying at a cabinet meeting on July 27 that "the Israeli public is sensitive to the price this is costing us. Thirty-two soldiers dead [to date]. It can also change feelings in the home front." Detailed orders were issued after Maroun a-Ras. Udi Adam forbade attacks on additional nature reserves. The units were not experienced in this, he said: "A nature reserve can swallow an entire battalion." A brigade commander who fought in Lebanon during the first two weeks says that "in the background there could still be heard the unequivocal declarations of the chief of staff that there was not going to be a significant ground offensive. It affected us. When you send in a regiment and there's a good chance you'll come back with a lot of [bodies on] stretchers, your thoughts become very finely honed. My officers asked me [all kinds of questions] about the target and what our final objective was." Meanwhile there was considerable tension among officers of various ranks, all of whom had different views of the war and the risks it entailed. It became clear that the army was not a determining factor in the campaign, and some officers began pushing for moves that their commanders considered too adventurous. In a televised interview on Israel's Channel 2 in late July, Halutz hinted at the criticism being lodged at him. Are you afraid of a commission of inquiry? he was asked. The chief of staff replied in English, his favorite language: "I really don't care."

STEEL WEBS, COBWEBS

Maroun a-Ras, whether the IDF stumbled on it by mistake or conquered it deliberately, symbolized the start of the incursions. Unfortunately, the Northern Command and GHQ had totally different concepts of their consequences. To the Northern Command, these were the first stage of the IDF's grand plan for a war in Lebanon—Elevated Waters. At GHQ, they were still hoping to avoid a major ground offensive and focused their efforts on concrete objectives, attacking a specific region from the air and, using ground forces and the IDF's superior technological capabilities, causing enormous damage to Hezbollah. This would assist the IDF in satisfying its obsessive need for symbols. Certain that by aiming directly at Hezbollah's emotions they could speed up the enemy's defeat and end the war, Major General Gantz, commander of the Liaison Unit for Lebanon during the 2000 withdrawal, first raised the option of attacking Bint J'Bayel as a preferred symbol on July 16. "Nasrallah delivered his victory speech in Bint J'Bayel," Gantz told Halutz. "We're going to have to take that place apart. It's a Shiite [stronghold] and we're [going to have to] send them north. I would even consider a limited ground offensive in that area." Halutz and his generals were called, not for the last time, to provide some public relations. "I'd place a film unit there, to describe the speech and its current results, that is to say—to record the story to the end," Gantz recommended.

The chief of staff started taking a greater interest in Bint J'Bayel on July 21, the day after the Egoz battle in Maroun a-Ras. That day, Halutz flew up to the Northern Command for a meeting with Adam and his senior officers. For the first time, Halutz told them outright that he was dissatisfied with their performance. He then ordered the Command to prepare to attack Bint J'Bayel starting on Sunday, July 23. He pointed to a spot on the map, at the northern corner of the town that he wanted the troops to make for. Adam and Ben-Reuven testified that they opposed the plan, which they saw as a distortion of the original plan: Instead of vertical flanking by one of the divisions and surprise movement from north to south, the movement was expected to come from south to north; instead of controlled fire from outside the villages, Israeli troops would enter and come into close contact with Hezbollah troops. In any case, the Northern Command's order to the troops appeared to be a compromise between its own position and the chief of staff's. Hirsch was ordered to advance the Golani and paratroop brigades up to the hilly regions around Bint J'Bayel and to cover key positions inside the town. Contradicting Halutz's intentions, the troops were not ordered to join up with each other in the North, in order to form a circle around the town and block any escape route (and the possibility of Hezbollah bringing in reinforcements) between Bint J'Bayel and the North. The operation was given the bombastic name Web of Steel, a belated response to Nasrallah's "spider's webs." The brigade commanders, Golani, the paratroops, and the armored corps 7th Brigade were given various opposing orders. At the final briefing before setting out on Sunday morning, Adam told them that this operation was limited to 48 hours. They were not capturing the town.

Hirsch intervened, saying, "It's a raid." Adam concurred, saying: "You are going in, killing as many terrorists as you can and then coming out."

On the Lebanese side, Hezbollah had read the map perfectly. Following the battle at Maroun a-Ras, they had reinforced their ranks in Bint J'Bayel. Around 60 Hezbollah regular activists were in the town on a permanent basis; 15 were employed in stores and weaponry and were responsible for the town's arsenals. Before the battle, Hezbollah had posted between 100 and 150 activists in the region between Bint J'Bayel and the adjacent village, Eynatta, including about 40 from the special force. At the end of the week before the IDF entered Bint J'Bayel, Hezbollah had reinforced its positions with several dozen more of its people, who took cover in abandoned houses.

The Israelis took their time setting out for the operation. GHQ had at first expected it to begin on Sunday morning, but the Golani troops, who were supposed to attack the town from the east, set out only in the evening. The paratroops, who were supposed to capture territory west of Bint J'Bayel, advanced at an even slower pace and started moving only on Monday morning. Golani and the paratroopers took control of houses on the outskirts of the town and encountered a few Hezbollah fighters. In one such encounter on Tuesday, Golani's 51st Battalion killed three enemy fighters. Adam strove to end the operation. Web of Steel had exhausted itself, he said to Halutz at a briefing on Tuesday afternoon. It's time to withdraw the troops. Kaplinsky, who sat next to him in the Northern Command, disagreed. There's no hurry, he said. "The paratroops have only just arrived at the town. You still haven't completed your assignment of harming the terrorists, taking prisoners, collecting weapons." Halutz decided on an interim solution: Some of the troops would withdraw, but some would stay to attack those Hezbollah activists who returned to the town. The Command relayed Halutz's orders to the forces, who were planning to withdraw from the outskirts of the town that night. But then Kaplinsky phoned the chief of staff and appealed the decision, telling Halutz that he didn't understand his reasoning. The campaign had to be completed. Eisenkott told Halutz the same thing, and he was thus persuaded. Tuesday evening, Halutz called Adam with a new order: Occupy Bint J'Bayel. Adam wanted to know what exactly Halutz meant by "occupy"—Bint J'Bayel is a town as big as Holon.[7] "It'll take about three or four brigades to occupy it," Adam said. "It's completely superfluous and hopeless and will take at least another three days." The chief of staff stuck to his position but did not provide details. He left

Adam with the draft of the order. (In the end, this included directions to the troops to intensify their hold on Bint J'Bayel or to advance a little into the town, especially in the area of the Qasbah, the old city, and to capture more houses.)

Shortly after the tense conversation between Halutz and Adam, Gal Hirsch convened a press conference to take credit for the successful campaign. Over the last few hours, he told the reporters, his forces had taken control of the town. Hirsch's terminology was relatively restrained. From a military/professional perspective, there is a difference between "control" and "occupation"; the latter term means clearing out all resistance in a region and occupying it from within. But it was the officer's tone of voice that stuck in the minds of the Israeli public, not his words. The public's already hostile attitude toward Hirsch after the kidnapping reached new heights the day after the press conference. There was no use producing a recording of the press conference to prove that Hirsch had not mentioned the word "occupation." The public held a grudge against him, even for things he had not said. The only officer who said on that day "Bint J'Bayel is in our hands" was another senior officer from the the Northern Command HQ, Brigadier General Alon Friedman, in an interview to the army radio station. Shortly after his press conference, Hirsch received a new order from GHQ. He ran to the war room. "Stop everything," he said, "we're staying put."

Golani's 51st Battalion did not encounter a Hezbollah ambush at Bint J'Bayel. Both sides were equally surprised. The Shiite fighters (who, according to Golani, numbered between 40 and 60) were positioned inside a group of houses at the edge of a valley leading north. In the battle, one of the officers found Katyusha launchers primed for firing. The IDF later assumed that the battalion had happened on a launching area. Apparently Hezbollah activists were staying in the houses and coming out occasionally to set off Katyushas; supplies and ammunition flowed in on the backs of donkeys from the North. But deputy battalion commander Roy Klein and his men found themselves on the outside of a building, the height of which provided the enemy with an advantage. And the Hezbollah-held buildings formed an almost complete half-circle around the houses held by C Company of the 51st Battalion. Hezbollah did not seek a frontal confrontation with the IDF. It would have been better for the guerrillas to keep a low profile and wait for the Israelis to leave the town. But once the battle began the two sides fought with determination. Hezbollah retreated from the area only after having suffered several dozen casualties.

Bint J'Bayel provided the ordinary soldier and the junior officer with an opportunity to display their courage. Their superiors did not abandon them: Battalion commander Yaniv Assor participated in the fight, and the regimental war room was involved in every stage of the battle. But conditions in the field prevented the IDF from using all its technological advantages and turned the confrontation into a battle of rifles, teeth, and fingernails. Shiran Amsilli, a tall, silent type, whose military service had been fraught with disciplinary issues, emerged a hero, fighting for hours almost single-handed, perched on top of a wall under heavy Hezbollah fire. Squad commander Avihai Ya'akov returned time after time to the death grove to carry out dead and wounded soldiers on his back. Captain Itamar Katz took over command of the section without even knowing the soldiers' names. Before loading the dead on helicopters, he personally identified them by their dog tags in order to save his soldiers from having to do this. "It was a suicide mission," said Avihai Ya'akov when describing his experience in the olive grove to a *Yediot Ahronot* reporter. "You knew that the chance of getting out alive was minimal. People went in to commit suicide for their friends. What else could we have done? In the end, all that was left was you and your friends. Everyone who stayed alive—you take out the bodies and take them back to their parents."

Eight soldiers of 51st Golani Battalion fell in battle at Bint J'Bayel.

A record 16 IDF soldiers and officers were awarded citations for their part in the battle, testimony to the exceptional courage and initiative of the Golani soldiers but also an indication of the deeply rooted military convention in which citations are handed out in cases where something went very wrong. After the war, Assor said that he was especially proud of the fact that his regiment withstood the turmoil and continued to fight. At times, it had appeared to him that the framework of the battalion would collapse under the pressure, but it didn't happen. He was 35, he said later, and the Lebanon war had been the most powerful experience of his life. No experience equals war. Everything he did before it was dwarfed by the enormity of this experience. One of the conclusions he took with him from Lebanon was that commanding officers have a tendency to prejudge their soldiers. It is hard to tell how soldiers will behave under fire—and most of the surprises are for the best. Troop motivation throughout the battles was high, and no special effort was needed to rally the 51st Battalion to the next mission, because they identified fully with the moral justice of the objective.

"BECAUSE OF YOU EIGHT SOLDIERS WERE KILLED"

On Friday night, July 28th, as the paratroop forces west of Bint J'Bayel were preparing to retreat, Hezbollah embarked on a counterattack. Dozens of the organization's special forces flowed into the town but attacked mostly empty buildings, which until the previous day had housed the Israeli paratroopers' reconnaissance battalion. After receiving an MI warning of the attack, soldiers of the paratroop regiment 101st Battalion killed 26 of the Hezbollah force and suffered no losses. Like Assor, the 101st's commander Colonel Ariel Yohanan emerged from Bint J'Bayel and the war in Lebanon in general with a feeling that each time his soldiers came face to face with Hezbollah, the Israelis had the upper hand. However authentic this feeling was, the Israeli public did not share it. The deaths at Bint J'Bayel reinforced the depression caused by the casualties at Maroun a-Ras. In GHQ, too, the atmosphere was subdued. Tel Aviv had expected to see a heavy blow backed by massive artillery fire. All the GHQ got was a West Bank-style crawl, with the Golani and paratroop regiments ambushing houses. Each unit was fighting virtually on its own. When the 51st was in trouble in Bint J'Bayel, the paratroops to the west were unable to offer effective aid. In any case, the force allocated to the operation appeared unable—considering its small size and the short time allocated to it—to conquer Bint J'Bayel. The large two-division campaign that the chief of staff envisioned never happened. In fact, nothing positive came of it. Another week of fighting wasted—with no significant achievements for the IDF.

In the Northern Command, a frustrated Major General Adam received news of the casualties at Bint J'Bayel. The chief of staff tried to console him over the phone. "Udi," Halutz said, "casualties are part of the game. We must go on and do what we are committed to doing." Major General Kaplinsky, who was listening in, thought that the conversation should be "[a compulsory course] in leadership school." On Friday the chief of staff flew to the Northern Command. In the presence of Generals Adam and Gantz, Eyal Ben-Reuven, usually a very self-controlled man, shouted at Halutz, "It's your fault. Because of you eight soldiers have been killed. The dead at Bint J'Bayel are down to you." They were fighting sideways and backward instead of forward, Ben-Reuven added. "We can't go on like this." After the war, Ben-Reuven would say that the Tuesday evening order to advance into the Qasbah caused the IDF to lose its relative advantage. He opined that the forces should have continued moving northward rather than wasting time in Bint J'Bayel.

If Ben-Reuven thought the conversation convinced Halutz, he was soon disillusioned. Over the next days, GHQ continued to order the Northern Command to conquer Bint J'Bayel. Similar directives were issued throughout the rest of the war—and in no instance did the Command carry them out in full. Several generals, including Adam and Udi Shani, suspected a connection between the order and a plan for Defense Minister Peretz to deliver a speech at Bint J'Bayel as a victorious response to Nasrallah's "cobwebs" speech, but there was no proof of this. Such an idea was indeed raised at one of Peretz's debates but did not get to a practical stage.

CHAPTER NINE

TO US, A TIE IS THE SAME AS DEFEAT

I T WAS ONLY on Sunday, July 23, that the Israeli Prime Minister's Office started seriously considering the possibility of a political end to the war. Following a stormy weekend during which over 200 Katyusha missiles fell on northern Israel, a special debate was convened in the PM's office. Foreign Minister Tzipi Livni and her senior staff presented a plan for withdrawing from the campaign. A presentation titled "Changing the Rules of the Game in Lebanon" detailed the points that had been drafted a week earlier with a single clear emphasis: It was not going to be possible to obtain the release of the kidnapped Israeli soldiers as part of a military campaign.

However, the Foreign Office reckoned that at least a partial removal of Hezbollah from southern Lebanon, as part of a political agreement to end the war, was possible. An embargo on the transfer of weapons to Hezbollah was also possible, as was multinational supervision of border crossings between Lebanon and Syria. That day the government appointed a team, led by Chief of Staff Yoram Turbovitz and including Olmert's political advisor, Shalom Turgeman, along with representatives of the foreign and defense ministries. The team was to oversee negotiations the next day, when Secretary of State Condoleezza Rice was due in the region.

"The first debate with the Americans on strategies for exiting Lebanon will take place on July 24," said one of the team's members. "Until then, all talks with Washington will be on the necessity to continue fighting and/or the need for an urgent supply of weapons to replace those we have used."[1]

Rice, who had begun her Middle East visit on Monday, July 24, devoted the afternoon to meetings in Beirut. First, she met with Prime Minister Siniora, who showed her a preliminary, seven-point plan for ending the war, which he had drafted with UN diplomats, his advisors, and his political colleagues in the Lebanese March 14 camp. Siniora's proposal had not yet been shown to Hezbollah or to their mediator, Nabih Beri. However, the Lebanese prime minister did know that France and Saudi Arabia had promised to support him. The salient points of the plan are:

1. The Israeli and Lebanese prisoners will be released under the auspices of the Red Cross.
2. The Israeli army will withdraw to its side of the blue line.
3. The UN Security Council will transfer the Sha'aba Farms and the nearby village of Sha'aba to the legal authority of the United Nations, until the border and Lebanese sovereignty are settled. Israel will hand over to the UN all maps of minefields remaining in Lebanon.
4. The Lebanese government will deploy the Lebanese army over all its territory, including the south of the country. There will be no weaponry or authority in the country besides the military forces.
5. The United Nations International Force in southern Lebanon will be improved and reinforced with the necessary personnel, equipment, mandate, and sphere of activity.
6. Together with the sides relevant to the agreement, the United Nations will take the necessary steps to reinstate the 1949 armistice line between Israel and Lebanon.
7. The international community will commit itself to assisting the rehabilitation and rebuilding of the Lebanese economy.

Rice expressed her agreement in principle with the seven-point plan but pointed out some problematic issues that still had to be discussed with Israel. From there, she went to the office of the Parliament chairman, Nabih Beri. The meeting between the two was tense. Rice, said Beri, demanded the release of the two Israeli soldiers, removal of Hezbollah to beyond the Litani River, deployment of the Lebanese army across the southern border, extended UNIFIL (United Nations Interim Force in Lebanon) activity, and, later, the introduction to the region of a new and reinforced international force. "I warned her of the danger of civil war and told her that first of all we would need a cease-fire," he said. Beri, who liaised with Hezbollah, was not aware that Siniora at that stage also accepted the general principles Rice had presented. The meeting ended with no results.

Rice arrived in Israel in the late evening and dined with Tzipi Livni at Jerusalem's David Citadel Hotel. In an adjacent room sat Livni's aides with the two emissaries, David Welch, from the State Department, Elliot Abrams, Deputy National Security Advisor, and State Department counselor Philip Zelikow. Livni presented the principles of the Israeli egress plan and was surprised to discover that Rice was in almost complete agreement with the plan's principles. "There is no point to another cease-fire, with no agreement that will change the situation in Lebanon," she said. This American position contradicted that of the UN, France, and Russia, all of which strove to reach an immediate cease-fire and to discuss a political agreement later. But Rice knew that Siniora and the anti-Syrian camp in Lebanon supported the American position together with the moderate Arab states, Britain, Australia, and Canada. The main argument with Israel remained the issue of the Sha'aba Farms. Voices were raised when Rice, Livni, and their advisors began discussing Siniora's demand that Israel hand the farms over to the UN.[2] Rice met with Olmert the following day; again, she heard Israel's vehemently negative position. "The farms will not come under United Nations sovereignty," said the prime minister.

ROME

On July 25, the eve of Siniora's departure for Rome to attend the international conference on the war in Lebanon, his government was still arguing about the seven-point plan. Muhammad Fanish, minister for water and energy and Hezbollah representative in the government, objected to the clause that related to the deployment of the Lebanese army along the border and the ban on non-government weapons possession. Health minister Muhammad Halifa, an associate of Amal's Beri, joined Fanish. Together, the two wanted to change Siniora's initiative and to prevent the debate on disarming Hezbollah from being transferred to the public arena. According to Ha'aretz analyst Zvi Barel, Siniora, who was afraid that such a stance would turn his plan into a joke, reminded Beri and the Hezbollah ministers that the Ta'if agreement mirrored some of his seven points. But Hezbollah would not budge. Nasrallah pointed out that "the Lebanese army was too weak to withstand an Israeli attack. [But Hezbollah] resistance had the means and the ability to face the Israelis." Siniora set out for Rome on July 25. On his way, he made it clear that he was not expecting a cease-fire in the near future.

Still, he threatened to resign if Amal and Hezbollah refused to accept his seven-point plan, saying, "Nasrallah can do his business opposite the Americans or whomever he likes." In previous years, the resignation of a Lebanese prime minister was a matter of routine; now, however, it was clear even to Siniora's enemies that, without him, the war could continue for many more weeks. Hezbollah agreed to curtail its verbal attacks on the plan.

In Israel expectations were equally low. France handed out the Security Council proposal for a cease-fire, including a political arrangement, compatible in all its clauses with Siniora's plan. The French proposal was coordinated ahead of time with the Lebanese government, although the two plans were presented separately. No one was surprised by the similarity between the two. In the Rome conference the Lebanese prime minister blamed Israel for destroying Lebanon. Siniora called on the international community to take advantage of the tragic events in order to help the Lebanese people, once and for all, find a fundamental solution to their problem—which he heavily hinted was Hezbollah. "So far over 400 have been killed and 2,000 wounded in the Israeli bombing," said Siniora. "Almost a million people, about a quarter of the population, have been dispersed. Try to imagine what would happen if a quarter of the population of your countries was forced to escape their homes with only the clothes on their backs. In short, ladies and gentlemen, this is the story of a country that has been torn apart by destruction, destitution, expulsion, desperation and death. It is the story of [unnecessary] human suffering. We are determined not to turn once again into a site of conflict and struggle."

From Rome came reports of fierce arguments over the wording of the conference's conclusion; the European and Arab states demanded the inclusion of a call for an immediate and unconditional cease-fire. But it was obvious to all that the United States would not agree to this. Moreover, after his return from Italy, a senior UN diplomat recalled that the Arab representatives asked him to pass on a secret message to Israel to carry on beating Hezbollah. In the end, it was agreed that the declaration should include a call "to take immediate action to reach an urgent cease-fire." Another clause demanded the establishment of a multinational force in southern Lebanon under the auspices of the United Nations to help in implementing decisions to disarm Hezbollah.

In the final press conference on July 26, Condoleezza Rice stressed that any cease-fire had to be stable and sustainable and that there would be no return to the former status quo. Rice was convinced that many components in the declaration provided a way to end the conflict. For her, the most important achievement of the Rome conference was the Lebanese statement of intent that authorized her to conduct negotiations with Israel on a cease-fire as part of a broader agreement.

THE QUESTION IS: DO WE WANT TO?

For Israel, the Rome conference was less important than the battle at Bint J'Bayel in which eight Israeli soldiers were killed on the same day. Since Halutz didn't immediately approve a major attack in response to the battle, General Adam began pressuring GHQ to allow an interim attack in preparation for a larger future offensive: taking control of a 10-kilometer belt in southern Lebanon. A constant focus on symbols only serves Hezbollah's interests, said Adam. He and other generals advised Halutz to hurry up and prepare for a larger assault. On July 25, Northern Command presented an updated version of Elevated Waters to the defense minister and GHQ.

Instead of taking control of territory up to the Litani and a little to the north, as dictated by the original plan, the theater was restricted to the area around the villages of Kapra and Ya'tar, to the south. Eyal Ben-Reuven called this plan Elevated Rain. (When it was postponed, Ben-Reuven presented an even more reduced plan with the ironic name Elevated Dew.) GHQ approved the plan on July 28, but it would take more time before the assault was even partially executed. The delay was due to uncertainties among the political hierarchy and GHQ, developments in the field, and progress on the diplomatic level. In fact, GHQ's approval appears to have been less than wholehearted. The following day, July 29, it was written in the general commands of the GHQ that "at this stage the IDF will not go on a large-scale offensive in southern Lebanon." Only now, Ben-Reuven said after the war, was he able to understand that GHQ did not want a major offensive. Northern Command, he said, had thoroughly prepared itself for an offensive. It was GHQ that stopped it by refusing to mobilize reserves, by wearing out the troops in unnecessary assignments and in searching for "symbols"—like the battle of Bint J'Bayel—that supposedly would defeat Hezbollah.

LISTS

And this, in essence, is the most emotionally charged issue in the battle of the generals that came after the war. With the exception of Halutz, who never provided a clear answer on the matter, not even to the Winograd Commission, and Eisenkott, who still believes that a ground offensive would have failed, if most of the generals supported in late July a big ground operation, the question is, who was it that held up the grand offensive? There is a consensus that it was Halutz's responsibility. The chief of staff admitted, albeit evasively, to his part in putting the brakes on mobilizing the reserves. But beneath him a passionate debate raged between two hawkish camps: the Northern Command (Adam and Ben-Reuven) on one side and GHQ seniors (Kaplinsky and Eisenkott) on the other.

In his Winograd Commission testimony, Adam made four serious allegations against the chief of staff. Halutz had given him the misleading impression that the Elevated Waters plan would take place in just a matter of days. In fact, behind his back and in discussions to which he had not even been invited, Halutz and his generals sought alternative, more compacted, plans, which meant eviscerating Elevated Waters. These things, he said, sabotaged the army's ability to function in the war. After the war, Adam claimed that Halutz and his generals planned an alternative operative plan without his knowledge, while he and Ben-Reuven were busy with Elevated Waters, which the chief of staff had no intention of approving. According to Adam, on July 18 Halutz banned preparations for Elevated Waters. The next day, he reassured Adam that he would soon be taking steps to ensure that the larger offensive would soon begin. On July 20, GHQ was involved in operative decisions (preparations for Bint J'Bayel) behind Adam's back, and on July 24 they formulated a plan that, from Adam's perspective, junked Elevated Waters. The real decisions were made without Adam; Adam's positions were merely recorded in the transcripts. And all the time, says Adam, his access to the government was blocked.

What part did Kaplinsky and Eisenkott play in the debacle? Their united line is that the Northern Command was weak and confused, while the chief of staff's arrogant dominance prevented the two senior land officers in GHQ from turning the campaign in the right direction. Although Halutz did declare on July 24 that "this team is the best there is in the Middle East for thinking," in fact, he forbade his senior officers from presenting positions that differed from his own to his political superiors. Kaplinsky also bases his claims on the structural reforms instigated by Halutz in GHQ, which divested his deputy of most of the authority for troop mobilization. In his testimony to the Winograd Commission, Kaplinsky compared the job of deputy chief of staff to that of a passenger in the first row behind the bus driver. So long as the driver does not turn the bus into a ravine, the passenger is not allowed to take over the driver's role. This approach enjoys considerable support in the army, especially as Kaplinsky and Eisenkott are highly respected by their subordinates (which cannot be said about Halutz or even Adam). There are those who describe Kaplinsky and Eisenkott as the war's tragic heroes, who gave the chief of staff all the right advice. He simply did not listen. But is this view of such senior officers too forgiving?

Another issue worthy of investigation is whether, if GHQ decided on mobilizing reserves or going for a ground offensive at an earlier stage in the war, the IDF would have achieved the necessary result. Would they have succeeded in reducing the number of Katyushas fired on northern Israel?

Halutz later admitted that the main objective of the campaign should have been to reduce the threat of missiles on Israel. Moreover, a major mobilization of reserve troops, together with some public saber rattling on Israel's part, might well have been enough to coax Hezbollah into a swift cease-fire, under conditions that Israel could accept.

HALUTZ CHANGES HIS MIND

Behind the scenes, Kaplinsky did have some influence on his boss. After almost a week of effort, on July 23 he presented Prime Minister Ehud Olmert with his team's strategy for ending the war. He also continued to pressure Halutz into mobilizing the reserves, believing that with the political campaign at an impasse, there was no alternative to a major ground offensive. In an unrecorded private discussion with Olmert on July 24, Halutz proposed calling up reserve divisions and pushing forward plans for a ground offensive. Olmert refused.[3] On July 26, the day on which some of the generals pressed Halutz for a ground offensive, Kaplinsky had a tense, private conversation with Halutz. "We can't go on like this," said the deputy chief of staff. "You must demand a ground offensive at tomorrow's cabinet meeting. I shall be there to hear you at that meeting, to make sure." Halutz promised to do so— and kept his promise.

Even today, it is difficult to decipher what Halutz was thinking at each stage of the war. In retrospect, the chief of staff's zigzag attitude to the issue of a ground offensive seemed to be a delaying tactic to buy time. Halutz trusted the air force and doubted the land forces. When the air campaign failed to achieve its objective and the raids took a heavy toll in soldiers' lives, cracks appeared in his self-confidence, especially after Bint J'Bayel. On July 28, he was hospitalized for fatigue, according to the Israeli TV channels. The IDF spokeswoman said he was in hospital due to a stomach ailment. He was released after a few hours only to be re-hospitalized on July 29 after further problems. At this stage, Halutz passed the ball to the cabinet's court by recommending a mobilization of the reserve units. Still, in his heart of hearts, he might have been hoping for a halt in the ground offensive. At no stage did the chief of staff appear completely frank with his generals about his intentions. In his testimony to the Winograd Commission, he appears to have kept some of his thoughts and ideas during the war to himself. Maybe one day, when he writes his memoirs, some of the mystery will be solved.

BANU LE'MILU'IM[4]

Throughout the war, the government's very limited participation in the decision-making process was obvious. The smaller forums, the cabinet, and the Seven played more significant roles at all the major crossroads of the war, such as the night of the Fajrs, the Dahia bombing, and approving the final campaign on August 9. The government provided a stage on which IDF officers could air incoherent accounts of developments in the field, Olmert delivered his rousing pep talks, and government ministers made patriotic speeches. But the cabinet, too, was not particularly dominant. It was not there that plans of action were defined; the plans were drafted by the IDF ahead of time—and key cardinal decisions were made after very brief consultations between the prime minister and chief of staff. Only occasionally did the defense minister make a token contribution. Against this background, the cabinet meeting on July 27 was quite unusual. For the first time in almost two weeks, the cabinet faced a real dilemma—and did not make do with copying down reports from Halutz and Eisenkott. Shimon Peres put it dramatically: "We must decide—it's either war and we take a risk, or it's peace and we pay the price." In other words, the cabinet had to decide whether to continue with the war while proceeding toward a major ground offensive—which, everyone knew, would involve heavy loss of life—or agree to a cease-fire before solving the Katyusha threat, fully aware of the adverse effect this would have on the country's future deterrence factor.

The cabinet decided to mobilize three divisions but, by insisting that "further force would be exerted only after additional approval by the government and the cabinet," it was agreeing in principle to carrying out the plan that would become known as Change in Direction 8—that is, recapturing the old security zone prior to an eventual advance toward the Litani River. But Olmert had instructed the army not to allow the cabinet to see maps. "We shall approve the plan in principle. When we want to, we shall go back to discussing them," he told the top-ranking officers. Halutz explained that only the unit commanders would be called up at first. "When the need arises, when the time comes, we'll call up the soldiers," he said. By the end of the war, the IDF had mobilized around 62,000 reservists.

Some reserve officers saw the cabinet's decision as good news, albeit overdue. After two weeks of heavy Katyusha fire, it seemed a positive step. The regular army, they believed, did not have enough troops to carry out a ground offensive that would wipe out Hezbollah. Now the real story would begin. Officers of the reserve infantry brigade Carmeli started pressuring a former company commander from the brigade, now government secretary, Israel Maimon. "Even if you haven't decided to go in, at least you should call up and train reservists. And if you are already calling up troops, call us." The order came the day after the cabinet meeting, but only for officers. Soldiers were mobilized on Sunday, July 30, three days after the cabinet meeting.

Notwithstanding the natural doubts as to their real capabilities, the reservists were charged by an ever-growing sense of commitment and knowledge that the country really needed them this time. Recruitment levels in all reserve units were particularly high. The reserve officers, as well as their counterparts in GHQ, considered their mobilization an incentive to carrying out a ground offensive. Although the cabinet had frozen its decision, the presence of thousands of reservists in the vicinity of the Lebanese border placed the political echelon under some real pressure. Continued barrages of Katyusha fire on northern Israel, coupled with the overall harm to the country's economy resulting from the mass call-up, were weighty ingredients that finally led to the big campaign. Yet there is something about troop mobilization—and, even more so, dead reserve soldiers—that is highly significant to Israelis and their politicians. Reservists being killed in action is a sure sign that it is time to stop the denials and pretense that it is only a regular military mission and recognize that it is a real war, with all the painful reminders of the 1973 Yom Kippur War and the first Lebanon war. Olmert, who was well aware of all this, continued to hesitate whether to assign the campaign to the mass of mobilized reservists.

SYRIA THREATENS

One of the Israeli campaign's defined objectives from the beginning was to prevent Syria from entering the conflict. Despite heavy hints from Washington on the practicality of attacking Syria, throughout the war Jerusalem continued to send out conciliatory messages to Damascus.[5] Doing this involved double trouble; on one hand it was impossible for Israel to pressure Syria to curb Hezbollah and bring about a cease-fire. On the other, in order to avoid frightening the Syrians (and a wish to avoid a hasty mobilization of reserves), the IDF refrained from troop reinforcement in the Golan Heights, except for a few additional reserve battalions in the Hermon theater. But GHQ's decision, reached with relatively little political intervention, was sharply criticized. Things changed toward the middle of the war when the Knesset Foreign Affairs and Defense Committee intervened.

Almost from the beginning of the war, Israeli statements and declarations often included the Syrian issue. Israeli spokespeople frequently blamed Syria for supporting Hezbollah. The July 16 attack—in which eight workers died—on the railway in Haifa, using a Syrian-made Katyusha rocket, was clear proof of this, and throughout the war, the IAF continued its attacks on truck convoys carrying rockets from Syria to Lebanon. (On August 4, a packing station on the Syrian side of the border was accidentally bombed; it was suspected that weapons were being prepared there for smuggling to Hezbollah. Thirty-four Syrian laborers were killed. Damascus showed restraint and did not respond.) From the second week of the war, Syria began sending threatening messages. On July 23, Syrian foreign minister Muhsan Balal said his "country would not sit by idly and would join in the conflict, if Israel [were to] launch a ground offensive in Lebanon." He explained that the IDF would then be only 20 kilometers from Damascus, and this would force the Syrian army to attack. "We have troops at the ready and if Israel goads us, Syria will take action," he said. Israeli Military Intelligence followed developments on the Syrian side, which included a level of high alert in certain Syrian army units.

General Amos Yadlin said on July 25 that "alert in the Syrian army is the highest it has been since 1983," and reckoned that "the situation is explosive. There is a potential for mistaken assessment, and the Syrians could misconstrue Israeli movement in Lebanon." Two days later, at the end of that cabinet meeting in which a troop call-up was approved, Peretz and Halutz made it clear yet again that Israel had no intention of attacking Syria.

Israel took a big risk both by delaying and restricting the mobilization of reserves, and by not preparing the home front for a potential Syrian attack. Another issue relates to what Syria had deduced from Israel's reservations about involving it in the war. Did this not raise the potential for a Syrian-initiated attack in future conflicts? Things were very tense between Israel and Syria for several months after the war. MI gauged that the Syrians might attack, whether as a result of renewed aggression in Lebanon or in response to a possible American attack on Iran's nuclear facilities. In October 2006, Syrian president Bashar Assad met a senior Western diplomat in Damascus to discuss his impressions of the war. The war with Hezbollah, said Assad, has proven to us what we have suspected for quite some time: Israel is no more than a paper tiger.

WILD ASSUMPTIONS IN BEIRUT

Most of the boutiques in Hamra [the Christian quarter] are either open or in the throes of closing down sales. Hey, Persian Gulf tourists! The bargains are phenomenal. Sure you wouldn't like to come back for some shopping? I am sure your distinguished royal families can organize a ceasefire in honor of the occasion. . . .

Ragusto, a restaurant bar in Hamra Street that I used to frequent, has at long last gone back to serving steaks for $5 and beer. I've become neurotic about the quality of the meat, especially because the dogs in my street are no longer barking. The child shoe-shiners are back at work on the street; men in suites sit reading the paper as they stretch out one leg for a shoeshine. The Philipino [sic] housemaids who stayed are now respectable Lebanese ladies. They shop, wander around, chatter. Rubble and garbage are piling up; entire streets have been turned into garbage dumps because the "Solkin" company, owned by Hariri and responsible for cleaning the streets, is suffering huge manpower problems after most of the Asian and Syrian laborers have left. Every other car has the letters TV on its roof or on any random window. Obviously they are not all pressmen. They are trying to cheat death! Well, the Israeli air force is cleverer.

—Emily, Friday, July 28, 10:52 a.m.

The day after the Rome conference, Hezbollah's representative in the Lebanese government, Muhammad Fanish, was quick to criticize Siniora's seven-point plan. "What they are asking is for the Lebanese army to deploy in the south, in order to prevent Hezbollah from carrying out its work—and we won't agree. There is still occupied territory," he said. He also had reservations about the demand for an international force. "The prime minister raised the idea at the Rome conference before presenting [the plan] to the Lebanese government. The issue has not been discussed in the government and, in any case, nothing has been agreed on it. We won't agree to the demands of Israel and the United States. The first thing [we demand] is a cease-fire and prisoner exchange. Afterwards we'll discuss [things] amongst ourselves, in Lebanon and decide what's best for our security."

Nabih Beri, who insisted that Siniora's plan would only weaken Lebanon, joined Fanish's attack. But, while publicly condemning the plan, Beri was secretly arbitrating between UN representatives and Hassan Nasrallah, secretary general of Hezbollah, on the Lebanese army's deployment in the south and Hezbollah's withdrawal to positions north of the Litani River. "United Nations representative in Lebanon Geir Pedersen became a major player," recalls a Western diplomat. "He mediated between Hezbollah and Israel and, to a certain extent, even between the Lebanese government and Nasrallah." UN representatives in Beirut held clandestine talks with Hezbollah operatives and sometimes sat together in cars in crowded places. Pedersen and his people pressured Hezbollah, which was suffering from Israeli air attacks, to agree to the seven points. The organization's forces in the south were exhausted, but, above all, Nasrallah was worried about what the Lebanese public thought of his decision to initiate an attack that had resulted in so harsh an Israeli reprisal. The Hezbollah secretary general knew that his rejection of the seven-point plan could lead to Siniora's resignation, which Israel would take as a signal to extend its attacks to most of Lebanon, this time with no inhibitions whatsoever. "Hezbollah was fully aware of public pressure and wanted to end the war," says the Western diplomat. "We persuaded their senior operatives to agree to military deployment in the army. They wanted to know what the authority would be of the Lebanese army vis-à-vis Hezbollah operatives. We explained to them gently that once Hezbollah left the area, there would be no friction between the sides. We also received their agreement to the arrival of an international force in the south, but we were obliged to promise them this force would have the authority to act in accordance with Clause 6 of the United Nations charter, that does not include permission to open fire, nor Clause 7, that grants permission to use force. Hezbollah also assumed that if the government became responsible for disarming the organization, as promised in Siniora's plan, there was no one in Lebanon daring enough to implement it."

On the evening of July 27, while the cabinet in Jerusalem was approving the mobilization of three reserve divisions, the Lebanese government, with the support of five Shiite ministers, agreed to adopt Siniora's plan as outlined in his speech at the Rome conference. Nasrallah's willingness to agree to such a decision was revolutionary and proof that Hezbollah was in deep trouble after the battles in Bint J'Bayel. What Israel conceived as an IDF failure was not a resounding victory for Hezbollah, although of course, in its public announcements, the Shiite organization described things quite differently. Two days after the Lebanese government's decision, Nasrallah explained, "It is our interest that the government be strong and take responsibility. We are determined to cooperate with the government and with all the political factions, so that Lebanon will be united." These words, in an interview with Al-Manar, aroused speculation in Lebanon. Hezbollah's famous fighting spirit seemed not far from breaking point.

NEAR MISS NUMBER 2

Following the Lebanese government's announcement, the end of war seemed at hand. Hezbollah was ready for historic compromises. More important, the governments of Lebanon and Israel had made progress in secret negotiations under the auspices of U.S. emissaries Welch and Abrams and the assistance of the U.S. ambassador in Beirut, Jeffrey Feltman. The emissaries had arrived in Lebanon immediately after the Rome conference and went from there to Israel. In their hands they had Lebanon's "egress plan" for ending the war. Their mission was to reduce the gap between the positions of the warring sides. On Friday, July 28, a day before Secretary of State Rice was due to visit the region, the Americans met with the Israeli team under the leadership of Chief of Staff Yoram Turbovitz. They presented the American plan for ending the war, a kind of compromise document, according to which the governments of Lebanon and Israel were interested in ending the hostilities between them and instilling Lebanese sovereignty over all of Lebanon. The clauses included:

1. In a letter on behalf of Prime Minister Siniora, Lebanon would request the admission of a stabilizing force, in accordance with United Nations Chapter 7, which would assist the Lebanese government to execute its commitments.
2. Israel would agree to admit the force and coordinate activity with it.[6]
3. Israel would withdraw its forces to (an unspecified) point on the arrival in the area of the international force.
4. Israel would cooperate with the international community in order to enable assistance to the needy population.
5. Israel would provide Lebanon with maps of mine fields.
6. Lebanon would deploy its forces up to the recognized international border with Israel (blue line), in accordance with UN Resolution 425 and prevent the entry of armed militias to the region.
7. An embargo would be imposed on the import, sale, or transfer of ammunition to Lebanon, except to the Lebanese army.
8. Lebanon would renew its commitment to implementing Security Council Resolution 1559 and the Ta'if Accord (Lebanon demanded the inclusion of this clause).

At this stage, Lebanon and Israel were still debating the issue of prisoners and kidnapped soldiers. Lebanon continued to demand a single clause combining the demand for the release of Lebanese prisoners with the release of the kidnapped Israeli soldiers, Miri Regev and Udi Goldwasser. According to the document: "The United States calls for the release of Israeli prisoners and has made a note of the release of Lebanese prisoners." Israel rejected this formula. Another point, which remained unfinalized, was the fate of the Sha'aba Farms. "There appeared a solution to the disagreement on the matter of the farms," says a high-ranking Israeli; "the Americans led us to believe that Siniora might exercise flexibility in his demand for Sha'aba to be transferred to UN custody." Secretary of State Rice and Prime Minister Olmert met in

Jerusalem on the Saturday night. Rice had good reason to feel optimistic. Not only were Olmert and Siniora close to an agreement on a joint formula, but the agreement would have undermined France's initiative for a UN decision calling for an immediate cease-fire. Such an achievement would once again require France to recognize America's superior status in the Middle East.

"Olmert has arranged with Condi for the campaign to continue a further 10 days at the most," recalls a member of the prime minister's inner circle. "Rice said that once she received a positive response from Siniora, to the document, a UN Security Council cease-fire resolution would be received within a week. A further 48 to 72 hours will be required for a complete cease-fire to go into effect, which is why 10 days have been agreed upon." A member of the Seven says, "We had a feeling that it was all agreed. . . . We addressed every word in the draft and knew that Ambassador Feltman was in direct contact with Siniora. It was clear to everyone that Rice was leaving Jerusalem for Beirut on Sunday, July 30, in order to close the deal with Lebanon."

HIDING QANA

On Sunday morning, Rice and Livni met for a congenial breakfast at the David Citadel Hotel, which, during the visit of the U.S. delegation, had become a veritable American stronghold. Toward the end of the meal, one of the Israelis received a text message on his mobile phone. "Incident in Kafr Qana in Lebanon. Dozens of dead." The Israeli called to confirm the message. "I wasn't sure if the report was genuine. I thought someone was horsing around and sending messages from Operation Grapes of Wrath in 1996," he said. He decided to keep silent, fearing that the information was misstated. After taking her leave of Livni, the secretary of state set out for a meeting with Foreign Minister Amir Peretz on another floor of the hotel, overlooking the walls of Jerusalem's old city.

Peretz and his advisors had arrived at the hotel about two hours before the planned meeting with Rice. The group included Peretz's military secretary Eitan Dangot, head of the Political Security Branch Amos Gilad, a Defense Ministry translator, Peretz's political advisor Hagai Alon, and an external advisor, Oriella Ben-Zvi, who had helped Peretz with the foreign press on his election campaign and was considered an expert on American affairs.[7] They talked among themselves about the length of time Peretz should ask for in order to continue the campaign in Lebanon. "Peretz's advisors [shouted at each other] as if they were in a market," recalls one of the participants. "Our impression was that the Americans wanted us to continue attacking and Israel needed at least 10 days more of fighting." Suddenly Dangot's cell phone rang. The military secretary answered and, at the end of a brief conversation, announced, "Something's happened in Qana." The group still didn't know what was going on. The report Dangot received was based on information provided by the Lebanese media, but a clearer picture emerged a few minutes later. However, when he met Rice right after the meeting with his advisors, Peretz apparently decided he was not going to be the first to tell her about the incident, although by then it had reached TV stations worldwide. When the Americans entered the conference room, Dangot took U.S. Ambassador Richard Jones aside and whispered a garbled sentence about the incident. Jones did not understand and had no time to update Rice.

Rice wished them all good morning and said, "OK, we'll do our usual," a signal to her entourage and Peretz's advisors to leave the room. While the two were talking in private, their advisors waited in the adjacent corridor. Picture the scene: Outside in the corridor, the Israelis are waiting with the distinguished American entourage, all the time knowing an explosion is inevitable. At any moment the bad news might arrive. An hour and a half had passed since the first report on Qana, and Peretz had not mentioned it, as if out of some childish hope that if no one said anything, the storm might blow over. A few minutes later, in the corridor, there was a tiny electronic bleep from Welch's BlackBerry. "We all knew what was coming," said one of the Israelis. Welch burst into the room and spoke to his boss. Later, when Peretz's advisors joined the conversation, it was obvious that the secretary of state's tone and attitude had changed completely. She rushed out of the room, giving Peretz a cursory handshake. There was no time for friendly good-byes. Israel's feeling that it could still deal a comprehensive blow to Lebanon was replaced by an understanding that America was worried and angry—very angry.

UPDATE FROM THE FIELD

When we arrived in Qana the international media were still there. Sixty people had been killed here,[8] when a missile hit an apartment block over the weekend [Sunday morning]. The house completely disappeared; the island of rubble rose to a height of seven meters. One or two surviving families told their stories. The journalists interviewed a young man whose cousins, aged between six months and ten years, were killed. In our presence alone he told his story to at least a dozen cameras. "Did you really dig through the rubble with your bare hands?" asked a Swedish journalist, pushing his video camera in the man's face. Among the concrete remains were shoes, baby pictures, sheets, teddy bears, women's underwear, handbags, yogurt containers, fridge handbooks, DVD receivers and piles of homework in French and Mathematics. A friend who works for the BBC arrived at the spot in the morning after the bombing and described how they pulled out one child after another, their mouths wide open and frozen, smeared with mud, out of the ruins. From the moment the bodies were extricated, all that was left was a shameful disregard for intimacy; exposed personal effects, the details of someone's life, left spread around a radius of what had once been his home; everyone able to see and rummage through, with every photographer able to step over [everything] and take photos.

—Emily, Monday, July 31, 10:48 p.m.

WHAT WENT WRONG?

The debacle in Qana was the result of one thing: frustration. Over the four days that separated the battle at Bint J'Bayel and the IAF's bombing of Qana, Hezbollah continued to fire an average of 100 Katyushas a day at northern Israel. Although the IAF constantly improved its ability to locate and hit the medium-range missile launchers, it remained helpless in the face of the short-range Katyusha rockets. In the absence of advance intelligence on the deployment of Katyushas, the IDF found it very hard to locate new objectives to attack. Believing that "something has to be done," the IDF improvised a new system. In late July, the IAF began to systematically attack houses on the outskirts of southern Lebanese villages, the region from where Katyushas were being launched over northern Israel. Objectives were defined as having "a circumstantial connection": identifying places from which rockets had been launched during previous days, combined with available intelligence. But the connection produced no more than an approximate location.

The killing of innocent people, it would seem, is part of the price of a war against an enemy that constantly attacks the Israeli home front while using its own civilians as human shields. But the killing in Qana was the direct result of a decision to bomb houses on the outskirts of the village—and, as in other instances where numbers of Palestinian civilians were accidentally killed in the occupied territories, Israel has never really spelled out its policies. Findings of the inquiry into the Qana incident were never published. Strangely, the Winograd Commission made no reference it its interim report on the killing of Lebanese civilians, of whom those in Qana were but a small percentage.

Israel's public relations on the Qana incident were doomed to fail. Only that evening, over ten hours after the first report came through, did head of IAF headquarters General Amir Eshel call a press conference on the day's events. After the mandatory expressions of sorrow, Eshel raised several doubts regarding the reports from Lebanon. Over the next days, the IDF would provide the media with some of the dozens of films taken by the IAF, recording Hezbollah operatives firing Katyushas toward Israel, then rushing off to take shelter within populated areas in southern Lebanon.[9] But the recordings could not counteract the pictures arriving from Qana: limbless, bleeding, soot-covered children and babies borne in the arms of local and Red Cross rescue personnel; alongside the ruined building, rows upon rows of bodies covered with white plastic sacks. Coining the incident "the second Kafr Qana massacre"—the first had taken place in 1996—the Arab stations reported 57 dead, including 21 children and many more bodies still buried under the rubble. Rescue forces said that their work was complicated by the dreadful devastation in the site. The death toll at the end of the day was much lower: 28, including 17 children. Not only Israel, but the Western media, too, suspected Hezbollah of deliberately exaggerating the numbers throughout the day. Convincing evidence was available that Hezbollah had brought in bodies of victims of other bombings in order to intensify the impact.

But the disparity in numbers made hardly any difference. "When Condoleezza comes here we'll show her pictures of the children," one of the villagers told al-Jazeera as he held up a photo album with pictures—so he said—of his dead children.

END OF THE PEACEKEEPING MISSION

Rice didn't make it to Lebanon that day. She was obliged to postpone her plan to return to Beirut on Sunday evening for a meeting with Siniora to discuss the American initiatives. President Bush's secretary of state, sometimes described as an "iron lady," was upset and angry. It is also said that she felt deceived by her Israeli hosts. On countless occasions, Ambassador Jones had pointed out to high-ranking Israelis the importance Washington attaches to not harming civilian populations. Rice herself had said so to Livni, Peretz, and Olmert. Israel's Ambassador to Washington, Dani Ayalon had heard similar American warnings from his counterparts in the State Department. But still the horror show took place. The IDF killed and wounded dozens of innocent civilians just moments before the culmination of a great achievement for the somewhat floundering American diplomacy in the Middle East—a cease-fire agreement under relatively comfortable conditions for Israel, Siniora, and the moderate branch of the Arab world.

Furious responses soon arrived from Lebanon. Parliament chairman Beri announced that Hezbollah's conditions for a prisoner exchange and cease-fire were no longer valid. There would be no more negotiations to achieve an agreement, he said, until Israel stops its one-sided bombing of Lebanese territory. Hezbollah understood that from then on the tide of Lebanese and international public opinion had turned in its favor. Lebanese parliament member and Hezbollah political ally General Michel Aoun was interviewed by al-Jazeera, where, in a patronizing and chauvinistic tone, he addressed Condoleezza Rice—though she was not actually present—saying, "I know that you are not married and that you have no children, but don't you feel any pain?" In the office of Israel's prime minister, they admit today that the killings in Qana failed the package deal that Rice had tried to sew. Pictures of dead civilians provided Nasrallah with plenty of propaganda material and added to his doggedness in the conflict with Israel. Even the Israeli chief of staff admitted to the Winograd Commission that the bombing had thwarted the possibility of a cease-fire agreement.

Siniora himself issued Rice a restraining order, forbidding her from visiting Lebanon. The Lebanese prime minister, who knew that the public opinion was against him, especially if he were to reach an agreement with Israel that would include some far-reaching compromises, made it clear that the U.S. secretary of state was not welcome in Lebanon at that time. "No negotiations will take place to end the conflict, unless Israel stops bombing," he explained. Rice was forced to stay away from Beirut, where the draft of the American agreement that was supposed to bring about an early end to the war was now obsolete.

CHAPTER TEN

FLOUNDERING

Aᴼᴛᴇʀ ᴛʜᴇ ǫᴀɴᴀ bombing, the chances for a quick end to the fighting through a settlement that was favorable to Israel were drastically reduced. What tolerance was left in the international community and moderate Arab countries for the Israel Defense Forces' operations abruptly died out. The United States and Britain reversed their positions as they came to the realization that France's intensive intervention was necessary and that Paris had to exert its influence on the Lebanese government to resolve the crisis. Condoleezza Rice, who was deeply pained by the Qana incident, orchestrated the change in American policy. One American news analyst claims that "Qana was the breaking point in Rice's relations with the Israeli government, and it even had the potential of being the breaking point in her relations with Bush, but the secretary of state was too loyal to the president to let that happen. Nevertheless the [civilian deaths] convinced Washington that the IDF could not succeed in Lebanon—and that America's war by proxy there against Iran was doomed to failure." Rice's entourage even began to suspect, after Defense Minister Amir Peretz's apparent attempt to shield the report on the Qana bombing from the secretary of state, that Israel had knowingly bombed an inhabited building. However, the conspiracy theory quickly disappeared from the agenda. Rice's staff came to the conclusion that the main cause of the IDF blunder was connected with the incredibly sloppy way Israel was handling the war.

A few hours after the bombing, Rice walked into Prime Minister Ehud Olmert's office. "We never saw her so mad," one of his aides recalls. She opened the meeting with a frontal attack. "I read in the papers that you wanted me to OK between 10 and 14 more days for the war," she fumed, referring to an article in *Ha'aretz* that morning that discussed the previous evening's meeting between the two. "I do not like private talks to be leaked." The prime minister held his ground. "I don't remember asking you for two weeks, only 10 days. Furthermore, I read in *Ha'aretz* that you wanted us to include the Sha'aba Farms in the resolution—according to American sources." Rice's face contorted and she turned to her assistant, David Welch, for an explanation. He affirmed that the leak had come from the American side. Rice then asked Olmert to make a goodwill gesture that would contribute to halting the escalation. After further discussion, the prime minister agreed to a 48-hour pause in bombing populated areas. Olmert and Rice agreed that Israel would announce a cessation of attacks on unspecified targets.[1] But when the lull went into effect, it turned out that the United States and Israel disagreed on the interpretation of the resolution. The Prime Minister's Office issued a statement to the effect that the Israeli Air Force had been instructed to proceed with operations against "targets that pose a threat to Israel and its forces, including rocket launchers, ammunition vehicles, Hezbollah fighters, arms warehouses, and Hezbollah positions" but would avoid attacking "suspicious buildings." A senior State Department official, however, was quoted as saying that Israel agreed to cease its air strikes for 48 hours in order to allow an investigation of the Qana killing. The White House spokesman added that Israel would coordinate a 24-hour "window" with the United Nations during which the UN would assist locals who wanted to leave southern Lebanon. Neither the UN nor Israel had heard of such an agreement. The letup in the bombings occurred in spite of the IDF's reservations. In consultation with Peretz that day, Deputy Chief of Staff Kaplinsky said that Israel had to do the opposite: Step up the air strikes. "If we maintain the same pace, Hezbollah will get the message that there's no way out for them and they'll shorten the war." Before leaving the region, Rice managed to convene a joint press conference with Peretz in which she appeared especially angry. On her way back to the United States, her entourage received a report that the IDF had resumed the bombings in southern Lebanon. In the plane's midway stop in Ireland, Rice told the American reporters accompanying her that "Israel had violated the cease-fire." She was scheduled to have supper with President Bush. According to reports from American journalists (reports that subsequently were denied by the State Department), Bush instructed Rice to lower her tone toward Israel. The president reminded her that the Israelis were American allies. Nevertheless, over the next few days, Rice continued pressuring the president to formulate a joint resolution with France that would bring the war to a quick conclusion. The head of the National Security Council, Steve Hadley, and his deputy, Elliot Abrams, disagreed with her. They set forth the White House's basic position: There is no reason to end the war without a fundamental change in the Lebanon reality.[2] Bush eventually accepted Rice's position that the Israeli attacks were causing more damage than benefit and endangering Siniora's survival; therefore, the IDF had to be taken out of southern Lebanon.

"The gap between Rice, on the one hand, and Hadley and Abrams, on the other, regarding Israel was very pronounced in this period," says an Israeli diplomat in Washington. "After Qana, the secretary of state lost her patience with us. Qana was a traumatic experience. Her good friend Dov Weissglas was not around to calm her down. Relations with Turbovitz and Turgeman were much more formal." An American diplomat criticized Rice for her hysterical response to Qana, claiming that "She gave the American ambassador in the United Nations, John Bolton, and his staff a direct order: Get the UN to pass a resolution, even if it means giving in to the French approach that we've been opposed to. First obtain a cease-fire, then a political settlement."

THE REAL VICTOR

To Nasrallah, the killing in Qana was a godsend. The tragedy enabled Hezbollah to avoid an agreement that might have been interpreted as ignominious surrender: the organization's unconditional expulsion from southern Lebanon, the introduction of an international force that was permitted to open fire according to Article 7 of the United Nations Charter, and an arms embargo on the country. Once again the Arab public, large sections of the Lebanese citizenry, and, to a certain degree, even the international community lent their support to Hezbollah. The American networks provided wide coverage of the killing—as they had not done for years with events connected with Israel. Israel had been missing from American TV screens since the United States went to war in Iraq. Now, because of Qana, Israel returned to prime time.

However, in Lebanon, the "Qana effect" faded away after a few days. Prime Minister Siniora and the speaker of parliament Nabih Beri, who on July 30 had refused to meet with Rice, were scheduled to meet with her envoy, David Welch, on Saturday, August 5. Only a few dozen people bothered to attend a demonstration in the city against the renewal of contacts with the

Americans. The press resumed its castigation of Nasrallah. "Lebanon suffers from schizophrenia," explains a diplomat who was there that week. "Christians, Sunnis, Druze—everybody wanted the war to end and for Beirut and vicinity to return to the good old days. While Israel was bombing Dahia, people were living it up in the discotheques. One evening I sat in a bar in Beirut. The idea of deploying an international force in the South seemed to be gathering momentum that week. Three Christian females at the bar said that you had to look on the positive side: 'There'll soon be thousands of European guys we can go out with.' In Rumana, 40 minutes from Beirut, wild parties were the rage. The main road was jammed with cars loaded with people out for a good time," the diplomat recalls. "The Christians wanted the war to be over as quickly as possible for another reason: They were afraid the Shiites would become squatters in the Christian areas of the North and not leave."

UN: U NOTHING

The Israeli ambassador to the United Nations, Dani Gillerman, was on his way to the NBC television studio to take part in the program *Meet the Press* when he received the first report on Qana. Sunday is a day off at the UN but the members of the Security Council convened with lightning speed for an emergency debate. Gillerman rushed to the UN headquarters without even taking off his makeup. His deputy, Dan Carmon, worried that Gillerman would not make it back on time, was sitting in the ambassador's seat. Carmon handed him a page with points on it that the Foreign Ministry wanted the ambassador to emphasize, but Gillerman preferred to improvise. Qana is a tragic incident, he said to the representatives of the Security Council. "There are people in Jerusalem who are saddened by this, but I am certain that quite a few people in Tehran, Damascus, and Lebanon are overjoyed. They were waiting for your meeting. Don't give them what they want. . . . If you go to bed with a missile, don't be surprised to wake up in the morning and discover it's exploded." Qatar wanted the council to vote on a resolution calling on the Secretary-General to condemn Israel, but the American threat of a veto effectively blocked the vote.

As the storm over Qana dissipated, the Israeli delegation noticed that the American ambassador, John Bolton, and his French colleague, Jean-Marc de La Sablière, who until now had acted with almost total transparency toward the Israeli diplomats, began keeping their distance. A few days later, de La

Sablière invited the Israelis to his office and asked their opinion of certain articles in the draft. The Israelis were very put out. "Don't you mean to ask us about the entire resolution proposal?" The French ambassador was evasive. On August 5, the riddle was solved. The draft was presented to the members of the Security Council, Israel, and Lebanon. Most of the principles in the resolution were acceptable to Israel (the French diplomats even accused Jerusalem of being overly enthusiastic about the contents, which might jeopardize getting Arab agreement on the resolution). The biggest problem lay in one article, around which a rare consensus developed between Jerusalem and Beirut. The two countries were at first opposed to the way the United States and France had separated the decision for a cease-fire ("refraining from hostile acts," according to the words of the proposal) and another resolution that called for a mandate for an international force to be sent to Lebanon only after Jerusalem and Beirut came to an agreement. This was the French idea that the United States adopted.[3] The next day, Siniora declared his opposition to this article (because of his fear that this kind of resolution would leave the IDF in Lebanon permanently). Siniora believed that the two states would have a hard time reaching a political settlement and that the inevitable postponement would prevent the deployment of an international force, resulting in the Israeli army staying in Lebanon. In a phone conversation with Hadley, Olmert stated his opposition to the same article, giving almost the same reasons as Siniora: the fear that the IDF would get stuck in the Lebanese quagmire while waiting for the decision to deploy the UN force. The Israeli Foreign Ministry reckoned that, by the phrasing in the draft, France was primarily guaranteeing its own interests. "The French had no desire to send their soldiers as a contingent in an international force, putting them in harm's way. Therefore they demanded first and foremost that a cease-fire and quiet prevail in the sector, which would be guaranteed by an Israeli-Lebanese accord," says an Israeli diplomat. The diplomat also claims that a few hours after handing the draft to the parties, the French ambassador in Beirut, Bernard Emie, sent a message to the Foreign Office in France, stating that if the Security Council resolution was ratified according to the proposed formula, the Siniora government would fall. A French diplomat says that Paris was a bit surprised by Siniora's intense opposition. "We consulted with him before this and were aware of his reservations, but we had to reach a compromise with the United States. When Siniora categorically rejected the proposal we realized that the Israelis too were opposed, and we were forced to withdraw the proposal from the UN's agenda." Siniora's opposition apparently sprang from a second reason: Without an international force, no element in Lebanon would succeed in getting Hezbollah to leave the South, whereas the continuation of the Israeli presence there would only strengthen the Shiite organization's hold on the region.

THE NEW MIDDLE EAST (1)

In a speech delivered the day after the Qana carnage, Olmert expressed "sorrow from the bottom of [my] heart" for the death of Lebanese civilians. "We did not intend to hurt them. We did not want their deaths." Having said this, he added, "There is no cease-fire, nor will there be one in the coming days." And he promised to hunt down Hezbollah's leadership "wherever it is, whenever we choose." In its ground operations, the IDF continued raiding villages relatively close to the border. Because of the limitations imposed on Israel Air Force strikes, artillery was increasingly used for infantry and armor support. "During this period we fired like crazy," admits a high-ranking officer in the Northern Command. But while the raids produced no substantial change in the fighting, Hezbollah's conduct reflected the real situation. The organization strictly observed the cease-fire during the two days it was in effect. Not one rocket was fired into Israel—and Hezbollah's leadership was proving control over the militants on the ground. Hezbollah cast in a somewhat ridiculous light the pronouncements of Israeli ministers and senior officers about the severe damage the IDF had inflicted on the enemy's command and control system. (The lull also gave Hezbollah an opportunity to reorganize.) It now became clear that the Katyusha shelling was not the local initiative of armed activists who lit off the rockets on the spur of the moment from their backyards but the result of instructions issued in an orderly manner in a well-disciplined hierarchy. Nasrallah still controlled the South despite heavy losses to his organization. Paradoxically, the cease-fire served as proof of the extent of Hezbollah's success. The senior command planned how many Katyusha rockets would be launched each day and selected the targets—and the activists in the South loyally carried out orders.

It would take the Prime Minister's Office some time to digest this information. On August 1, Olmert attended in the National Defense College's graduation ceremony at Glilot, outside Tel Aviv. Over the years, the prime minister's speech had become a ritual occasion to outline Israel's political and security horizon. Olmert deviated from the standard procedure, refusing to write the text beforehand with his advisors. The anxiety reflected on the face of Olmert's media advisor, Asi Shariv, was enough to say that here was a conjunction of circumstances destined to end in catastrophe. There were practical reasons for Shariv's deep concern. On the twenty-first day of the fighting, while the civilians in the North were taking advantage of the lull in the shelling, thanks to Nasrallah, and stepping outside for a breath of fresh air, Olmert decided to trumpet the positive sides of the crisis. In a flight of imagination he announced, "Today we can say that Israel is winning this campaign and has made outstanding, perhaps unprecedented gains. We can already say with certainty that the face of the Middle East has changed in the wake of Israel's, the army's, the people of Israel's magnificent achievement." Without discerning between short-range and long-range rockets, he described the IDF's prodigious success in crippling Hezbollah's rocket layout. He also reminded his listeners that Israel had lived in the shadow of the missile threat for years, but as of three weeks ago, it had decided that it would never live this way again. "Twenty-one days later the threat is no longer what it was. No one will ever threaten this nation again by firing on missiles on it because this nation will deal with the missiles and triumph over them. The truth is—we will never bend again," the prime minister proclaimed.

Excluding the dubious logic (it was good thing that the missiles hit us so that now we're not afraid of them), Olmert exhibited a regrettable lack of understanding of the enormity of the damage and suffering that shelling for days on end had caused the home front. His words also failed to correspond with events in southern Lebanon. Most of the senior commanders were absent from the ceremony at Glilot. They were fighting in the North. The audience consisted mainly of staff officers and the commanders of the various military branches, men who were not directly involved in combat. Nevertheless, when Olmert enumerated the achievements of the campaign, the officers could be seen fidgeting in their chairs. "Is it possible that he's looking at the same war that we see?" they asked each other. To them, Olmert sounded enraptured by his own rhetoric.[4] This was not the first time that a worrisome discrepancy was seen between the prime minister's public declarations and what was really happening in the field. A Western diplomat who watched a telecast of the speech in Beirut says he could not believe his ears. "Olmert boasted that he had succeeded in halting the Katyusha fire, when it was clear that this is not what happened. The next morning, immediately after the cease-fire, Hezbollah unleashed 250 Katyushas—a record number in the war—to prove that it still had the capability to bleed Israel. Olmert had displayed a total misunderstanding of Hezbollah's ability. He was detached from the situation on the ground."

Olmert's speech at the National Defense College was far different from what he was saying behind closed doors, however. In the third week of the war, Olmert met with an old friend, former defense minister Moshe Arens, who was very disturbed about the direction of the campaign. According to what Intelligence tells me, Olmert said, Hezbollah has only a few hundred fighters left south of the Litani River. Arens retorted that if this was true, then given its equipment, technology, and vast manpower, the IDF had an advantage, so much so that no shortcomings in the ground forces' readiness could explain why the army wasn't crushing Hezbollah resistance in southern Lebanon. Olmert explained that if the IDF attempted a ground offensive, the masses would take to the streets in Jerusalem and Tel Aviv in protest against the government. Officers such as Kaplinsky and Gadi Shamni told him that such a move would cost the IDF around 400 deaths, he added. They warned him against a bloodbath. "What about Gabi Ashkenazi?" Arens asked.[5] (Ashkenazi, the former deputy chief of staff, would succeed Halutz as chief of staff after the war ended.) Even he wasn't keen on a ground operation, Olmert answered. Arens's impression was that the prime minister was scared of returning to the Lebanon 1982 period, when Israeli soldiers got stuck on enemy land for years. The fear of getting bogged down in the Lebanese quagmire paralyzed him, Arens thought.

Shamni, the military secretary, had a commanding influence over Olmert. A paratroop officer—whose appointment to the prime minister's office in the autumn of 2005 was regarded as a somewhat bland choice compared to his predecessors, the domineering Kaplinsky and Yoav Galant—became the pillar of military authority in the entourage. Shamni served as the main link between Olmert and general headquarters (though Halutz and Kaplinsky sometimes used their direct line to the prime minister) and was the only advisor with invaluable experience. Unlike Ariel Sharon, Olmert needed military experts around him. (Turbovitz had nothing to contribute in this area.) Shamni, who was skeptical from the start about a major ground operation, did not hide his views from Olmert. He and Eisenkott also had reservations about an operation carried out by elite Matkal and Shaldag reconnaissance units, which landed from helicopters in the Lebanese town of Baalbek, near the Syrian border. The operation took place on August 1. The attack surprised Hezbollah but did not change the course of the war. The day after the defense college speech, Shamni discussed a possible end to the war with another officer. The other officer outlined three possibilities: an Israeli victory; floundering and attrition; or failure, which would force Israel to reach a compromise. Shamni took the paper and erased the possibility of victory. "We're left with 10 to 12 days of fighting—right now we're somewhere between the two remaining situations," he said.

ANOTHER CHANGE IN DIRECTION

On August 1, as the end of the cease-fire approached, the Northern Command received permission to implement Change of Direction 8, the plan for capturing "the Step"—the old security zone. The IDF began introducing more troops into southern Lebanon, including, for the first time, reservists. The IAF's massive bombing of the long- and intermediate-range rocket launchers gained a respite for Haifa, but Hezbollah's pressure on the cities closer to the border also intensified. Acco, Ma'alot, and Kiryat Shmonah at times were targeted by scores of Katyushas in a single day. Israeli losses mounted and residents gradually fled the northern cities. People who remained usually were those who had nowhere else to go. Inside the bomb shelters, the citizens complained that they were approaching the end of their rope.

But in southern Lebanon, the IDF still floundered. Progress was sluggish. Top priority was given to killing Hezbollah fighters of the Nasser Unit operating in the South rather than locating and knocking out the Katyusha launchers. On July 29, before commencing operations in the Lebanese town of Taibe, the commander of the Nahal infantry brigade, Colonel Micky Edelstein, heard the chief of staff give a detailed assessment. According to intelligence reports, Halutz said, they would have to kill another 170 Hezbollah fighters in order to create a tangible effect on Nasrallah. Their assignment in Taibe would be to kill 110 terrorists. Edelstein felt that the order was unlike anything he had ever been given but decided not to argue with the chief of staff. The Northern Command's reservist paratroop brigade entered the fighting theater on Saturday night, August 4. Lieutenant Colonel Amos Brizel's battalion received an order to replace the Nahal forces that had pulled out of the Taibe area in order to take part in another operation. Brizel's battalion was given 72 hours to occupy eight houses in Taibe. Go in and go out. Brizel, whose superiors pressed him to enter Lebanon as soon as possible, took with him intelligence reports only on Taibe and the adjacent village, Rav a-Taltin. This turned out to be a mistake. His battalion exited Lebanon only 10 days later and Brizel had no other maps with him. When it entered houses in Rav a-Taltin the next day, in broad daylight, the operations room of the 162nd Division dressed him down: "Didn't they tell you that we don't operate in daylight?" The battalion commander said he had never heard of such a command and continued fighting in daylight. The following night, the battalion took over Taibe, the town the Nahal troops had recently left. There was low-level friction with Hezbollah. "They fired missiles at us from a distance. Each time we advanced, they retreated." On Monday evening, the first supplies arrived: Major Tomer Bouhadana, a company commander from another battalion in the brigade, brought them in heavily armored Achzarit-type personnel carriers (APCs). The soldiers discovered when they opened the packs that they had been sent supplies for another battalion—and had received only a third of the packs that the battalion HQ officer had loaded near the border.

Less than a kilometer from Israeli territory, relentless fighting continued in the village of Eyta a-Sha'ab, close to where the kidnapping had taken place on the first day of the war. A regular army paratroopers brigade had entered the village on the night of July 30, shortly before Israel announced a letup in the air strikes. Although two and a half weeks had passed since the abduction, and the village was only one and a half kilometers from the border, the IDF still had not overcome Hezbollah resistance there. The paratroops' ingress had not resulted in a substantial change in the situation. During the next four days, four of the brigade's men were killed by small-arms fire and by a weapon that now became the nemesis of the infantry: antitank missiles. The military concept that had served the IDF so effectively against the Palestinians in the occupied territories proved exceedingly difficult to apply in southern Lebanon. In the West Bank and Gaza Strip, the army positioned snipers and sharpshooters in houses inside the qasbahs and refugee camps, who zeroed in on armed but untrained Palestinians. The Palestinians' relatively simple antitank weapons had a hard time penetrating the Merkava tanks or hitting infantry troops protected by a sophisticated "envelope" of control and observation equipment. In Lebanon, however, the paratroops discovered a different kind of enemy: Hezbollah fighters who did not up and flee. They had excellent command of their own territory and were not afraid to die. (In some cases, they shaved their body hair and heads in preparation for a "holy death" during battle). The houses in Palestinian villages and cities that the regular army units had occupied temporarily for ambushes were relatively safe hideaways, while in Lebanon these houses became death traps. Hezbollah's advanced antitank missiles, such as the Coronet and MATIS, penetrated the houses and caused fatalities. Another reservist brigade, Carmeli, which later entered the same village, also failed to complete its mission, and the brigade commander even ordered one battalion to withdraw after a soldier was killed. He was bitterly criticized for this after the war. Eyta a-Sha'ab was another symbol of Israel's performance in the war, the village where it all began, where the IDF thrashed about for four weeks and never succeeded in taking. At home, Israelis found it difficult to understand how this was possible.

On August 9, General Eisenkott presented the government with an update on the ground fighting. The head of the operations branch had to inform the ministers that Eyta a-Sha'ab had still not been captured, even though the mission was supposed to have been completed a day earlier. Olmert demanded an explanation. Eisenkott promised to find out the reason. The ministers were skeptical and bemused. Eyta a-Sha'ab was not the only place from which the IDF had retreated and then become bogged down in battle again in the fourth week of the operation. The army had not recuperated yet from the events at Bint J'Bayel; the wound refused to heal. Although Operation Change of Direction 8 called for the IDF's deployment on the line of the Step, on August 6 the Northern Command was ordered to return and take control of the town located to the south of it. Gal Hirsch protested that Hezbollah's Zone 3 (a large force stationed in the center of South Lebanon), which was operating in the area, was about to collapse if only GHQ would allow the troops to continue their movement north. As in the previous battle, Hirsch and Udi Adam decided to limit GHQ's original plan, but the general staff in Tel Aviv ordered them to get the tank column moving into the town. Despite this, the two commanders instructed the paratroop brigade to capture the compound where an IDF Brigade had been positioned up until the Israeli withdrawal from the area in 2000, a strategic point dominating the junction at the town's northern entrance. The Command's order to the 91st Division's headquarters contained a curious item: The forces were instructed to raise the Israeli flag in the locality's headquarters. (Raising the flag was not in itself unusual, but that it would be included with the list of commands was.) Adam speculated that the order came directly from the chief of staff. The Northern Command contends that "Halutz was perpetually involved with perception and symbols." "He talks about perception and takes the IDF spokeswomen Miri Regev with him on every tour. Time after time the chief of staff told us: 'But you promised they'd raise a flag.' We didn't think this was vital." The paratroopers' brigade commander, Hagai Mordechai, who was sent back to Bint J'Bayel after his force had advanced north, discovered that his mission—the capture of the compound—was more complicated than he had estimated. His battalions were exhausted after consecutive days of fighting and supply foul-ups. On August 8, Mordechai sent two battalions to the crossroads, from the east and west. A force from the brigade's reconnaissance battalion found itself in serious trouble. The men came under concentrated fire from a large house—nicknamed "the monster"—that overlooked the junction. Two soldiers were killed. At Mordechai's request, a jet fighter dropped a one-ton bomb 200 meters from the force. A few Hezbollah fighters were killed. In the meantime, Mordechai decided to abandon the idea of flying a flag from the headquarters building. The assignment that had seemed bewildering to him from the first was just too risky. Instead, the flag was photographed flying from an adjacent building. The paratroopers quit Bint J'Bayel after they accomplished what they felt was their primary mission, gaining control of the junction. "Flying the flag," Mordechai later charged, "was not the main thing [we were supposed to do]. I had no intention of endangering the lives of my men for it. If this is how the soldiers understood it, then it means we didn't explain ourselves properly." The quest for a victory picture did not end here—and was destined to involve more tragedy.

There was no sense of urgency in all the ground moves in the first ten days of August. After the war, the basic principle in David Ben-Gurion's security concept was repeated ad nauseum: Given Israel's inferiority in population size and territorial dimensions, the IDF had to make every effort to limit the length of a military campaign and transfer the fighting to the enemy's territory as quickly as possible. Nothing like this happened (nor was it discussed) during the second Lebanon war. The political echelon made it clear during most of the war that the IDF had all the time it needed. The chief of staff failed to make a determined decision regarding a large-scale ground offensive. Both echelons were terrified of incurring heavy losses. In most cases, the units operating in southern Lebanon received no specific targets and were not given strict schedules for carrying out their missions. Until the last stages of the war, the cessation of Katyusha fire almost never appeared as the objective. Under these circumstances, little wonder that the troops in the field had a hard time figuring out what was expected of them and were unable to discern the key differences between the approach to war and the approach to a regular security operation.

The frequent changes in missions had an extremely negative effect on the lower links in the chain, those who had to switch their positions and missions every two days without knowing what had caused the change. The army's decision to pull out units from Lebanon for rest and recreation (R&R) only added to the confusion. Sometimes units returned to the border the same way they had left only two or three days earlier: under fire. At the same time, the troops sent to relieve them had no clue as to why so complicated a transfer was necessary if Israeli forces were already in the sector. To the men in regular army units who were used to daily security operations, the fact that the fighting ended with casualties seemed a failure and a defeat. No one at headquarters took the trouble to explain that proportions are often different in wartime, or how their duty in Lebanon actually served the war's aims. Many of the egresses to R&R were accompanied by emotional encounters between the soldiers and their parents. Although some of the men undoubtedly derived strength and resolve from the contact with home, infantry brigade officers also tell of parents who beseeched them: "Just keep my son safe." This was a hefty psychological load for a platoon or company commander who would be returning to Lebanon a day later and whose superior officers expected him to carry out his assignments at almost any price.

The situation in the reserve units was not much different. "You sit outside and realize that this is a war of choice," one officer said. "After all, we started it. The enemy is not about to wipe us off the map. You don't have the sense of a real emergency: It's not the Yom Kippur War. The reserves were shocked by the thought of ingresses and egresses from the territory. All the dynamics that entering and exiting entailed were problematic. If you're in, you kill two terrorists and get out. It's natural for people to ask: Is this the reason that human lives are being endangered, to get a battalion into a mess?"

The fighting in Lebanon sparked uncomfortable questions about things that the IDF considered sacred cows, such as adhering to the objectives. Carmeli pulled a battalion out of Eyta a-Sha'ab after the death of one of its men—not the only case of "tactical retreat." Such incidents repeated themselves in the following days in the Yiftach Armored Brigade in Marj-Ayoun and in the 551st Reservist Paratrooper Brigade in Reshef. These events were connected to an ongoing debate over semantics and values: Had the IDF forgotten how to win, or had it simply convinced itself, as the chief of staff claimed, that "victory against terrorism is an irrelevant term?" A senior IAF officer who inspected various divisional headquarters in the North noticed the gap between the blue (air force) and green (land forces) headquarters. In the air force, orders were issued simply and clearly because their objective—delivering a bomb to its target—was always the same; on land, however, words rang empty. Everything was "sort of," approximately.

The IDF still had not broken through the few kilometers north of the border in the strip that Hezbollah had armed with bunkers, explosives, anti-tank missiles, and Katyushas. General Kaplinsky, who frequently toured the North, "was shocked to see a division thrown into the field and nothing happening," lamented an officer who served with him. "Naturally, the divisions always had loads of excuses."

LOGISTICAL CONSTERNATION

The declining morale in the reserve units combined with serious problems in logistics. The media picked up the first complaints from the reservists in the first week of August and they were related to two different issues: the quality of the equipment they had received at the mobilization camps, and the lack of food and water once they crossed into Lebanon. The IDF's own investigation after the war showed that the shortages had two main causes: reorganization in the IDF in the years preceding the war, and the Northern Command's controversial decisions. In retrospect, it seems that the lack of food and water was more serious than the quality of the equipment.

In recent years, the IDF had gambled that the probability of war was low—and that if war erupted, there would be ample time to organize. The state of preparedness of the emergency layout fell into disrepair because of the IDF's ongoing struggle against Palestinian terror, its involvement in the disengagement process, and its wide-scale, chaotic organizational overhaul. But the most difficult problems came to light only when the army was deployed in Lebanese territory. Organizational procedures for approving plans and emergency preparedness were nonexistent in the prewar years. General Adam's decision to bar the entry of supply convoys into Lebanon created a major problem for the forward units. The Northern Command's prewar plans did take into account infantry movement in the first stages of a major action, but afterward, a large-scale operation was supposed to open passages and enable convoys to roll into the area. Adam's blanket prohibition on the entry of vehicles (excluding tanks and Achzarit APCs) and the infuriatingly slow pace in forging the passages severed the link between the advanced forces and the supply. The IDF, which had come to perceive itself as a modern, technological army, now operated in the field at almost the same level as the Hezbollah fighters. In fact, the latter's situation was probably better, as many villages and bunkers had amassed stockpiles of food and water capable of sustaining Hezbollah forces for weeks at a time. The troops of the most modern army in the Middle East scavenged the villages, desperate for food and water, and the heat of July and August only exacerbated their predicament. Sometimes the soldiers were forced to break into village grocery shops and markets to stock up on water. After the war, scathing criticism was hurled at the Northern Command's decisions regarding basic troop supplies. "Logistical units know how to work in combat conditions," says a senior officer. "Perhaps a few oil drums and water tanks would have been lost to roadside bombs, but that happens to armored tanks, too. This is the price of war. Make no doubt about it, we had to build logistical corridors and get the convoys to the troops, but most of the time the divisional commanders weren't aware of how important this issue was, mainly because they hadn't trained for it for years. Instead of convoys, we were stuck with llamas."[6]

None of the senior officers in GHQ warned Halutz in time about the implications of his prohibition on convoys. The Logistics Branch, whose senior officers almost never entered Lebanon, was unaware of the severity of the situation. Investigations discovered that the Northern Command and the 91st Division kept no documents in real time of the amount of equipment that the field forces lacked. In the absence of orderly records, the Logistics Branch concentrated its efforts on improvising solutions mostly based on how close the forces were to the border, company strength, or the commanders' ability to make direct contact with relevant quartermaster officers. On more than one occasion the chaos led to excessive amounts of equipment being sent to the wrong places, especially on the Israeli side of the border. Even the troops in the strongholds along the border often lacked of food because of logistical bungling. The situation was very disturbing, especially since the IDF had failed in a campaign against a terrorist organization that was employing Katyushas, and not even against a country like Syria that was capable of launching thousands of rockets—and more technologically superior ones at that—in one day into the home front.

Units that entered Lebanon with enough supplies for two days found themselves stuck in the field for a week, with quite a few hungry and thirsty soldiers wandering around looking for food between battles. As usual, the air force came to the ground forces' assistance. In the last days of the war, the IDF came up with a new solution: Blackhawk helicopters, and later Hercules cargo planes, took enormous risks in low-flying missions, dropping equipment and supplies to the forces. No less that 360 tons of supplies reached the field units this way. This impressive, spur-of-the-moment undertaking entailed a great effort—performed in order to get supplies to troops who in most cases were operating only 5 to 10 kilometers north of the Israeli border.

THE TEARS FALL BY THEMSELVES

The Arab foreign ministers have met in Lebanon today to discuss the current crisis. Owing to the event, the Lebanese minister of the interior, Ahmad Fatfat, honored the democratic regimes of Saudi Arabia and Egypt by prohibiting public demonstrations during the day. There's a kilometer-long line of cars waiting for gasoline on Hamra's [a western Beirut neighborhood] streets. Some of the drivers are pushing their cars; others are getting coffee and a sandwich while they wait; last night the hospitals announced that there's enough oil for only another few weeks. The owners of the Yunis coffee shop have only one week's supply of coffee left. Prime Minister Siniora is crying on television again. Why doesn't somebody tell him there's a shortage of handkerchiefs and we expect many more bereaved mothers who will have a greater need for this tiny commodity.

Emily, Monday, August 7, 2006, 10:41 a.m.

Siniora burst into tears at the Arab foreign ministers' summit meeting in Beirut. From the outset of the war, whenever he mentioned the Lebanese dead, the tears started to flow. "We know that we're not the only ones facing this catastrophe. Our brothers in Palestine and Iraq also suffer from the occupation," he bewailed. After the speech, he called on the Arab states for help and began weeping again. "It is your obligation and responsibility to stand by us." The Arab foreign ministers appeared moved and gave him a drawn-out applause. Only the Syrian minister, Walid Muallem, stormed out of the summit in anger ten minutes after it began. Muallem, who arrived in Beirut a day earlier, maintained a high profile in the media and staged four press conferences in less than 24 hours. He described the proposals for a resolution being drafted in the UN Security Council as a "recipe for perpetuating the war." The foreign minister, who by Damascus standards was considered to have pro-Western views, had no qualms about expressing Syria's unlimited support of Hezbollah. "We are ready to join the organization's ranks and stand shoulder to shoulder with Hassan Nasrallah and the defense of Lebanon," he declared. Deviating from the Syrian position, Muallem announced, "The Sha'aba Farms are Lebanese." But the Syrian minister's statements also elicited an angry response in Lebanon. Siniora's supporters suspected that the change in the Syrian position on the Sha'aba Farms issue was intended to radicalize Lebanon in the negotiations with Israel on the formula of the Security Council resolution and prevent the Arab summit from arriving at practical decisions. As was his custom, the Druze leader Walid Junbalatt, did not mince words. "Assad is a lion in Lebanon and a rabbit on the Golan. If it wasn't for the [Arab] tradition of acting the host, we would have stoned him [Muallem] to death," he fumed.

Syria was the only Arab state that openly backed Hezbollah. In the second week of August, the Israeli daily *Ha'aretz* reported: "In Syria, if until now only pictures of the president, Basher Assad, were hung on the streets and from balconies, the picture has now changed. Next to Assad a new figure has made its entrance in the Syrian public: Hassan Nasrallah. According to reports from Damascus, the city is flooded with Hezbollah paraphernalia. Hezbollah flags are draped over porch fronts and Nasrallah's profile adorns car windows. The souvenir industry connected to Hezbollah and the Nasrallah cult is booming." These sentiments overflowed into the Arab street in other countries, too, but unlike Syria, the authorities did not take an active part in the ritual. Even secular demonstrators brandished pictures of Hezbollah's leader in demonstrations in Amman and Cairo. The Palestinians in the occupied territories held daily parades in support of Hezbollah, and kiosks sold cassettes with songs extolling the chairman's honor.

But Nasrallah did not help Bashar Assad out of his long-standing political isolation. France's foreign minister met with the Iranian foreign minister in Beirut but continued to avoid official contact with Syria. The French, like their Lebanese friends of the anti-Syrian March 14 camp, regarded the Syrians as inexorable subversives who wanted to take over Lebanon. Indeed, Damascus used Hezbollah not only as an effective means of pricking Israel but also for the preservation of Syria's political and military influence in Lebanon. The moderate Arab states viewed Syria as Iran's fifth column in the Arab League. During the summit, when Muallem wanted to change the wording of Siniora's seven-point plan, which had been adopted by the Arab foreign ministers, by including in it support of Hezbollah, the Lebanese prime minister bitterly criticized him. After the representatives of Egypt, Saudi Arabia, Jordan, and Libya joined in the criticism, the Syrians declared they were leaving the summit in protest. A delegation of Arab foreign ministers flew to New York at the end of the summit in order to "present the Arab position to the Security Council"—in other words, to change the wording of the decision for a cease-fire that France and the United States were hammering out.

Siniora made his most successful political maneuver a few hours later, on the evening of August 7. He managed to get the government to approve the deployment of 15,000 Lebanese army troops in the South. Hezbollah and Amal ministers supported the proposal. UN officials in Lebanon, the speaker of parliament Nabih Beri, and even Nasrallah himself took part in formulating the resolution. Siniora understood that such a move would win the hearts of the Americans and French, demonstrate his seriousness and determination, and hamstring Hezbollah. "Once again he surprised us," admits a Western diplomat serving in Israel. "The deployment of the Lebanese army in the South was not specifically mentioned in the American-French draft, but Siniora exploited Hezbollah's military adversity in order to obtain a resolution better than the one we expected." Until the outbreak of the war, France and other countries persistently pressured Siniora to make a similar decision, only to see their efforts ignored. The announcement that Lebanese forces would be dispatched to the South after the cease-fire and Israeli withdrawal was designed to bolster Siniora's bartering strength vis-à-vis the United States and France over the wording of the draft. The Lebanese government's decision resulted in a breakthrough in the negotiations between the two Western partners on the draft's text. Thanks to the decision, France agreed for the first time to send an international force to the South immediately after the cease-fire went into effect and to arrange the force's mandate within the framework of the UN's first resolution.

Why did Nasrallah agree to have the army stationed in the South? Two days after the government's decision, Hezbollah's Secretary General sounded like the army's greatest admirer—the same army that he had earlier adamantly refused entry into the South. "True, in the past we were opposed to the army's deployment, not because we suspected it, heaven forbid. Our objection stemmed from our fear for the army's safety," Nasrallah said in an interview on Al-Manar. "We believed that when the army headed south, to the border, its job would be to defend Lebanon and the homeland and not protect the enemy. Now the Lebanese government has decided that the army's main role is to defend the homeland. As I see it, the army's deployment is a politically honorable exit plan that will lead to a halt in the [Israeli] attacks because it will be a national army acting in accordance with the instructions of the elected Lebanese government." Hezbollah's agreement to having the army in the South was based not only on a desire to boost national pride; Nasrallah may have also felt that the Lebanese army, most of whose soldiers were Shiites, would avoid clashing with Hezbollah's troops. The bottom line was that the organization had suffered serious setbacks on the military level and feared a defeat. In order to arrive at a cease-fire peacefully, Nasrallah had to swallow a few frogs, one of which was the dispatch of the Lebanese army to the South.

HALF-TRUTH

On the Israeli side, the continuous floundering in southern Lebanon increased consternation at the political level. Amir Peretz came under heavy pressure and seemed to be influenced by the last person who spoke with him on any given day. He gradually came to realize that the only solution was a large-scale ground operation. On August 3, his office released a startling statement to the press. The defense minister, it read, had ordered the IDF to prepare for a rapid takeover of the entire region south of the Litani River against all launch sites. Officially, such a move depended on the cabinet's approval, but Peretz managed to outflank Olmert on the right. The public and the media perceived the minister as someone who invariably recognized the correct direction: while he was for an operation from the start, it was the prime minister holding him back. In reality, Peretz seemed less inclined to act than his office portrayed him. But, in an exceptional step, he not only exposed internal differences of opinion while the war was still raging but also unwittingly provided Hezbollah with a great deal of information. Later the media

184 — 34 DAYS —

became the target—and justifiably so—of criticism for its early publication of
the IDF's moves, but it was the politicians who were responsible for the first
leaks.

On August 7, Olmert accompanied Peretz and Halutz to the Northern
Command. This was the prime minister's second and last visit to the headquarters during the war. Olmert met reserve officers from units that had been
mobilized. One complained about the equipment, and a colleague cut him
short, saying, "There's always an equipment shortage. Let's go in already."
Olmert was the symbol of fortitude, telling the officers: "War involves
fatalities, pain, tears, trauma. But this is the hour we must rise to meet the
challenge. We're not going to stop. We have to end the Katyusha fire." He
repeated the same words in other talks with senior officers in GHQ and the
Northern Command. "The whole time Olmert banged on the table: 'hit
them, destroy them,'" one of the participants recalled. "It was pathetic. He
reminded us of his caricature on the popular TV satire show *Eretz Nehederet*
[A Wonderful Country]. On the other hand, he spent a lot of time asking
about the cost of the impending attack. 'How much will it cost us [in human
life]?' he wanted to know." Adam, like Kaplinsky two days earlier, felt that the
question and the way it was asked were not fair. This is a cruel question, he
thought; how are we supposed to know? The head of Northern Command
had other reservations. "We're dealing exclusively with Hezbollah. This is
our mistake," Adam claimed. "When the electricity in restaurants in southern
Beirut falls from 100 watts to 40, then they'll begin to hurt. Then we'll see
results." Adam wanted to know why the air force had stopped its massive
attacks on Beirut, why the ground offensive had been postponed. "Udi, Udi,
Tony Blair is speaking with me about the situation in Lebanon," replied
Olmert. "Do you want to bomb Beirut right now? The entire international
community will start jumping up and down." General Benny Ganz joined in
the criticism. "I respect your firm decision after the abduction for attacking,"
he said to Olmert, "but we need to do something else now. We need to bring
in large forces and strike at the heart of Hezbollah's operations, in the territory south of the Litani." Then Olmert said something that shocked Adam
and Ganz: "Until today's meeting," the prime minister claimed, "nobody
showed me any plans for taking control of the territory south of the Litani.
Every plan that the army has showed me, I've approved." Olmert turned to
Halutz to confirm what he just said. The chief of staff kept silent. The political echelon, the prime minister continued, doesn't determine military moves.

It receives recommendations and decides whether or not to accept them. Already aware of the danger of an investigation committee that was already hovering over his head at this stage of the war, Olmert described the problematic division of labor between the cabinet and GHQ. But the cabinet had to be much more involved in the war (it is doubtful whether Rabin or Sharon would have made such a statement). Adam was flabbergasted over another matter. The war had begun almost four weeks ago, and here was the prime minister saying that none of the plans for a ground offensive had been presented to the political echelon. It was at this point that a realization hit him: Halutz may have blocked them. But he had no way of knowing at the time that Olmert had revealed only half the truth to the officers and that for a long time Olmert had eschewed a detailed discussion of the plans (although it was true that Halutz was not enthusiastic about discussing them). The last time Olmert had discussed these plans was just two days ago.

But now Adam had other problems to deal with.

DISMISSAL

Dan Halutz had considered firing Adam for a long time. The roots of the tension between the chief of staff and the head of Northern Command have already been described. Halutz found Adam indecisive, unfocused, and insufficiently assertive. Adam felt that the chief of staff was conceited, infuriatingly cemented to his air concept, and disingenuous when it came to backing his subordinates. The prolongation of the fighting, without any real gains, only exacerbated the crisis between the Kirya, the military headquarters in Tel Aviv, and Safed, the city where Northern Command HQ was located. The ongoing dispute over Bint J'Bayel intensified the mutual hostility between the two commanders, as did their divergent positions on the timing and scope of the ground operation. Halutz must have realized (as Olmert certainly did) that the campaign was approaching its end, and that this war would not produce many victory parades. Halutz knew that sometime in the next few days the IDF would probably launch the ground offensive that he had been trying to avoid for three weeks. Perhaps Halutz decided to fire Adam because he hoped that the infusion of fresh blood into the Northern Command would enhance the last and most critical phase of the war. A less generous interpretation is that Halutz already saw the criticism against the IDF after the war. Getting rid of Adam may have been his attempt to pass the guilt onto his subordinate for all the delays and blunders in the war. That morning, before the discussion with Olmert, Halutz entered Adam's office and told him bluntly, "I've decided to bring in Benny Ganz as my representative."[7] Adam responded angrily, "No problem. I'll go home. If I'm not up to it, you can fire me, but Ganz won't be coming here." Don't try me, Halutz said. Adam wanted to find out why Halutz was so angry with him. The chief of staff replied that the command had not carried out its missions. "We're about to commence a major operation. I need a GHQ rep here," he said. "Then you sit here," Adam suggested. Later that day the chief of staff returned with an alternative suggestion. "What about Kaplan [Kaplinsky]?" Adam said that if Kaplinsky was Halutz's representative, then he (Adam) could live with that. Adam felt that bringing in Kaplinsky was slightly less insulting than Ganz, who, as commander of the geouns forces, was in a position equal to his and had previously served as the head of Northern Command. In fact, Adam had been very critical of the condition of Command when he took over from Ganz. There was an additional palliative in having Kaplinsky come in as Halutz's representative—the deputy chief of staff would be there as the chief of staff's eyes and ears, not as Adam's superior. The exact division of authorities between the two was not made clear.

Very few people were privy to these plans, but in less than 24 hours, the decision was leaked to the media. Adam's phone was inundated with calls from officers and friends expressing sympathy and understanding for his plight. He set out to visit one of his units where he was scheduled to give a television interview. His reaction didn't conform to the official line from the chief of staff. "If I'm being fired, then I take this very seriously. It's a vote of no confidence." One of the officers accompanying the general realized that Adam, in effect, was resigning live on TV. Adam and the interviewer were about to take their leave when the officer convinced the general to rerecord the interview, this time in a milder vein. In the jeep ride back to the Northern Command, the general gave vent to his rage, telling his staff: "I'm a tanker. I've always been a loyal officer, but Halutz lied to me." However, in later responses to the networks, he made sure to assume a statesmanlike pose. "I feel the burden of responsibility," he said. "Right now there are soldiers fighting valiantly and courageously. This is war—some things are more important than [bringing in Kaplinsky]. I don't see this as a dismissal and I don't see myself as the guard at the gate."

With Kaplinsky's mollifying presence, Adam was left as a group player (at least until the end of the war). Kaplinsky took care to treat Adam with dignity and, in the following days, managed to neutralize most of the potential points of friction between the two. "He's a good guy," Adam said of the deputy chief of staff. "You can't be angry with him. If somebody had to come in, fortunately it was Kaplan."

The affair had a catastrophic effect on the public. The media stopped cutting the army slack. Daily opinion polls and the IDF's spokesman showed that the public, like the newsmen, viewed the move as Adam being given his walking papers—and doubted the army's ability to defeat Hezbollah. Kaplinsky, who was following orders, did so with many doubts. In the end, no one was more suited for the uninviting task. The deputy chief of staff was "Mr. Lebanon" in Halutz's headquarters, but Kaplinsky had no illusions; despite the hopes pinned on him, the change in command structure was too late to produce a turnabout in the war. That evening, after the publicity, he spoke with an officer who had once served under him. "From this kind of a move," the officer told Kaplinsky, "you either end up prime minister or the head of the Gedera town council."[8] Halutz, whose relations with his deputy were already frazzled at this point, probably knew that the appointment would sling some of the mud associated with the war's failure on Kaplinsky, too. After the war, the deputy chief of staff must have speculated what would have happened if Halutz had listened to his advice at the beginning of the war and appointed Gabi Ashkenazi to work with Adam. Would Ashkenazi still be Halutz's successor now?

A KATYUSHA IN KFAR GILADI

The turning point in public opinion, which until then had solidly backed the government's policy in Lebanon, came in fact two days before Adam's ouster. A number of Olmert's advisors refer to August 6 as the day the prime minister lost the war.

The morning began fairly propitiously. Olmert sounded self-confident in the weekly government meeting, even a little too cocksure. The previous evening, the helitransport of paratrooper units had been canceled. In a few days, the American envoys, Welch and Abrams, would be arriving in Israel with the final wording of the proposed draft for the Security Council resolution. The prime minister showered praise on his ministers, the government, and himself for having made the decision to embark on a campaign that had set back Iran's and Hezbollah's plans to attack Israel in the future. "A great miracle has been rendered to us by the Lord Almighty, who created a situation that was revealed today and not, Heaven forbid, in two or three years from now. . . . If this hadn't happened [the abduction of the soldiers], no one in the military establishment would have suggested such an operation. I know that here are those who ask why this or that prime minister did or didn't do something, but it is easy to ask such questions. . . . The army received full support, receives full support, and has chalked up some splendid achievements. No state in the modern world has accomplished so much in the War on Terror."[9] But reality, as usually happens, returned and intruded in a most ugly way into the prime minister's forecast. While he was speaking, his aides brought him a note: catastrophe at Kfar Giladi.

The Katyusha explosion at Kfar Giladi that morning was the most lethal event in the war: 12 soldiers, all paratroop reservists bivouacked in the Kfar Giladi quarry, were killed. The dust from the quarry, in addition to the oppressive heat, irritated the soldiers, and they asked to be allowed to enter the adjacent kibbutz. Until permission was granted, they waited next to the kibbutz cemetery. The Katyusha scored a direct hit on one of the vehicles filled with soldiers, killing all of the passengers and other reservists standing nearby. The media set up a direct transmission from the scene of the carnage. Hezbollah, too, listened to the broadcasts and continued shelling the direct area. The TV's open channel proved a boon to Hezbollah and reflected the difficulty of waging a war where the front and rear were practically intertwined. True as this was, from the start of the war, the IDF displayed exasperating apathy toward defending its camps. While the citizens in the North were instructed to remain in bomb shelters, the soldiers in the nearby bases paid little heed to warnings—not even wearing protective vests and helmets. Often the units' assembly and staging areas were located in the middle of fields exposed to Katyusha fire. The fact that all the casualties were reservists, many of them fathers, had an immense impact on public morale. Thus, on August 6, even before the major ground offensive had commenced, the cost of the war was painfully and tangibly felt. The men had been killed inside Israeli territory by a short-range Katyusha missile, the same weapon that the chief of staff had dismissingly defined at the opening of hostilities as "an irrelevant threat."

But the soldiers' deaths were not the end of the prime minister's troubles that day. One minute before the 8 p.m. news, information came of a deadly rocket falling on Haifa, killing three civilians. Only a day before, the IDF had boasted that air force's efforts had put the city out of rocket fire range. "This is the moment when public opinion switched," confessed one of Olmert's staff members. "Two days earlier, there was a feeling that the whole country was united. But on August 6, a sense of distaste and disgust sunk in. People had the impression that we were 'catching it' on every corner, almost like the destruction of the Third Temple." Olmert, who up till then had enjoyed close to 70 percent of the public's support, witnessed his popularity decline steeply in the following days. The IDF spokesman's surveys also showed that public confidence in the army, which had peaked after the first week of the war, had plummeted from grade C to grade F.

PERETZ STILL VACILLATES

The participants in the discussion on Tuesday evening, August 8, in the defense minister's office, were surprised by Peretz's opening statement. The group of outside advisors gathered in the Kirya was supposed to give its opinion of a large-scale ground offensive, the one that Peretz had promised five days earlier. But the defense minister expected something else from them. "Forget about the strategic discussion," he said, "what interests me now is do I or do I not give the army my backing, under what conditions, and how can I survive politically?" Most of the speakers explained that on the political level, it was hard to see how he would get out of the war without being seriously hurt. Then they turned to the strategic context. After being shown the outline of the operation, some of the advisors, former generals, expressed their support for a ground offensive designed to take control of southern Lebanon. Others felt that the war must not be allowed to end without a crippling blow to Hezbollah; still others strenuously opposed this. Peretz's political advisors, Uzi Baram, Hagai Alon, and Oriella Ben-Zvi, voiced their reservations over the operation. The retired generals asked Peretz how much time the IDF wanted for the job. "The army says it needs more than three days, less than five," answered the defense minister. Former chief of staff Amnon Lipkin-Shahak said that "if the army's working assumption is that gaining control of the territory will reduce the volume of Katyusha fire and there's time for it—then we have to go into action. But if there's not enough time, then we mustn't go in." Peretz got what he wanted: backing for his feeling that a ground offensive was necessary. "The retired generals gave him an alibi," says a former member of Peretz's inner circle. (Most of the inner circle staff became *former* members because of their differences with him by the end of the war.) "Later, when Peretz was criticized for his decision, his answer was: 'What do you want from me? All the generals spoke in favor of a ground offensive.' He only neglected to mention that they warned him not to begin the operation if there wasn't enough time to finish it."

CHAPTER ELEVEN

THE CABINET

F OR THE FIRST ten days of August, before the massive ground offensive, the war seemed to be going nowhere. The Israel Defense Forces acted like an injured beast: It writhed in pain and wound up hurting itself. If one insists on tracing the IDF's moves on a map, it is hard to discern where the army fought and what Hezbollah did. The army invested enormous effort over the years in acquiring and producing technologies for destroying the enemy at a distance while limiting the number of Israeli casualties. Naturally the IDF made copious use of air strikes and artillery barrages. But reality proved that this was not enough and that close combat in the field was needed to defeat Hezbollah—a tactic that was avoided almost at all costs. Most officers at the senior level were in favor of practical moves that would "somehow pass the time" until the cease-fire, which was being worked out in political channels, went into effect. Hezbollah's strategy during the first third of August added to Israel's consternation. Hezbollah secretary general Nasrallah continuously signaled to the Israeli public and army reservists that theirs was not a war of survival but of Hezbollah's response to Israel's moves. The reservists' commanders found a glaring discrepancy between their troops' willingness to sacrifice as far as the border and their attitude toward sacrifice north of it. The gap was even greater after the Qana ceasefire, when it became clear that Nasrallah was prepared to cease hostilities if Israel followed suit. Hezbollah's message "if you want—we'll stop shooting" influenced the fighting spirit of Israeli society, which was not at its peak in the summer of 2006.

Most of the fighting took place in built-up areas. This created a paradox. In order to have the freedom to fight in such an area, civilians had to be evacuated. This occurred in South Lebanon, when the majority of the inhabitants fled their homes because of the Israeli bombings. But their flight failed to influence the Lebanese consciousness in the way that Israel expected. Israel misread Lebanon on this point. It is not a unified country, and the degree of obligation by the government and population in Beirut to the suffering of the inhabitants of the South, many of them Shiite, is limited. The Shiites were not a small, weak minority that the other ethnic communities in Lebanon could bend to their will. Israel's official spokespersons constructed a theory according to which Lebanon was a sovereign state. But it is one thing to tout this publicly; to believe in it and act accordingly is another. Hezbollah continued its shooting spree because only Israel's massive ground forces, which were not applied early in the war, might have been able to stop it. Until the Katyusha launchers were knocked out, Hezbollah continued its rain of missiles. Hezbollah fighters who remained in South Lebanon knew the terrain inside out and seemed to vanish into thin air after shooting the rockets. The IDF was unable to overpower a large number of them, and the Israelis were surprised by the Hezbollah guerrillas' fighting capacity, determination, command of forward units, and relatively high level of military intelligence. The large prisoner-of-war camps that the IDF had prepared in the Galilee remained unoccupied. Almost no Hezbollah guerrilla surrendered. The few who were taken prisoner usually had been surprised at home while sleeping.

After the war, General (Res.) Giora Rom wrote that the IDF "failed to understand the deep-seated feeling in the heart of the Israeli public. Then it happened. One day something snapped in the public: from the sense that victory was possible to the growing malaise of uncertainty regarding the likely outcome. The IDF may have judged the Katyusha phenomenon through the equation of civilian losses: Hezbollah missiles vis-à-vis the number of civilian deaths from Palestinian suicide attacks. Based on this parameter, Israel's decision-makers seem to have assumed that the Katyusha ordeal could be tolerated for a long time." Hezbollah, however, perceived that this was likely to be the "finest hour" of its Katyusha layout, which had been organized and prepared with military precision and discipline. The organization's ground force defended the Katyusha launch sites and was reinforced with firing positions, bunkers, improvised explosives (IEDs), and antitank units. In many cases, Hezbollah also developed a rapid response capability to IDF activity, based on tracking Israeli communications networks and military cell phone calls. Wherever ground fighting took place, it was waged according to Hezbollah's rules of the game, greatly limiting the IDF's relative advantage as an army capable of operating in a large framework with massive firepower.

THE GOOD, THE BAD, AND
THE UGLY PLAN

During the war, transportation minister Shaul Mofaz acted as a kind of tacit opposition to the government's moves. Mofaz, who had been alienated from the defense ministry in May as a result of the coalitional deal woven by Prime Minister Olmert and Defense Minister Peretz, was aware of the IDF's weaknesses in ground fighting. (To a great degree he was also responsible for them because of certain decisions he made in the years preceding the war.) After the first week of the bombings, he had grave doubts over the advantage of prolonging the war; he also harbored reservations about getting bogged down in Bint J'Bayel; and he was especially skeptical over the introduction of massive ground forces into Lebanon. But it seems unlikely that the former defense minister and former chief of staff Mofaz, the most experienced player in military affairs at the government table, can chalk up any success for himself during the war. While Olmert, on a number of occasions, consulted with him discreetly (lest Peretz take umbrage), in practice the prime minister preferred not to take Mofaz's advice. Prior to the ingress to Bint J'Bayel, Mofaz warned Olmert not to make the move ("I was area commander. The place is a huge city where a division can easily get lost"), but Golani infantrymen already had penetrated deep in the town. When Mofaz proposed an alternative—a quick move to Tyre, the source of the rocket fire on Haifa—Olmert was surprised: "Oh really? On Haifa?" he asked his military secretary. Gadi Shamni had to admit that Mofaz was right. But Olmert did not heed his transportation minister's suggestion; and Mofaz apparently did not go the "extra mile" to exert his influence. Although he voiced his reservations in private conversations, he generally adhered to the official line.

Mofaz's main chance to influence the war occurred on the morning of August 8. Shamni called, saying "The prime minister wants to see you. Yesterday he OKed the Northern Command's plans and wants you to take a look at them." Olmert and Mofaz met in Jerusalem at noon. Shamni, Mofaz's former subordinate in the paratroops, opposed a large-scale ground operation and seems to have been behind the idea to ask Mofaz his opinion on the plan in the hope that he would find fault with the IDF's proposal.[1] Olmert and Shamni briefly presented the plan: Gal Hirsch's 91st Division would continue north; forces from Eyal Eisenberg's Fire Formation would be helicoptered north to the 91st Division, south of the Litani River; Guy Tzur's 162nd Division would cross the Saluki River from the east and proceed west, where it would join up with Eisenberg's forces and deploy along the Litani. Mofaz's opinion was unequivocal: "Don't implement the plan." Olmert asked him why. "We're now in the twenty-eighth day of the war," Mofaz replied. "Under the best of circumstances the operation will be launched two days from now. If you accept this plan, you can look forward to another two months of ground operations. Cloud formations begin in the beginning of September. This'll make it extremely difficult to get air support, carry out air observations, and go on air rescue missions. In Lebanon the rainy season begins in early October. I think it would be unwise to put four divisions in the field under present conditions. Do you really believe [our] population in the North can withstand two or three more months in bomb shelters?"

Mofaz had a different solution. "Forget about the IDF plan," he said. "Take two divisions. Go to the 'Step' above [north of] Tyre and seize the dominating areas overlooking the Litani. Do this and you've surrounded Hezbollah. They can't get out. Any Hezbollah guerrilla that sees two divisions at his rear will think twice before continuing the fighting. You want to eliminate the Katyushas? Afterwards, put two brigades in the south to deal with the pockets of resistance." The transportation minister was in effect providing a truncated, "user-friendlier" version of the army's plan. Instead of two months—two days, while employing half of the force that the IDF intended and limiting contact with the enemy. The move would be concentrated not at the border but deeper into Lebanon, where the Shiite organization's layout was thinner, and would avoid a major engagement between the Israeli troops heading north and Hezbollah's fighting force. Olmert, who had grave doubts about the army's ability to carry out its original plan, waxed enthusiastic over the idea of "Elevated Waters Lite."

Mofaz's plan seemed to offer the best of all possible worlds (relatively speaking). Israel would give Hezbollah and the Arab world a taste of its strength, but the number of casualties would be low and the fighting would end quickly. "In this way," Mofaz avowed, "the whole world will know that the IDF has reached the Litani and that Hezbollah has [been] surrounded. This'll get the political process moving. If they tell us to evacuate, we'll pull out within forty-eight hours on condition that [Hezbollah] halts the Katyushas. If we have enough time, we'll send some troops further south [for mopping up operations]. Let them begin operations in the evening of the day after tomorrow [August 10]. I can't guarantee there won't be any casualties, but we'll have established a new strategic situation. It'll be an alternative to not having eliminated Nasrallah. By Friday you'll have the trump card in your hand." Shamni and Chief of Staff Yoram Turbovitz, who took part in the meeting, also accepted the plan's inherent logic. "Tell Halutz, no . . . tell Peretz," Olmert corrected himself, "to prepare a second modus operandi based on Mofaz's plan and to present it to the cabinet tomorrow." Apparently suspicious that Mofaz was undermining him, Peretz strongly objected when he was approached by members of the Prime Minister's Office. There was no time to change plans, he charged; they'd been diddling with the army too long already. Chief of Staff Halutz readily agreed with him. When the IDF wanted to dismiss a rival plan, it always had excuses. Peretz and Halutz, like Olmert, had been leery about a ground operation throughout most of the war. Now they seemed to become the most tenacious supporters of the "grand plan."

The next day, Wednesday, August 9, the cabinet convened in Jerusalem at 10:00 a.m. for the most decisive meeting of the war. Facing the ministers, General Eisenkott outlined the military movements of the past few days. He had to admit that Change of Direction 8 had not been completed and that Hezbollah guerrillas were still in Eyta a-Sha'ab and Bint J'Bayel. Operational control in the old security area, the general acknowledged, is not complete, and several pockets of resistance are still left there. Eisenkott and Halutz presented the next plan: Change of Direction 11. "We've reached the point where we have to make a large-scale military effort in the direction of the Litani," the chief of staff announced. "This maneuver cannot be measured by the sole question: how many casualties will it entail. This is the price that has to be paid so that the operation will have an impact on the entire campaign. The political level's directive—reduce the short-range Katyushas—cannot be implemented without a ground operation." At this late hour, Halutz was merely expressing what had been obvious at least two weeks earlier. "If you want to carry out an operation, then you have to do everything [so that it will succeed] or do nothing," he concluded, with a nod toward Mofaz's proposal (which had not been introduced to the ministers yet). Foreign Minister Livni raised the same question that she posed in the meeting on the first day of the war: How do you define victory? The chief of staff's answer: "To arrive at political negotiations in a better position. The proposed move, as I stated, is a comprehensive operation. Let me add—if you don't want it carried out, then say so loud and clear. No halfway measures: We're not going to go half way, or a quarter or a third [of the way]. . . ." Halutz pointed out that the army needed another month for mopping-up operations, "but without house-to-house fighting. That would take two years." Didn't the army have a faster way of getting the job done?, Livni asked. Halutz replied in the negative. Livni shot back that the army left the political level no room for maneuvering. "If we don't approve the plan, we'll look like enemies of the state," she claimed. Some of those present thought that the chief of staff was considering tendering his resignation if the army's plan was not approved in its entirety.

Peretz gave Halutz his full backing. A ground operation has to be made, he declared—recalling his visit with reservists at the front. Minister Rafi Eitan declared his support for the transportation minister's proposal. "It's a brilliant idea," he beamed. Binyamin Ben Eliezer agreed with him. But while the proposal was gathering support from other ministers, Mofaz realized that the prime minister no longer backed him. During the meeting, Olmert conveyed a note to Eitan: "Don't back Shaul's move. It will be a blow to the security establishment." Olmert, who just one day earlier believed that Mofaz had discovered the magic bullet, now retreated. Minister Yitzhak Cohen from the Shas party, who was present in the cabinet meetings, took Turbovitz aside. "Mofaz's plan seems better," Cohen said. The head of the prime minister's staff explained that Olmert simply had no choice. "What do you want us to do?" he asked. "The chief of staff and the generals came with their plan. Can we send them home and express our lack of confidence in them?"

Probably the last thing the prime minister wanted was for even a glimmer of contention between him and GHQ, or among the cabinet ministers themselves, to be leaked to the public. Unity in the ranks was the determining factor. Even Mofaz expeditiously withdrew his proposal. When Halutz pointed out that the transportation minister's plan in effect approximated the army's proposal, Mofaz was quick to agree, although, as we have seen, there were major differences between the two plans. Olmert removed Mofaz's recommendation from the agenda and brought the IDF's plan up for a vote. None of the ministers protested or demanded explanation. Nine ministers, including the prime minister, voted in favor of the army's plan. Three ministers abstained. The plan was not approved for immediate implementation. It was agreed that the cabinet would authorize the prime minister and defense minister to decide when to issue the IDF its orders to attack.

The rejection seems to have reflected Olmert's hopes that a military operation could still be averted. Olmert left the conference room at 2:45 p.m. and phoned U.S. Secretary of State Condoleezza Rice, who informed him that the United Nations was about to reach an agreement and promised that Israel "would 'love' the resolution. You'll get everything you wanted." She said that she needed another "24 to [maximum] 48 hours" to clinch the deal. Olmert told her that he would not agree to another version of the UN's Interim Force in Lebanon, to troops from countries like Fiji. Rice promised an upgraded force with the authority to lay down the law, with backing from European states. Apparently military operations were not discussed in detail. The development of events in the course of the six-hour cabinet meeting was nothing short of astounding. As one cabinet member put it, "You had to be a moron not to recognize that [Mofaz's plan] was preferable to the army's," yet the plan disappeared as if it had never been presented. The prime minister, who had been in favor of it, reneged, as did Mofaz himself, though both men understood that they were opting for a worse choice. Peretz and minister of interior security Avi Dichter opposed the Mofaz plan from the beginning. But most of the other ministers who preferred Mofaz's proposal also backed down and voted in favor of the army's plan. They supported Halutz's and Peretz's plan, even though they doubted its feasibility. (Today some of the ministers confess that they felt already at this stage that "we lost the war.") At the end of the day, political reality won out. The ministers were careful not to be seen as purposely undermining the prime minister and defense minister, fearing that, without a military operation, Israel would be perceived as having conceded to Hezbollah. Halutz and the IDF, as usual, had an enormous influence on the vote. Few politicians had the courage to stand in the way of so crucial a matter by going against the chief of staff's opinion, even if the suspicion that Halutz's term of office was approaching its end was afloat.

The view on Olmert is still divided. Some of his advisors believe that the meeting was the biggest slipup of the war, that the prime minister still finds it difficult to explain, even to himself, why he did not proceed with his gut feelings (and what he felt during most of the war) and choose Mofaz's plan. Others allege that Mofaz's proposal was only a general layout, too rudimentary to be presented before the cabinet. The chief of staff, they claim, is a top-notch professional. When Halutz decided that Mofaz's proposal wouldn't succeed, no one could force it down his or the army's throats. Furthermore, the cabinet was not the forum for cooking up alterative military plans. Mofaz, too, had to give a reckoning of himself. After the war he claimed that "from the public's point of view, you can't vote against the security establishment in the middle of a war. Any minister who goes against the army's plans looks as though he's trying to subvert the war effort, and especially me, because I was the defense minister up until three months ago. It would have appeared as very bad." But is this not the true test of an outstanding professional figure in the cabinet? Mofaz offers a legitimate explanation at the political level, but it leaves much to be desired at the ethical level.

When the cabinet meeting was over, Mofaz accompanied Olmert on his way out. "Ehud, this isn't a good decision," he said. "Take Peretz and Halutz into a room and try to convince them [to change their minds]." That night Mofaz phoned Olmert, again pleading with him that "there's still time." As in the previous conversation, Olmert kept silent. Mofaz figured that he was still hoping that political progress would be made, thus relieving him of the onus of having to decide on a military operation.

The IDF was on tenterhooks throughout the day, waiting for the cabinet's announcement. The officers believed that they would get the green light, and even determined 8:00 p.m. as H-hour for ground operations. At 3:00 p.m., the commander of the 162nd Division, Brigadier General Tzur, ordered his engineering battalion to advance to the Saluki, the river his division was scheduled to cross. Tzur wanted to save time and lighten the gridlock that was bound to be created on the way to the river once the signal was given to commence operations. The battalion commander, Lieutenant Colonel Oshri Lugasi, who had crossed the Saluki several days earlier and was then called back, was now instructed to seize the western bank of the river and prepare the area for tank movement that night. Lugasi went down to the river where he suddenly lost radio contact because of bad reception. At 8:00 p.m., radio contact had been reestablished with the engineers who, in the meantime, had reached the river without any problems. But at almost the same time, Tzur was informed that the operation was being postponed for another 24 hours. The division commander begged his superiors to allow him to bring more forces to the western side and to helicopter a Nachal recon battalion into the villages of Farun and Randoria overlooking the Saluki. The answer was negative, and he received instructions to order the engineer battalion back to areas under IDF control. On their return, the troops' movement was observed by Hezbollah, who apparently fired antitank missiles at them, though the rockets missed. Lugasi's report was held up at the 401st Brigade's headquarters; the rest of the forces in the sector knew nothing of the incident.

The engineer battalion's officers reckoned that the missiles were fired from the Kantara area (though they probably came from Randoria). This incident, which the senior commanders hardly took notice of, would have dire consequences two and a half days later.

"RUN, EHUD, RUN"

The Northern Command and the 91st Division regarded the forward movement of the Alexandroni (reservist) infantry brigade in the western sector of South Lebanon as one of the successful maneuvers of the war. The brigade, the first large reservist force to enter the campaign, began its northward advance in the evening of August 1. In the following days, the brigade, under the command of Colonel Shlomi Cohen, took over the villages in the area with relatively few losses, but faced logistical problems in supplying the troops with food and water. On August 7, Nachum Barnea, Israel's most influential columnist with the major Israeli daily *Yediot Ahronot*, spent two days with Alexandroni soldiers in village of Ras-Biada, a few kilometers north of the Israeli border. Barnea's column recounting this experience appeared on page one of Thursday morning's edition (August 10), the day after the cabinet decision. The title was aimed directly at the prime minister: "Run, Ehud, Run." Barnea recommended that Olmert cut his losses and "hightail it" out of Lebanon. The IDF, he wrote, was not winning the war and would not win it in the coming days.

Olmert, who had known Barnea for over 30 years, undoubtedly took his words to heart. Opposition to a ground move at this late stage was also prevalent in the IDF and security establishment. But the General Staff felt it had to be done. After the head of the Northern Command was fired, after the casualties at Kfar Giladi and an almost month-long floundering, most of the generals hankered for an operation that would redress the IDF's previous poor showing. The army seems to have wanted a ground operation at almost any cost. According to one senior minister, the IDF was itching for a crack at Hezbollah even if the plan was a bad one. In the fighting up to that point, the defense minister served as the generals' impassioned mouthpiece, only rarely disputing the logic of their arguments and prognoses. On Wednesday evening, while Eisenberg's lead paratroop brigade was again on helicopters waiting to move out, head of Northern Command General Udi Adam received the cabinet's decision to postpone the operation. Furious, he told the chief of staff, "You're killing the men. They're completely exposed in the field, let them advance." This time Halutz was of like mind but could only remind Adam that they had to obey cabinet orders. The army set a new date for the operation: Thursday evening.

On Thursday at noon, Peretz met with senior GHQ officers in the Northern Command's pit and reported that David Welch, the U.S. envoy, was very optimistic about the prospects of obtaining a decision favorable to Israel. The officers were distraught when they heard that that the operation might be further delayed, and Halutz himself seethed. "It's impossible to continue postponing the operation," he raised his voice. "I'm not willing to waste any more time on your consultations—not till 16:00 [4:00 p.m.] or 17:00 [5:00]. We're going to move now!" Deputy chief of staff Kaplinsky and Adam fully supported Halutz. Five brigades are in the field, they said, under enemy fire and just sitting on their asses. Adam fumed, "The men are fed up, they're asking if this is or isn't a war. Either [we fight] or we leave." Halutz told Peretz, "We'll make the decision. Phone [Olmert] and we'll decide. It's perfectly legitimate for the prime minister to decide what he wants. But we can't continue this way without a decision. The price is too high." Peretz agreed. "I'd give the order to go ahead right now," he said, "even if [the UN] already agreed on everything. We'd make our move with flags flying after [Hezbollah committed] an aggressive act." Udi Adam kept the pressure going. "It'll be an irreparable waste of soldiers and officers if we don't attack now. You can't leave them there any longer. One thing is perfectly clear—we have to go on the offensive, [otherwise] Israel is retreating. That's how this will look." In an announcement that would prove wrong two days later, Halutz warned: "I refuse to sacrifice soldiers on an operation only to have them withdraw a day or two later." The defense minister went into the next room to call the prime minister. Peretz wanted the operation to commence. But Olmert told him there was still time, also basing this on phone calls he made to the division commanders. "The army says it can wait." Peretz came back to the room crestfallen. Halutz summed up the situation: "No-go today. We're willing to wait another 24 hours."

It was not by chance that at this critical stage Peretz repeated the symbolic importance of flag-raising. The notion of burning the enemy's consciousness again lifted its ugly head in the last days of the war, when it received a far different meaning from what its originator—the former chief of staff, Moshe (Bogie) Ya'alon—ever intended. Discussion in the IDF and at the political level over a large-scale ground operation revolved endlessly around the question of "staging a victory," that is, how to inculcate in the minds of the Arabs—no less than of the Israelis—the sense that the IDF emerged from the war as the victor despite all that occurred in the last four weeks. Olmert even found time on August 6, the day the Katyusha fell in Kfar Giladi, to call dozens of spokesmen and public relations people into his office for a gung-ho pep talk. Rare was the voice that dared criticize the lunacy of the imagery. Shortly before the last move of the war, Halutz held a meeting in his office to discuss how to convince the public that Israel had actually won. Various weird and bizarre ideas were broached for "winning the minds-and-hearts operations" and "victory pictures." The head of the GHQ planning branch, Major General Yitzhak (Khaki) Harel, was opposed to all of them. "Are you guys crazy?" he reproached his colleagues. "What are we trying to do? Rewrite history?"

NEGOTIATIONS ON THE FORTY-FOURTH FLOOR

The French delegation to the United Nations is located on the forty-fourth floor of an office building in New York on the corner of Second Avenue and Forty-eighth Street. Every morning during the last days of the war, Jean-Marc de La Sablière, the French ambassador to the UN, and his American colleague, John Bolton, met at 9:00 sharp in the delegation's conference room. Only four people took part in these meetings, which were taped: the two ambassadors and one aide apiece. In early August, talks between Washington and Paris on the Security Council resolution were done over the phone. But when the foreign offices of both countries realized that intense negotiating could only take place face to face, it was decided that from August 4, the two ambassadors to the UN would meet and report directly to their superiors.

One participant recalls that Bolton preferred the meetings in de La Sablière's office, "mainly because the coffee was better. The two of them were rather formidable characters, and critical negotiating was accompanied by raised voices as well as a lot of banter." Bolton was not considered a member of Secretary of State Rice's inner circle. He was a neoconservative, and like others in this camp, he had reservations about Rice's predilection toward the French in the talks dealing with the wording of the Security Council resolution.

The French wondered if Bolton occasionally sought advice without Rice's knowledge, sounding out ideas with his friends in the White House: John Hannah, Vice President Dick Cheney's political advisor, and two senior officials on the National Security Council, Steve Hadley and Elliot Abrams. Nevertheless, those close to Bolton claim that despite the differences of opinion with the secretary of state, he carried out her instructions loyally. De La Sablière, however, belonged to the French Foreign Office elite. His father had been France's ambassador in Tel Aviv in the 1960s and de La Sablière spent several years of his youth in Israel. According to one French diplomat, although Jerusalem believed that de La Sablière acted in Lebanon's interest, the truth is he always felt warmly toward Israel.

On Thursday, August 10, 9:00 a.m. New York time (4:00 p.m. Israel time), the two ambassadors met for their daily tête-à-tête in the meeting room under a satellite photo of France. Two days earlier, the talks had almost exploded when each side threatened to introduce a separate draft proposal for the Security Council resolution. The draft that Bolton and de La Sablière presented jointly on August 5 had been rejected by both Lebanon and Israel. Now the two ambassadors decided to hammer out a joint Franco-American resolution that would be acceptable to both Beirut and Jerusalem. But a few key issues remained unresolved: Lebanon and France (Lebanon's proxy in the talks) demanded that the resolution specifically mention the Sha'aba Farms and their transfer to UN jurisdiction. Bolton adamantly refused. The government of Prime Minister Fouad Siniora had decided on August 5 to dispatch the Lebanese army to the South once the cease-fire went into effect, winning France's heart, and, to a lesser degree, gaining Rice's sympathy. Siniora convinced Paris that the Security Council resolution regarding the deployment of a multinational force in South Lebanon had to be implemented according to Chapter 6 of the UN Charter—that is, without permitting the force to open fire in order to carry out its duty. The Americans said the resolution had to state that the force would be allowed to employ all means necessary to perform its mission. As the final clincher, France opposed Israel's demand to place an embargo on the transfer of weapons to Lebanon by deploying an international supervisory mechanism on the Syrian and Lebanese border. The Americans believed that Siniora would accept this arrangement. But when Damascus threatened that such a solution would be considered a hostile act, the French feared that its soldiers would pay the price by coming under attack in Lebanon. The fourth unresolved issue concerned the timing for the deployment of the multinational force vis-à-vis the IDF's withdrawal. (Israel and the United States demanded that the two moves occur simultaneously.) On one point, however, de La Sablière agreed with the U.S.-Israeli approach, but only after lengthy bargaining: The UN resolution would call for a cessation of *all* hostile activity—a cessation of all Hezbollah attacks and offensive operations by Israel. According to this formula, it sounded like Israeli troops would still be allowed to defend themselves after the cease-fire went into effect. The negotiations continued throughout the day. Bolton and de La Sablière came and left for telephone consultations with Washington and Paris and their representatives in Beirut and Jerusalem. Moscow, somewhat frustrated that—like the other members of the Security Council—it also had been relegated to the sidelines of the negotiations, proffered its own draft to the Security Council, calling for a 72-hour "humanitarian" cease-fire. This was Russia's attempt to pressure the United States and France to work at a faster pace. At the same time, the Arab League's foreign ministers arrived in New York: the minister of Qatar, Hamad Bin Jassam; the United Arab Emirates minister, Abdullah ben Zaid; and the secretary-general of the league, Amr Moussa. Bolton asserts that these representatives exerted a "negative influence" on Rice. "She wanted to reach a decision on a cease-fire in the United Nations the next day and listened too much to the demands of the three Arab diplomats." At around 4:00 p.m. in Jerusalem (9:00 a.m. in New York) Rice's envoy, David Welch, together with the State Department's legal advisor, Jonathan Schwartz, entered the prime minister's office after conducting a round of talks with Siniora and his staff in Lebanon. The two were joined by Dick Jones, the U.S. ambassador in Tel Aviv. (Elliott Abrams was absent this time.) At the beginning of the meeting, Welch presented his formula for the Security Council resolution to Chief of Staff Yoram Turbovitz's team. The Israelis were unpleasantly surprised. "It reminded us of the French proposals of late July," recalls a member of the Israeli team. "Welch's draft on each of the unresolved issues was closer to the Lebanese approach." But the formula was amended more to the Israelis' liking after a few hours of intensive negotiating (which included phone calls to Hadley and Abrams in Washington, State Department official Nick Burns, and the UN ambassadors). "Welch came in and out of the room, speaking with whom he had to—and by late evening a proposal was hammered out that was acceptable to us," says the senior Israeli official. "We realized that this was a nonbinding understanding. The Americans in the room, like their colleagues in Washington, made it clear that they would do everything they could to make sure that this was the final wording, but they couldn't guarantee that it would be."

The Israeli team in Jerusalem decided that the international force would operate under Chapter 7 of the UN Charter, although opinions on the Israeli team were divided. Turbovitz and Shalom Turgeman were not keen on having the force receive its mandate according to this chapter because it would greatly reduce the IDF's freedom of movement (for example, the multinational force would be allowed to open fire on Israeli aircraft). The Israelis accepted the non-binding American formula on the Sha'aba Farms conundrum: The Security Council would call on the Secretary-General of the UN to present a report with proposals for delineating Lebanon's international borders, especially in ambiguous areas, and include a mechanism for dealing with Sha'aba Farms. Welch and his staff agreed to Israel's demand that the resolution include an embargo on arms shipments to Lebanon that would be forcibly upheld. They told their Israeli interlocutors that they would present a draft of the resolution to the Security Council on the next day and that it would come up for a vote on Saturday.[2] "We went to sleep before midnight rather pleased," relates a senior Israeli official. "A few hours later we woke up with a shock."

At 11:00 p.m. Jerusalem time, the prime minister decided to "get even" with his foreign minister whom, according to Livni's people, he accused of working behind his back since the beginning of the war. When Livni concluded her meeting with Welch and Schwartz, she called Olmert and informed him that she was planning on leaving for New York within the hour in order to participate in the Security Council debate on the cease-fire. Both the Israeli ambassador to the UN, Dani Gillerman, and David Welch had asked Livni to fly to New York. The diplomats realized that the negotiations on the UN resolution would probably continue till the last minute. Livni also planned to make use of her good relationship with Rice, who was supposed to be arriving in New York the next day. But Olmert had his own agenda and forbade the foreign minister to go. "The prime minister opposed Livni's mission on two counts," an insider claims. "The Americans and French were liable to exploit her presence in New York in order to pressure her, and it was feared that Livni might clinch a deal with them that ran counter to the army's position. Also, Olmert felt that the public had the impression that it was Livni who obtained the peace, while he, the prime minister, was depicted as having embarked upon on war." Livni's objections were overruled, and the foreign minister remained in Israel.

"RICE SOLD YOU OUT TO THE FRENCH"

At 7:00 p.m. New York time (2:00 a.m. Israel time), the negotiations resumed between Ambassadors de La Sablière and Bolton. But when Bolton received his instructions from Rice over the phone in the evening of August 10 regarding the unresolved sections in the draft, they were far from the understandings that Welch and the Israeli team had reached in Jerusalem only a few hours earlier. An Israeli diplomat believes that Siniora vetoed the Jerusalem proposal with France's backing. The meeting began that evening in a gloomy atmosphere with major inconsistencies between the sides. In an interview with Shlomo Shamir, a *Ha'aretz* correspondent based in New York, de La Sablière stated that two points were still in dispute: a reference in the document to the Sha'aba Farms and the timetable for the IDF withdrawal vis-à-vis the deployment of the multinational force. "I was very rigid on the Shaba'a matter," the French ambassador said. "Obviously Siniora wouldn't agree to a solution unless it included a reference to this issue, but Bolton wanted to expunge the Farms from the draft." According to de La Sablière, Bolton also avowed that Israel would never agree to a comprehensive and immediate withdrawal as a step toward advancing the deployment of the multinational force, as France demanded. "When our foreign minister got on the plane in Paris on his way to New York, no resolution had been reached yet. When he landed in Kennedy Airport, the formula was almost completed. It took an hour. We inserted sundry formulas into the paper and arrived at a draft that contained a reference to the Shaba'a Farms in a way that was acceptable to Bolton." De La Sablière, who supported the idea of the simultaneous IDF withdrawal and multinational deployment, further stated that parallel to this, the American position was also accepted—that the resolution would call for a gradual IDF withdrawal *after* the multinational force deployed.

What led to the breakthrough? According to Bolton it wasn't a real breakthrough but a process that lasted a week. Bolton claims that the relatively rapid conclusion stemmed from Rice's concession to French and Arab pressure. "Siniora rejected the concessions," a State Department official stated, "and repeatedly warned that his government would cave in. Under this pressure, we complied with France on many of the sections. The French wanted an expanded UNIFIL force instead of a massive multinational force—and we agreed. The French feared a military clash with Hezbollah and consented to having the force's mandate more or less in accordance with the formula that they wanted. The Lebanese did not wish to discuss Hezbollah's disarmament, and we agreed to this, too. As for the embargo, we accepted a very mild formula, according to Rice's instructions. The formula stated that the Lebanese government could, in the later stages, enforce the embargo without a supervisory mechanism." But in any case, a close examination of the changes in the draft made in New York that evening reveals that the final formula was not concluded. The compromise that the State Department official described as an "American concession" was incomplete. A number of points still remained unresolved, and the two ambassadors preferred to leave them that way until the next day when Rice—who was still in Washington—arrived in New York. In effect, Bolton and de La Sablière closed the evening's meeting leaving all the unresolved issues marked in parentheses: The problematic sections appeared in the document in parentheses with the French and American positions juxtaposed.[3] Now diplomatic pressure was needed in order to change the formula in Israel's favor. But the pressure—"panic" would be the more appropriate word—was especially felt in Jerusalem. The Prime Minister's Office and Foreign Ministry staffs were in a high state of agitation, also because of a message that had been received, ironically, from an American diplomat. Condoleezza Rice, the diplomat divulged, had betrayed Israel.

At 9:00 p.m. New York time (4:00 a.m. Israel time), the Israeli delegation to the UN obtained the new draft from the Bolton-de La Sablière foundry. In the following days and months, this draft became Olmert's explanation for his decision to approve the last ground operation. An almost tragic atmosphere prevailed in Olmert's office concerning this paper, even though it was clear that this was not the final version of the draft and there was still time to alter the resolution. (Olmert and Peretz concluded that the best way to influence the draft's wording was to launch a major military operation rather than merely threaten one. This is a very controversial conclusion, to say the least.) It is difficult to explain the Judgment Day angst that overtook the prime minister's advisors when they read the draft. "At five in the morning, when the draft was in our hands, we realized that this was a matter of life or death," Olmert insiders insist today, also claiming that the changes inserted into the draft on the previous evening were radical and included the transfer of the Sha'aba Farms to the UN custodianship. "Why was the version changed to our detriment?" asked officials in Olmert's office. "The State Department, which handled the talks, wanted to conclude matters quickly with the Europeans. This required adopting the French position in support of

Lebanon. As we see it, the Americans, mainly Rice and State, did not come through with the goods. Instead of standing as a bulwark against the Europeans and reaching a reasonable solution, they signed a mutual pact. When we saw the draft, we realized that hope was gone and a military action unavoidable."

But a document prepared for Turbovitz's team, citing the discrepancies between Welch's draft of Thursday afternoon (Israel time) and the Bolton-de La Sablière draft 12 hours later, shows that Olmert's people are incorrect. The new formula did not specifically state that the Sha'aba Farms would pass into Lebanese hands, but it did include the French proposal in parentheses (in other words, it was unacceptable to the Americans) and determined that "a marginal note would be added to the text stating that the secretary-general would send a letter to the prime minister of Lebanon declaring his [the secretary-general's] willingness to weigh the Shaba'a option which had been included in the seven point plan [the transfer of the Shaba'a Farms to UN custodianship]." Other changes that Olmert's entourage describes as a "disaster" do not appear in the "document of discrepancies" drawn up in the Foreign Ministry in Jerusalem on Friday morning. Olmert's staff still insists that the draft, which was formulated in New York, included the deployment of an international force with very limited authority that would operate according to Chapter 6 of the UN Charter, not according to Chapter 7. But for some strange reason the staff forgets to point out that the draft had not decided the issue yet and specifically mentioned that France and the United States disagreed on the issue. The prime minister's staff also ignores that Olmert's two senior assistants, Turbovitz and Turgeman, had reservations about Chapter 7. In the end, they preferred the draft to include an expanded version of Chapter 6 that contained parts of Chapter 7.

At this point, it seems that the French and American diplomats and the senior ministers in the Israeli government were all correct in claiming that some of the histrionics over the draft were a cover for justifying the grand operation. An anonymous official in the Israeli Foreign Ministry says that the sense of impending "political collapse" (in his words) was not shared by the Israeli delegation to the UN, whose staff was the first to review the new formula. "Were the changes in the draft really so critical that evening, really so cataclysmic for Israel?" he asked. According to the official, the changes (some of which were removed from the final version the next day) did not justify a large-scale ground operation when it was already known that a decision on the cease-fire was expected that evening. The phone call that Israeli ambassador to the UN Dani Gillerman received that evening probably contributed to the panic in Jerusalem. At just about the same time that Gillerman was handed the Bolton-de La Sablière draft, Ambassador Bolton himself called Gillerman, and according to reports claimed "Condi has sold you guys out to the French," he announced. "You better speak with Olmert and Livni; things have changed for the worse—and State's agreed to this." Gillerman was impressed by the gesture. The American, he told his staff, "called for fire on his troops. He got us involved in order to block his superior's initiative." Gillerman thanked the American diplomat and immediately phoned Livni and the director of her office, Aharon Avramovitch.

After Avramovitch received a fax at his home with the new formula, he phoned Livni. "We didn't discuss this with Welch and the Americans," he said. Then he called Turbovitz and Turgeman and told his own staff to prepare a paper summarizing the gaps between the "Welch draft" and the Bolton-de La Sablière formula. On Friday, August 11, at 9:00 a.m., Avramovitch convened the "directorate forum" in his Jerusalem office to discuss the differences in the drafts and decide whether they were as critical as he believed. An hour later, he met with Olmert's top advisors Turbovitz and Turgeman. They had three hours to formulate a position for Olmert's and Livni's approval. They planned to call their American colleagues and resume discussion on the draft at 2:00 p.m. Israeli time (7:00 a.m. in New York). From Israel's point of view, the formula for the four key issues—the arms embargo, the reference to the Sha'aba Farms, the mandate for an international force, and, in this context, the application of Chapter 6 or 7 of the UN Charter—was insufficient.

"OLMERT HAS TO GO"

Olmert's office also dealt with the political ramifications of the crisis. That morning, Ari Shavit published a response in *Ha'aretz* to Barnea's column of the previous day. The article appeared on the first page of the paper and bore the aggressive headline: "Olmert Has to Go." According to Shavit, the prime minister "is allowed to decide on unconditional surrender to Hezbollah. This is his right. Olmert is a prime minister that the press invented, that the press defends, and whose regime the press protects. Now the press says to him 'get the hell out.' This too is legitimate. Not smart—but legitimate. But one thing must be clear—if Olmert leaves during the war that he initiated, he cannot continue as prime minister for one day more. There's a limit to his chicanery. You can't lead the whole nation into war with the promise of victory, and then suffer a humiliating defeat and remain in power."

Shavit's article, like Barnea's, was very carefully read in the top floors of the government ministries. Throughout Friday, Peretz pondered the political implications of obtaining an agreement without the final ground offensive. On the day that Olmert made the most fateful decision of his career as prime minister, he also found time to consult with Kalman Geier, an expert poll-taker. In the late morning, Peretz held a Labor Party ministers powwow in Tel Aviv in which he tried to present the inherent benefits of the UN document. His staff distributed an explicatory page to the ministers based on Welch's draft rather than on the more recent understandings contained in the Bolton-de La Sablière document. The page even claimed that "the abducted soldiers would be released immediately"—a mistake that appeared in none of the drafts. Some of the Labor ministers were wary about buying Peretz's interpretation. Ben Eliezer pounced on the Labor Party chairman, saying, "This is a catastrophe. It's an agreement that will have disastrous consequences. You should know that if this is how the war is going to end, you're dead meat." Ben Eliezer was especially angry over the sections dealing with the Sha'aba Farms and the release of Lebanese prisoners. Peretz cut the meeting short and refused to listen to any other ministers. He then drove to Jerusalem to the prime minister's residence, seemingly determined to convince Olmert to give immediate approval for the ground operation.

When Peretz arrived in Jerusalem, Olmert was in his workroom in the middle of a meeting that had begun at 11:00 a.m. The prime minister had called in four external advisors, none of whom held an official position or bore any responsibility for the war's moves.[4] The forum convened for the first time that day, even though some of its members had spoken separately with the prime minister earlier during the war. The discussion lasted for two hours, and Olmert, reported Aluf Ben of *Ha'aretz*, showed the participants the IDF's plan and a draft of the agreement that he received by fax. "The army wants me to give it another month," he stated. "One week for capturing the area up to the Litani; two weeks for mopping-up operations; and another week for the exit." Each of the advisors was against a lengthy campaign and warned that

Israel was liable to get stuck in Lebanon for a good many years. Nevertheless, they supported a military move as a means of exerting pressure for an agreement. If the military establishment decides on an easy way out, they told Olmert, you have to stop the army's advance immediately. At one point, Olmert went into a side room to talk briefly with Peretz. The defense minister had no idea that a few steps away in the other room, a crucial meeting was taking place, again without Olmert inviting him to take part in it.

THE TASTE OF LONELINESS

Shortly after 1:00 p.m., Olmert began a round of consultations with his closest aides. Peretz waited outside the room with his military secretary, Eitan Dangot, entering and exiting in order to keep up the pressure on the prime minister. "If there was one minute in all of my sixty-one years that I can point [to] as the most difficult—then this was it," Olmert testified before the Winograd Commission. "Afterwards I understood what the historians and pundits had been writing about: the taste of loneliness when all the responsibility is borne on your shoulders. That was not a problem. The chief of staff supported [the operation]. The defense minister supported it. But it was I who had to make the decision. I remember pacing the room during those two hours, agonizing over the consequences, seeing the faces of the kids who might not becoming back, recognizing some of them, my friends' sons. . . . Hanging in my office is Harry Truman's famous slogan—'the buck stops here.' I realized that I . . . was alone. I had to decide the fate of Benny's, David's, and Haim's sons . . . I knew that they're all [in the army] and some of them wouldn't be returning."

The Israeli political system made an all-out diplomatic effort to change the draft's wording. The Israelis explained to their American colleagues why they could not accept the formula as it stood. Turbovitz and Turgeman spoke with Nick Burns and Steve Hadley, while Livni conversed with Rice, then on her way to New York. The line was disconnected and picked up only after Rice was being driven to her hotel, the Waldorf-Astoria, where she continued negotiating the final draft. "We can't live with it," Livni told her American counterpart. The parts that troubled Livni dealt with the marginal notes on Sha'aba Farms, the nonbinding statement about strengthening UNIFIL (without the guarantee of a "strong mandate"), and the lack of a supervisory mechanism on the Syrian-Lebanese border. Another general section that

Olmert's staff and the Foreign Ministry were displeased with was the link between the abducted soldiers and the Lebanese prisoners in Israeli jails. But Rice surprised Livni with a positive response. Either the members of the National Security Council or Burns from the State Department had updated her on the sections that Israel opposed. "We know [about them]," Rice reassured Livni, "they've been taken care of." Rice was referring to two of the four outstanding issues: the UNIFIL force's mandate, which she promised would be upgraded; and the question of Chapter 6 or Chapter 7, in which she explained Chapter 6 would incorporate sections from Chapter 7 that were more binding but without specifically mentioning it, just as Israel had demanded. At the end of the conversation, Livni felt that a solution was in the offing. All that was needed now, she believed, was to continue applying political pressure on the two other issues: the Sha'aba Farms and the embargo. Olmert insiders still see things differently. "An Israeli action was inevitable. It was supposed to send a signal loud and clear that we would not accept the unsatisfactory formula in the draft and that the Lebanese government had to be pressured into flexibility. Even the Americans told us two days before that it was a good thing we were threatening to initiate a military operation, but then they asked us to put it on hold. The Bush administration was happy to see the French sweat a little and grow jittery over a large ground operation." In the meantime, Israel also exerted pressure on France to agree to a change. Vice Prime Minister Shimon Peres spoke with President Jacques Chirac, who was on vacation. At the same time Dominique Boucher and Maurice Gourdault-Montagne, Chirac's top political advisors, maintained continuous contact with the Israeli embassy in Paris.

At 9:00 a.m. New York time (4:00 p.m. Israel time), John Bolton returned to de La Sablière's office. Bolton had already received instructions from Rice to amend the formula in Israel's favor. His French colleague, who realized that Israel would never accept the draft that had been formulated in his office just 12 hours earlier, was prepared to concede a number of points. The French proposal that appeared in parentheses and included the marginal note on the Sha'aba Farms was deleted; in its place, the two ambassadors agreed to a nonbinding reference in the resolution's introduction stating that the Security Council takes note that the proposals appear in the seven-point plan regarding the Sha'aba Farms area. In addition, the practical section of the resolution requested that the UN Secretary-General develop a mechanism for implementing Resolution 1559 that would resolve the still-disputed border areas, including the Sha'aba Farms. But even these alterations were insufficient to curb Israel's military juggernaut.

At about 4:50 p.m., Olmert made the final decision for the operation. He had mulled over the problem until the last minute. The heavy pressure exerted on him by Peretz, who was deeply concerned that the war might end with the image of Israel as the losing side, seems to have been a powerful influence. What exactly went on between the two leaders sub rosa has yet to be divulged. But people close to Peretz, who were with him in Olmert's office that afternoon, say that he left "in a flurry with eyes glowing, radiating the aura of a great masterstroke having been achieved." Olmert contacted Halutz, who was going over a situation assessment with the senior staff officers. He left the room to take the call, and a short exchange took place. The prime minister informed Halutz that the army had 60 hours until the cease-fire went into effect. Halutz returned to the meeting and announced to his generals: "We got the green light. We have to be able . . . to stop the moves within six to eight hours. There's nothing we can do about it, this is part of the game. We're going for it, so let's get cracking. . . . Each of you knows what to do." Udi Adam, participating by video conversation from the North, was the first to leave: "All right, got to go now," he exclaimed. The air force commander, Eliezer Shkedi, remained for a moment to get instructions from Halutz on two targets, and then the meeting broke up. The senior-most IDF forum did not devote even a minute to discussing the campaign's objectives that had finally been approved, the changes that had to be made because of the ultra-tight time limit imposed by Olmert, or the final lines that the forces were sup-posed to be posted on. After the war, Adam testified before the Winograd Committee that the generals were not given details of what was happening in the UN, nor had Halutz informed them that he and Olmert had decided on a 60-hour operation, when in reality the Northern Command figured that 96 hours would be needed (Halutz asked the prime minister for 72). Thirty-one days after setting out to war, the Israeli army embarked on the belated large-scale ground operation that had been first broached on July 12. The decision, which might have been carried out successfully in the first two weeks, was made on the last possible date, just as a cease-fire was about to go into effect. The cabinet had approved a longer and larger move two days earlier, based on a different situation assessment of the UN debates. But no one asked for its opinion. Olmert, like Halutz, no longer had the time or patience for delving into nitty-gritty details. According to his statement to the

Winograd Commission, it was up to him, and him alone, to decide. After updating Halutz, Olmert and his staff held a round of phone talks with cabinet members to fill them in on the latest developments, but without involving them in the essential deliberations. Livni asked the prime minister how much time the army would need to halt the troops if need be. Olmert's answer: "The officers tell me that eight hours [should be enough]." Some of the ministers figured, without Olmert having revealed anything specific to them, that the whole operation was only a pressure ploy: The forces would head north to assure that the Security Council made the right decision. In divisional headquarters where the order to move out was received, the commanders perceived things in an entirely different light: The major operation of the war finally was beginning.

At 5:50 p.m., Olmert contacted Minister of Transportation Shaul Mofaz, who was at home in Kochav Yair. "We've just given the IDF the OK for a large operation. The Mofaz plan is included in it." Mofaz could not believe his ears. "Now on the thirty-first day of the war, you're sending them on an eight-week campaign?" By no means, Olmert corrected him. "It'll only be for 60 hours. On Monday at 07:00 [7:00 a.m.], the cease-fire is supposed to go into effect, and the UN document is unfavorable to us. We hope to better it." "Ehud, it takes many hours just to get a division moving," Mofaz warned. "What do you expect to accomplish in 60 hours? You're not going to gain anything except get a lot of good men killed. What will you say to the bereaved families?" Olmert replied: "The army has been telling me 60 hours is enough." Mofaz repeated his admonition: "I don't recommend this." But Olmert could only respond, "Orders have already been issued." After the conversation, Mofaz switched on the TV. The news announcer reported that the IDF had received permission to commence a large-scale operation up to the Litani. "This can't be happening," the transportation minister said to his wife, Orit. "They've completely lost their minds. Hezbollah guerrillas will return from their vacation straight into their [fixed] positions." Questions were being raised elsewhere, too. That afternoon, the IDF attaché in Washington, General Dan Harel, spoke on the phone with one of his colleagues in the GHQ. Harel bitterly criticized the ground offensive. "History will never forgive you," he warned. "There was an agreement and the forces must be stopped. There's absolutely no sense in getting more soldiers killed."

THE VISAGE OF DEPRESSION

On Friday afternoon a family celebration was due to take place at the prime minister's residence. It was a birthday party for Aliza Olmert, the prime minister's wife, who was turning sixty. Although the family—whose political views were much further to the left than Olmert's own—argued openly over the way Olmert was waging the war, Aliza and the children provided him with unflagging emotional support. As family members made their way to Jerusalem, they called home on their cell phones and got the impression that something positive was brewing: that the UN agreement was close to being finalized. But when they arrived home, Olmert greeted them with a downcast look on his face. He said that he had received the formula of the draft and it was disappointing. "Has everything really collapsed?" they asked. Their father answered affirmatively. French influence on the draft, he said, was stronger than they had imagined. "There's nothing we can do but tell the army to go in," he lamented. Aliza Olmert could not hide her feelings. She took some large pieces of paper, tacked them on the wall, and began drawing together with the grandchildren. The prime minister went into an adjacent room several times, and spoke on the phone in English. Now and then the family heard him shouting. When he came back from one of his calls to Rice he said to them, "My God, I never spoke to her like that." There were no advisors with Olmert that evening. His conversations with them were only over the phone. The family understood that the decision was his responsibility alone. The phone marathon continued. Later that evening the prime minister told his family that another draft of the proposal had been received, and it appeared more favorable to Israel. Nevertheless, he hastened to add, the army will be entering Lebanon. Somebody asked why. Olmert replied: "So that if everything falls apart, the IDF will be in a better position. I'm not sure that the draft will stay as it is." Political considerations, if ever there were any, were not mentioned. An air of despondency pervaded the Olmert household.

CHAPTER TWELVE

CASUALTY COUNT
IN SALUKI

Some one had blunder'd:
Theirs not to make reply,
Theirs not to reason why,
Theirs but to do & die,
Into the valley of Death
Rode the six hundred

—Alfred, Lord Tennyson, "The Charge of the Light Brigade"

THE NORTHERN COMMAND'S divisions received the order to move out to attack shortly after 5:00 p.m., Friday, August 11. Half an hour later, the order reached the brigades and battalions. The change in the schedule surprised the commanders. They had been told that 2:00 p.m. was the deadline for the attack. The Nahal Brigade's HQ, which was part of the 162nd Division, prepared for the new mission: Instead of crossing the Saluki River from the west, the brigade would enter Hezbollah's nature reserve close to the border. The officers realized there was no way they could accomplish the original plan in the hours left to them. The news on radio and television was the same: A UN-brokered cease-fire agreement was imminent. According to the 162nd's timetable, an attack on the western side of the Saluki had to begin that night, and it was already too late. Lieutenant Colonel Oshri Lugasi's engineering battalion had been withdrawn from the Saluki two days earlier and sent to the Golan Heights for the Sabbath. Now a frantic message arrived in battalion HQs: Stop everything. The offensive is a go.

THE IMMINENT AGREEMENT

At 11:00 a.m. New York time (6:00 p.m. Israeli time), the sides inched toward an agreement. After several heated hours of talks between UN ambassadors Bolton and de La Sablière, which included phone calls to Jerusalem, Beirut, Paris, and Texas (where President Bush and Steve Hadley were staying), the ambassadors resolved some of the knottier issues. The White House's fingerprints were all over the new formula. By the terms of the compromise, acceptable to both the Israelis and the Lebanese, at least 15,000 troops would comprise an international force that would operate according to Chapter 7 of the UN Charter (without the chapter being specifically mentioned). The section on the Sha'aba Farms that Israel found problematic was removed. Still, no mechanism was decided on for enforcing or overseeing the arms embargo. Secretary of State Rice received and approved the text. Another outstanding issue took an hour and a half to resolve in a meeting among Rice, the ambassadors, and the Arab foreign ministers in the UN building. All the parties agreed that the resolution should state: "immediately following the termination of hostile activity, the Lebanese government would deploy its forces in the south and simultaneously the Israel would withdraw its forces."

At about 7.30 p.m. (12:30 pm East Coast time), Hadley contacted Turbovitz and updated him on the negotiations. "You'll see," he said, "I did a great job with you guys." Hadley informed the head of the Israeli team about the final draft of the resolution, and Turbovitz was amazed at the new formula. Olmert insiders note, however, that Hadley specifically mentioned that it was still unclear whether Lebanon would ratify the UN resolution in its government meeting the next day, Saturday. Actually, Fouad Siniora had already conveyed his agreement via the French, though it is unclear if Hadley knew this. Soon after Siniora's approval, the chairman of the parliament, Nabih Beri, relayed general secretary of Hezbollah Hassan Nasrallah's positive reply. A little after 12:30 p.m. New York time (7:30 Israeli time), the longed-awaited agreement was presented "in blue" (the final version).

At exactly 8:20 p.m., the final draft of Resolution 1701 reached the Foreign Ministry in Jerusalem. The ministry's director, Aharon Abramovitch, notified

Turbovitz that the "blue formula" had arrived. Nevertheless, Olmert's office did not call off the operation. "There were a number of reasons why we did-n't cancel the operation," explains one of the prime minister's staff members. "We didn't know if Lebanon would endorse the formula, or if the Russians would place obstacles in the Security Council, or when Hezbollah would stop shooting. At this point, Hezbollah still demanded understandings allowing it to continue attacking Israel Defense Forces troops in Lebanon. We couldn't halt the troops smack in the middle of enemy territory and leave them defenseless." The civilian leadership still hoped that the IDF would clinch a military victory in the field. "Before starting the operation, the officers assured us that the army had learned its lesson and that things would be different this time; furthermore, this was a golden opportunity to expel Hezbollah from a larger area in the South. But, as it turned out, again the IDF failed to come through with the goods."

Between 8:00 and 9:00 p.m. (Israeli time), Livni and Rice had two phone conversations. Rice wanted to know if Israel accepted the draft. Foreign Minister Livni asked her advisor, Tal Becker, to formulate an answer as soon as possible. Forty minutes later, he came back with a positive reply. After con-sulting with Olmert, Livni contacted Rice in New York. "We have a deal," she announced. The time was approximately 9:00 p.m. In Lebanon, the first hel-icopters were unloading paratroopers from Eyal Eisenberg's reservist divi-sion. The first units of the 162nd also began moving out but still had a few hours to go until crossing the Saluki.

In her conversation with Livni, Rice requested that Israel publish a state-ment supporting the Security Council's resolution. Livni got in touch with Turbovitz and Olmert's media advisor, Asi Shariv, to coordinate the announcement. To her surprise, Shariv asked to obtain a postponement of the cease-fire from Rice and UN Secretary-General Kofi Annan until Monday morning—60 hours after the start of the ground operation. "Why?" Livni asked (as Mofaz had a few hours earlier). "We discussed 8 hours [not 60]. What will we tell the families? The public won't understand this." Turbovitz explained that the IDF needed this time to establish itself in defensible positions. "Otherwise the soldiers will become sitting ducks.'" The foreign minister spoke with Olmert again. "We don't understand it, and if I don't understand this business of 60 hours, nobody else will." Olmert insisted. "This is exactly the operation that Mofaz suggested," he claimed, referring to the transportation minister's two-day-old plan. "The troops will reach the

Litani." Livni conveyed the message to Rice and Annan. The Secretary-General agreed also to have the cease-fire go into effect 48 hours after the decision, and didn't demand an immediate halt. Annan's position may be attributed to the U.S. decision not to rush things or press for an immediate end to the fighting. Rice asked the Israeli government to convene on Saturday and approve the settlement. Olmert refused, explaining that the sanctity of the Sabbath had to be taken into consideration and assuring Rice that the meeting would be held on Sunday morning as scheduled. "We didn't want to make a government decision before Siniora made a similar one," claims one of Olmert's advisors. In the late hours of Friday evening (Israel time), the prime minister spoke with President Bush for the first time since the beginning of the war.

On Friday, 7:52 p.m. New York time (Saturday, 2:52 a.m. Israeli time), the Security Council voted on Resolution 1701. The French and American delegations took an exceptional step in circumventing the Council's bylaws, which state that a resolution has to be circulated 24 hours before the vote. All 15 members of the Security Council voted in favor of the resolution. The Israeli ambassador to the UN, Dani Gillerman, delivered a pathos-laden speech on the Sabbath Queen unfurling her wings this moment in Jerusalem, Haifa, and Beirut." He concluded with a blessing of "Shabat Shalom [Good Sabbath]." In a conversation with the authors, the French ambassador, de La Sablière, said that "the Security Council resolution intended to achieve three main goals: end the war, create a new reality south of the Litani without Hezbollah's presence, and guarantee a long-term arrangement." According to Gillerman, the IDF's ground operation changed nothing in the resolution's formula. "There had been lengthy negotiating, and the operation had no influence on it," he claims. His American colleague, Bolton, spoke in a similar vein. However, all the senior Israeli officials who were privy to the political moves felt that the threat of an IDF operation, which would have led to a further deterioration in Lebanon, catalyzed the contacts in the UN and resulted in a formula that was more favorable to Israel. From the noontime in New York, when the IDF was given permission to commence operations in Lebanon, the International political system entered a state of high agitation, which culminated in that evening's vote on the draft. However, there was a wide gap between the threat of a military incursion and the operation itself. At 9:00 p.m. Israeli time (just as Rice and Livni agreed on the final formula), and for the next six hours until the vote in NY was taken, the resolution's formula was left as it was. Israeli forces continued to advance. Heavy exchanges of fire began only close to the time of the Security Council vote. After the war, Israel, France, and Lebanon separately pointed to papers that had been written at the beginning of the war as the platform for Resolution 1701's final formula. Each country wished to prove that its strategic objectives at the start of the campaign appeared in the final document. The Israelis refer to the document as the Foreign Ministry's "strategic exit" of July 14; the French claim that the document contains their compromise from the eighteenth of the month; the Lebanese see it as Siniora's seven-point plan of July 24. Elements from all of these papers appear in Resolution 1701. However, an entirely different conclusion may be drawn: Israel, Lebanon's moderate March 14 camp, France, and the United States all shared one aim: the struggle against Hezbollah. Thirty-two days of combat had to pass before they could translate this common interest into a written document—and two more days until a cease-fire was reached.

TANKS ON THE WAY TO THE SALUKI

The 401st Armored Brigade's Ninth Battalion had been holed up in the North for almost three weeks until it finally received orders to proceed to the Saluki. During the first days of the war, the battalion's commander, Lieutenant Colonel Effie Defrin, had noticed certain things that accompanied the entire campaign: the low training level of his tank crews, the overall haphazard handling of the war, and the soldiers' and officers' determination to meet Hezbollah's challenge despite the first two shortcomings. The battalion's men, who had been performing routine security duty in the Jericho area when war broke out, had been away from tanks for months. Just as the battalion and the Nahal Brigade were about to commence (subsequently canceled) operations at El-Hiam, Defrin discovered that the infantry company lacked hand grenades. The tanks received smoke canisters, but most of the officers had a hard time mounting them because they had no experience in that. Canisters had not been used in training for years due to budgetary cutbacks. Tanks became incapacitated because of tread shedding even in relatively easy maneuvers—a sign of inexperience on the part of drivers and tank commanders.

On Wednesday, August 9, the day the Israeli cabinet voted to postpone the grand operation, Defrin left Lebanon after 12 days. During a meeting near the border with his brigade commander, Colonel Motti Kidor, he received the initial details of the division's operation to the Saluki. He was also ordered to prepare to move out in a few hours, the moment the cabinet gave the green light.

On Friday morning, Defrin called his battalion officers for a last briefing. His estimate was that operations would commence in a few hours. "Our mission is to climb the Saluki at night, but if we have to—we'll do it daylight, too, tomorrow morning," he said. A reservist officer from the battalion's infantry company protested: "No way! That's a death trap. We'll catch shit out there." Defrin answered that he couldn't promise that that wouldn't happen. "During the crossing a tank or two might get hit. We'll push on. This is a battle of advance—and this is war," he concluded.

The batallion's artillery coordinating officer, Captain (Res.) Ami Ben David, was also a *Ma'ariv* newspaper crime correspondent. He inundated Defrin with regular updates of what was happening in Jerusalem and the United Nations: confusing messages of good tidings from the rear. His newspaper colleagues told him that Condoleezza Rice was on her way to the region, that Jerusalem had already received the UN draft, and that Olmert was about to announce Israel's acceptance of it. The battalion commander, caught between conflicting feelings, decided that this was the time to detach himself from everything going on behind his back. He conveyed a final text massage to Carmel, his wife, and clicked off his cell phone with heavy heart. Then he read the final orders to the company commanders, gathered behind his tank. He had them memorize the route they would be taking: Rab a-Taltin, Khirbet Kseif, Kantara, Saluki, Randoria, and from there west, to the area east of Tyre. After the war, he recalled that he had consciously stopped worrying himself over political goings-on. Whatever happens in the "upper spheres," he realized, was beyond his control. From then on, he would be a mother hen, concerned only with defending the tanks in front and behind him. The late command to move out naturally caused an expected delay in getting the forces started. At 9:00 p.m. Israeli time, when Livni informed Rice that Israel agreed to the final formula of the resolution, the Ninth Battalion's tanks were revving up near the Pereg Stronghold in Israeli territory. The battalion rumbled into Lebanon after midnight. The engineering battalion that had been called back from the Golan Heights reached Kantara only at 10:30 p.m.; according to the original plan, it should have crossed the Saluki two hours earlier. At 3:00 a.m. Saturday, immediately after the UN vote, the 931st Nahal Battalion ascended Randoria and engaged in a firefight with

Hezbollah guerrillas who were solidly dug in around the village. At 4:00 a.m., the engineering battalion commander, Lieutenant Lugasi, reported that the Saluki crossing was open for tank movement. Effie Defrin's tanks, waiting on the eastern side of the river, still had not entered the fray.

TWO PASSAGES

In the morning hours, Defrin received permission to advance his tank column to a point 500 meters from the crossing area. The tanks waited in the shade of bushes and terebinth trees on the road that passed through the wadi and that farther on connected with the Saluki. "In another half hour, move out according to plan," the battalion commander told his officers over the radio. "And you? Your position?" company commander Shai Bernstein asked. There was none of the usual humor in the company commander's voice. Defrin was in the eighth tank in the column, but it seemed that Bernstein was signaling that he needed him closer. Defrin changed the order of movement and positioned his tank fourth. "Move to mission," he ordered Bernstein. The tanks ground into gear and headed into the wide funnel connecting the wadi to the Saluki. Unlike their advance until now, the crossing was carried out on low ground, in open light, easily observed from houses in the overlooking villages of Farun and Randoria. Defrin called in a smoke screen from artillery support to conceal the tanks during the crossing. The shells were fired but the smoke dissipated a few minutes after the column began moving. In the last five years, the IDF had not held smoke screen exercises; now the screen was not laid down correctly and the tanks were left exposed as they climbed the road into the killing zone.

The armored vehicles moved with twenty-meter spaces between them. Bernstein reported to Defrin that the first three tanks had crossed and were climbing the mountain. Just as Defrin was about to cross, his tank lurched with a powerful jolt. "Ido, did you fire?" he asked his gunner. Ido replied negatively. Orders forbade firing while moving on the axis. The second slam into his vehicle left no room for doubt. Another Kornet anti-tank missile had struck the tank. The driver said that he thought the engine was hit. Defrin opened the top hatch, stuck his head out and saw brush fire to the rear where one of missiles had landed. Then he was knocked flat by an explosive shudder "like a kick in the balls." He felt he couldn't breathe, and a few seconds later he lost consciousness. The third missile had crashed into the turret, but had not completely penetrated the Merkava Mark IV. Later, Defrin mused that if he had stuck his body out a little further he would have been zapped on the spot. At the same time, the tank in front of him, with the platoon commander, Haim Gelfand, suffered a hit that blew the cannon off the turret. The battalion's general staff officer radioed: "Number One down." Defrin's men were certain their battalion commander was killed. It was 11:00, eight hours after the UN vote.

Bernstein continued to lead the column through the missile attack. He headed west on the road, which verged to the left, and started the ascent to Randoria according to instructions. This was a mistake: the main axis that the Nahal Brigade commander, Colonel Micky Edelstein, planned, was located a few hundred meters to the east, in a wadi that cut between Farun and Randoria. This is where Avi Dahan's 931st Battalion (which belongs to the Nahal Brigade) had climbed. Edelstein, who surveyed the area a few days earlier, felt the western axis was too exposed to missile attacks from Farun to be negotiated, whereas the eastern axis was relatively protected. The 401st Brigade commander, Motti Kidor, had not realized the mistake that Defrin's tank column was making. Such a misunderstanding was the all but inevitable result of the way the war was being run: continuous racing against time, exhaustion, hasty battle procedures that were frequently and unexpectedly altered, and impromptu patched-on solutions. The last time the division commander and his brigade commanders coordinated their movement plans had been on Wednesday night in a dugout next to Kantara, when the officers were still in full battle gear and combat helmets. Some of them were too tired to follow the minute details. Even Defrin was barely familiar with the route he was supposed to take. He assumed that the engineering battalion commander would mark the path with stick lights, which Lugasi did—but only up to the Saluki crossing, not beyond it. After Lugasi prepared the armor crossing, the engineering battalion was ordered to withdraw. The advancing tanks did not even have a bulldozer with them that could have pushed obstructions out of the way. The most basic tactical procedure calls for a bulldozer to be in the spearhead of an armor column.

At the top of the road Bernstein's force ran into a house that had collapsed from an air force strike and now blocked the axis. Bernstein and behind him the tank of Gelfend (the platoon commander with the smashed cannon) pulled off the road to the right in order to find an alternative route. Without realizing it, Bernstein headed in the direction of the wadi where the original route was located. In the meantime the road behind him collapsed when an

IED exploded underneath a third tank, lightly wounding the crew. The rest of the force was cut off, on the mountain behind him. Gelfand's tank tried to return to assist the third tank, but rolled down the hill into the wadi and shed a tread. Eight men were in the vehicle—four crewmembers and four reservist infantrymen from the support company. Bernstein's tank went down to the orchard to pull out Gelfand while the third tank maintained a steady rain of fire on the houses from where Hezbollah was zeroing in on the tanks. Gelfand saw the company commander get off his vehicle on foot and go to fix the tread. "If Bernstein got off, then what am I supposed to do?" he thought—and ran over to his company commander under fire to help in the work. The reservists waiting in the tank later told Shai's girlfriend, Sivan Rafeli, they were sure that this was the end, "but the minute that 1.90m (6'2") Shai, peeked into the tank, winked, and said, 'OK guys, keep it cool, it's gonna be alright', we knew we'd get out of this in one piece." Just as Bernstein and Gelfand finished realigning the tread, two anti-tank missiles hit the vehicle's flank. Shai ran back to his vehicle to see if the crew managed to fix the source of fire. At the same time, more missiles slammed into another two of the company's tanks that had been left on the top of the road. The tanks started to go up in flames and the soldiers abandoned them. The company commander radioed "my tanks are getting mauled!" and then the radio went dead. Gelfand ran to Bernstein's tank and saw his commander sprawled on the ground twenty meters from the tank. A missile had slammed into the tank when Shai was half-way out of the turret—he was killed on the spot. The three other crew members were stuck inside. Gelfand and the reservists worked furiously to get the men out. Two succumbed to their wounds within a few minutes. The third soldier, who was critically injured, was extricated safely and eventually recovered.

The crew and infantrymen who had abandoned the burning tanks gradually made their way to the "bathtub," the relatively low area surrounding an olive grove. There were not enough stretchers to carry all of the wounded, since much of the medical equipment had been incinerated in the tanks. "All this time we were asking the battalion for support and they kept saying that the rescuers would arrive any minute," Hanani Mizrachi, the commander of the reservist platoon, told *Ha'aretz*. But after repeated delays, Mizrachi decided to take the initiative. In the houses above them, he heard the guerrillas talking. Mizrachi knew some Arabic and understood that they were planning to abduct a soldier or a body. Later, the rescue force arrived, and Mizrachi, who had been carrying Bernstein's body on his back, went back down to the low area under murderous Hezbollah fire, in order to rescue the body. The tank crews moved out in a dolorous file and continuously asked where Shai was, even after they had seen Mizrachi lugging the only 6'2"–tall officer in the unit on his back.

STOPPED IN THEIR TRACKS

That afternoon, Motti Kidor sent the commander of the brigade's 52nd Battalion, Lieutenant Colonel Tzachi Segev, to the head of the tank column (which had been stopped) to lead its advance. Segev took the originally planned, right-hand track this time and made relatively quick progress. One of the tanks ran over an IED but no injuries were sustained. At 3:00 in the morning on Sunday, the first tanks pulled into the village of Randoria and joined up with the 931st Nahal Battalion.

Eleven officers and soldiers were killed in the Saluki-Randoria battle, including two company commanders from the 401st Brigade. Over 50 soldiers were wounded. In the last two days of the war, six men from the 162nd Division died in the Kantara area while on assignments indirectly connected to the Saluki crossing. On Sunday morning, Nahal infantrymen and armored forces deployed in the area between Farun and Randoria. That night they were supposed to move west in the direction of the original objective, the Joya area, east of the city of Tyre, but a few hours before H-hour, division ordered them to halt and wait for the cease-fire.

The divisional investigation that Major General (Res.) Moshe Ivri-Sukenik conducted after the war showed serious flaws in the 162nd's performance. The choice of passage for crossing the Saluki was marked as a major error. The problem was not just with the route of movement but with the entire plan—and with the poor coordination between the various headquarters. When Effie Defrin's Ninth Battalion began the crossing, it was supposed to receive the protection of the Nahal troops in the overhead villages. But the low ground where the Saluki flows prevented radio reception (a condition that was known beforehand), and Defrin was unable to make contact with the Nahal battalion commanders in Farun and Randoria. If he had spoken with Lieutenant Colonel Avi Dahan, one of the Nahal battalion commanders, Dahan could have told him that the armored column was traveling on the wrong passage. The investigation also discovered that the Nahal commanders were unaware of the critical importance of their role in the tank crossing. They were seriously engaged in house-to-house combat in the two villages and had little time to pay attention to the tank movement below them. Under these circumstances, Hezbollah teams continued firing missiles into the tanks at the river crossing. Even though the two brigade commanders— Kidor (armor) and Edelstein (Nahal)—were ensconced in the same house in Kantara, where their command groups had been set up, coordination between them was sorely deficient. On Saturday morning, Brigadier General Guy Tzur gave Kidor permission to advance the Ninth Battalion, but the order came over an encrypted cell phone. Edelstein did not know that Defrin's tanks were under attack. Nor did he know that the tanks had taken the wrong passage (the right-hand one) or that Defrin was out of contact with the Nahal battalion commanders who were supposed to be covering his advance.

There were more glitches. One of the main screw-ups had to do with the division's advance, which had failed to consider the elevation lines or sufficiently appreciate that the tanks at the Saluki would be exposed to missile strikes from all of the villages up to a range of about five kilometers. Had the infantry seized some of the villages earlier, fewer tanks and personnel might have been lost. Coordination among the various units crossing the Saluki— infantry, engineers, and armor—was not as close as it should have been. The chief of staff told the investigation committee that he could not understand why the division had delayed crossing the Saluki. Brigadier General Tzur and Major General Udi Adam called the engineer battalion back on Wednesday because they thought that the chief of staff had ordered it back; Halutz claimed that he never issued such an order. If the force had dug in on the western side of the Saluki, Hezbollah might have had a much more difficult time taking up positions there. Too many important decisions were made informally by cell phone, while divisional and brigade headquarters were not updated on the details worked out by the various HQs. Ivri-Sukenik concluded that the division failed to accomplish its mission according to the timetable. He found the senior commanders lackadaisical about reaching Randoria in time—and he attributed this, partially at least, to the officers' feeling that they were liable to be halted at any moment because of the ceasefire. When he presented his report to the general headquarters forum, some of the generals sat bolt upright in their seats in shock. "Despite everything that I heard after the fighting, I never imagined that the army's performance was so shoddy," one of them admitted.

Throughout the war, there were glaring deficiencies in basic soldiering: The infantry forgot how to coordinate its work with the armored division; tank crews were unskilled in night maneuvers (not a single battalion commander had practiced them in years) and in rudimentary operations. The army blamed the troops' rustiness on the need to deal with the conflict in the occupied territories, which had led to drastic cutbacks in training, but this did not furnish a full explanation to the frustrating question: Why did the army— the Israeli army, which had demonstrated such tenacity, initiative, and aptitude in quelling Palestinian terror—prove so inadequate in the Lebanese test?[1] The Nahal Brigade commander Edelstein, who assumed his post a few weeks before the war, had been a brilliant officer in the Ramallah (West Bank) area but had very little experience in leading a large combat formation in more conventional fighting. None of his or 401st commander Kidor's commanders had ever commanded a battalion in full-scale exercises. In April 2007, when the Nahal Brigade conducted its first brigade exercise in seven years (on the Golan Heights), Edelstein admitted to Brigadier General Tzur that this was his first brigade exercise. The division commander brushed it off until Edelstein made himself clearer: This was the first exercise he had *ever* participated in since enlisting 22 years ago. Another basic issue was almost completely absent from military considerations: practicing a breakthrough in such exigencies as a direct attack made by an Arab army on Israeli positions, which would require an Israeli breakthrough to achieve an early victory. The operational outline for the Saluki was entirely different. The main similarity between the two scenarios was that an obstacle (in this case, a narrow river) had to be traversed. We may state, cautiously albeit, that the army forced a known operational solution onto reality. A conditioned response may have been at play here, of the type that says "We'll do what we're familiar with." In the first scenario (a confrontation with a conventional army), it is entirely justified to risk—and even sacrifice—the lives of dozens of soldiers in order to attain a genuine victory. However, Edelstein's and Kidor's men could only achieve the goal of taking a victory picture on the Litani if they succeeded in getting to the river, which is what the chief of staff wanted; and this in the unlikely event that the brigade kept to the timetable. It is very doubtful that the enemy was waiting for them beyond Farun and Randoria. In fact, some of the Katyushas that were fired in the last days of the war were launched from the Nabatiah Heights, north of the Litani, which were not included in the operational plan.

On Monday, August 14, a short time after the cease-fire was announced, Brigadier General Tzur held a press briefing in the division's headquarters outside of Safed. With the cessation of hostilities in Lebanon, the army waged a defensive battle in the Israeli media against criticism of its mismanagement of the fighting and the war's results. For two days, *Ha'aretz* published preliminary analyses of the Saluki fiasco. At the same time, the divisions eagerly publicized their "exploits" in the campaign, whether for the sake of the soldiers or of the divisional commanders', it cannot be determined. Dozens of sweaty, exhausted journalists crowded into the small conference room, barely able to concentrate on Tzur's erudite summary. He displayed photos of "Cornet" missiles, still in its original packing, and spoils of war captured by Nahal infantrymen in Randoria.[2] The Saluki crossing, he said, was one of the main battles of the war. It was a heroic fight, waged under complicated conditions, and in the end it played a crucial part in the war. Without it, the IDF would have been unable to continue westward and capture the strip of land along the Litani. Suddenly some of the reporters perked up. "What exactly was gained here?" they asked. "Let's take a look at it. Immediately after crossing the obstacle with considerable losses, you ordered a halt. And now, there's a cease-fire and the IDF is going to pull out of the forward positions that it captured, so what the hell did the soldiers die for?" Tzur refused to answer, making do by saying that those were questions they would have to ask those above him.

Over a year has passed since the Saluki battle—and the chief of staff, like the prime minister and defense minister, has still not provided solid answers to these key, incisive questions. The officers responsible for the forces at Saluki, just like the British cavalrymen who charged the cannons in Crimea, did not stop to reason why. But, in retrospect, they have a hard time justifying the moves in the last days of the war. "I didn't know then what I know now about the contacts in the United Nations in those hours," laments one officer who played a key role in the battle. "We could have stopped the tanks at almost any stage if we'd been ordered to—and saved at least some of the men. The time frame was also critical: We weren't sufficiently aware that the advance was supposed to stop in its tracks on Monday morning. Given such a timetable, the tanks didn't have enough time to have much of an effect on the campaign. It would have been better to advance with the infantry alone, which did indeed suffer fewer casualties." Three days after the cease-fire, the chief of staff met with the senior commanders of the 162nd Division. Motti

Kidor found the courage to ask whether the last move had really been necessary. Halutz was adamant: The move had favorably influenced the agreement
that was being drafted in the UN. Like other officers who took part in the
fighting, Kidor remained unconvinced. With the passage of time, his doubts
still linger. "Today when I think about this, I feel that we didn't do enough to
halt the last move," says an officer in the reserves who served in the division's
headquarters during the war. "It almost justified a revolt. Every time
I remember the dead who fell in the last two days of the war, I get goose
bumps."

During the postwar debate, the prime minister and chief of staff tried to
justify the last move. As mentioned, Olmert's entourage still claims that the
army assured him that it could seize key positions in the 60 hours left until the
cease-fire went into effect. They insist that he wanted to be ready in case
the cease-fire collapsed, by deploying the IDF on a more forward line so it
would be conveniently situated for resuming the fighting against Hezbollah.
Some have even stated that a moving division could not be halted in time and
that the actual purpose of the advance was to save the soldiers' lives.

However, as time passes, the clearer it becomes to what extent these
explanations are refutable. Today, staff generals agree that it is doubtful
whether the decision to go on the offensive on Friday evening was justified,
and the troops' movement could certainly have been halted the next morning.
Not a single tank lost the use of its brakes in the descent to the Saluki. With
the timetable that the army was saddled with, they say, the chances of stabilizing the troops' positions on the Litani were nigh to impossible. Even the fear
of Hezbollah's violation of the cease-fire and the resumption of hostilities was
unsubstantiated. Area Three—one of the organization's major command area
in the South, in the Bint-J'Bayel sector—was about to fall. Nasrallah had all
the reasons in the world to respect the Security Council resolution. If the
positions seized by the IDF were so vital, as is was claimed, and the fear of
Hezbollah's violation so tangible, then why were the troops ordered to halt on
Sunday and withdraw immediately the next day? The history of Israel's wars
is replete with mistakes, mismanaged battles, and losses that sometimes can
be described as cannon fodder. In the past—during the Yom Kippur War and
first Lebanon war, for example—last-minute moves were made in order to
gain extra ground prior to a cease-fire. In this light, Saluki may not be unique.
Olmert and Peretz may have been motivated not only by concern over their
political positions but also by the genuine fear of losing the limited gains from

the campaign. One would have to believe that Halutz and the generals and division commanders who incessantly pressed for the last move while the Security Council was about to make the decisive vote in New York were truly and honestly concerned about Israel's regional standing at the conclusion of hostilities, not about the looming threat to their careers. Nevertheless, all of the problems that characterized the running of the war came to extreme expression toward the end of the fighting: the political level's isolation from events on the front; the vacillation of the politicians who were overly influenced by their impressions of the zigzags in public opinion; General Headquarters' lack of a deep understanding of developments in the political arena; the army's intolerable training cutbacks that had an averse effect on the professional competence of mid-level commanders. The braggadocio of a speedy victory from the beginning of the war had little to show for in the last week. The politicians' level and GHQ were willing to risk soldiers' lives for a goal whose benefit and chances of attainment were negligible from the start. Ex-chief of staff Moshe "Bogie" Ya'alon termed this an exercise in "corrupt spin." He may have exaggerated somewhat. In IDF slang, the expression "death number" is held in awe. It is an especially loathsome procedure in the military: When a unit gets an unexpected, last-moment detail and has to decide which soldiers cannot go on leave, the commander draws lots—and the soldier whose luck runs out has to remain on base while his buddies go home. It was the bad luck of this generation of soldiers to have to pay the heaviest price of all because of the mistakes of the national leaders and officers who sent them on their missions. Since August 14 (the day the cease-fire went into effect), it has been hard to overcome the thought that the 33 officers and soldiers killed in the last two days of the war—Nahal infantrymen in Randoria and Farun and the tank crews on the Saluki ascent—are the death numbers of the second Lebanon war. As Shai Bernstein said on his return from a raid on the village of Talousa: This was the war that none of the guys in the regular army believed would break out during their military service. Because of their decision to volunteer for a combat unit (today nothing is easier in Israel than getting out of service in such a unit), some of the soldiers went to their deaths or received severe wounds in the last two days of the war. A quarter of all the men in each age group are exempt from military service while others find cushy jobs in the rear. The reservists who were sent to Lebanon while so many men of their age finagled their way out of military duty definitely had reason to feel bitter. In school and later in the army, Israeli youth are indoctrinated with the mantra that "Those above know what they're doing." This dubious presumption did not prove itself in the summer of 2006.

THERE'S NEVER BEEN A FLIGHT LIKE THIS IN HISTORY

While the officers in the field had only the vaguest notion of events in the United Nations, the officers in the divisional headquarters obtained a more comprehensive picture, ironically, from the plasma screens, in which they saw the forces on the field (through UAV) and the TV channels. Throughout the sad weekend of August 11, one screen in the war room displayed a picture of the front taken by a drone while a second screen was hooked up Channel 2. When the first screen documented paratrooper movement toward the Litani, the sound on the second television set was muted, but no one could ignore the subtitles on the bottom of the screen: "The Security Council has decided on a cease-fire." In the week since the Katyusha hit on Kfar Gilaldi, over 30 reservists were killed in Lebanon, the highest number since the first Israeli war in Lebanon. Doubts arose: Was there any sense advancing to the Litani in the remaining time? How many more casualties would it cost? Considering the IDF's performance so far in the war, do we really believe it was capable of achieving anything?

Amir Peretz did not share these doubts. On Friday evening, forces from Eyal Eisenberg's division were airlifted in a large operation. The reservists in the main paratroop brigade under the command of Colonel Itai Virob were choppered close to the villages of Kafra and Yatar. The landing was made about five kilometers from the front lines (and much farther south than the original plan). The big move that had been ballyhooed since the first week of the war was at last under way. In the second flight the following evening, soldiers from the regular army paratroop brigade were supposed to link up with the reservist paratroopers. At 11:00 p.m., the defense minister in the pit at the Northern Command called the prime minister's home in Jerusalem. "Listen, Hezbollah's in trouble," Peretz said excitedly to Olmert. "Believe me, there's never been a flight like this in history. Everything's going great. If it continues like this, it'll be spectacular." The two briefly discussed the possibility of postponing Israel's acceptance of the cease-fire until after Monday morning in order to allow the IDF to chalk up some additional gains. But Olmert vetoed the plan. Peretz stressed the importance of public relations. "We have to think about [how] we can connect the UN resolution to the military operation," he advised the prime minister. "So it will appear as though they're stopping us." Olmert agreed. Peretz sounded almost elated. For the first time in several days, he felt satisfied. Israel was finally doing what he had been urging it to do for the past several weeks. Now, he thought, the IDF will show its real mettle.

The optimism at the political level evaporated on Saturday as more reports flowed in on fatalities in other combat zones. The main concern was Saluki, but bad news was coming in from other areas too. For a while, it seemed that everything that could go wrong did go wrong. In the central sector, a Merkava tank accidentally drove over soldiers of the 51st Golani Battalion. Two of the men from the force that had fought in the first battle at Bint-J'Bayel were killed. Also in the central sector, near Kantara, in two separate incidents, two paratroopers from the northern brigade (reserves) were killed by friendly fire. "This was the Black Sabbath, a goddamned Sabbath," says an officer who was part of the war room at the Northern Command. "Every minute the teleprinter spat out another report on the operation: A tank detonated an IED, four killed. Casualties in Saluki. Another soldier killed by friendly fire. Every line like this pushed us deeper into the ground."

The slow advance with many losses strengthened the estimate of the chief of the operations branch, General Gadi Eisenkott, that the move to the Litani should be terminated as soon as possible. News agencies from Beirut reported that the Lebanese government was expected to endorse the cease-fire resolution at 6:00 p.m. on Saturday. The Israeli government would debate the matter the next morning. At 4:00 p.m., Eisenkott convened and chaired a GHQ situation estimate in Tel-Aviv (Halutz and Kaplinsky were at the Northern Command). Supported by the head of Military Intelligence's Research Division, Brigadier General Yossi Beidetz, Eisenkott stated that there was no sense in carrying out any more night flights of Eisenberg's division. The political revenue had already been earned with the UN resolution following the Lebanese announcement. It was better to halt the mission. The chief of staff and his deputy, who were informed of the recommendation through a video call at the Safed headquarters, rejected it. Peretz's military secretary, Eitan Dangot, witnessed the conversation and quickly updated the minister. Peretz, back in Tel Aviv, no longer had much respect for the top brass at GHQ. Eisenkott, a sober general and not given to tirades, remained his favorite. On Dangot's suggestion, the minister asked Eisenkott and the head of MI, Amos Yadlin, to come to his office earlier than scheduled (a quarter of an hour before the situation estimate meeting began). "Gadi, what do you think?" Peretz asked. Eisenkott refused to answer. "You know my position," he said to the minister, "but it would be improper for me to repeat it here. Once the chief of staff sums up the situation, I have to give you the army's position." The head of the Operations Branch suggested that the minister talk on the phone with the chief of staff and try to resolve the dilemma, but Peretz's office couldn't locate Halutz. Peretz contacted Kaplinsky, who repeated: Proceed with the operation. The defense minister accepted the military's judgment, as he did in most of the critical junctures of the war.

"The greatest flight in history" was also touted to the media by the politicians and GHQ. The wives of the helicopter pilots, whose husbands were ordered to return on Saturday evening to the same makeshift landing pads where they had unloaded the paratroopers the previous evening, were shocked to hear the newscaster at noon announce that "the IDF will be continuing with the biggest troop landing since the recapture of Mt. Hermon in the Yom Kippur War." Halutz mentioned this, briefly albeit, in a conversation with the journalists in the North. His words were broadcast even before the helicopters lifted off. Hezbollah must have been listening to the Israeli transmissions. The second flight included over 20 choppers that were supposed to land roughly two battalions. The operation began much later than planned. Confusion reigned at the place where more of the helicopters had assembled. The regular army paratroop brigade was late in getting started. The delay would prove fatal; it meant the helicopters had to discharge their cargo after the moon was up, leaving them exposed to antiaircraft fire. The veteran military correspondent Ron Ben-Yishai, who joined the operation, was unimpressed by the paratroopers' hustle-bustle. "Nobody dragged their feet, but there was no sense of urgency." In the pre-operations briefing, the intelligence officer reminded them that Hezbollah was equipped with antiaircraft missiles. Some paratroop officers asked why they were returning to last night's landing spots. The answer: They were relatively secure. When the aircraft finally took off, an hour and a half behind schedule, the paratroop officers in the Sikorsky CH-53 helicopter told Ben-Yishai that the delay worried them. In addition to the brigade commander Colonel Hagai Mordechai, and the men of the 890th Battalion, the helicopter also carried a huge amount of Gil (personal antitank) missiles and ammunition. "It's bad for your health just to think about what would happen if we're hit," Ben-Yishai jotted down in his notebook. All of the chopper's interior and exterior lights were shut off, but the journalist had little difficulty scribbling on his notepad; the full moon afforded him ample illumination.

After dropping the paratroopers onto a terrace close to the village of Yatar, the heavy chopper immediately took off. Ben-Yishai saw that he was smack in the middle of a tobacco field and bent down to pick a leaf. Above him he heard a loud swoosh. When he looked up, he noted a red point flying toward a second helicopter that had just landed another paratroop force next to the brigade commander's aircraft, the one that he came with. An SA-7 anti-aircraft missile scored a direct hit on the second chopper, which was still hovering in the air, only a few hundred meters from the paratroopers. The chopper began to tilt. The troops on the ground froze, hypnotized. A second or two later the helicopter slumped over, crashed onto the mountainside, and disappeared. Ben-Yishai later wrote that this was a shocking, spine-tingling scene. "I had never in my whole life seen such a thing, except perhaps in the film *Apocalypse Now*. For over an hour the whole area reverberated with the explosions of the decoy flares that the chopper had been carrying."

The five-member crew, which included a woman mechanic, Keren Tendler (the only female soldier killed in the war), perished on the spot. If the CH-53 had been hit before landing, an entire platoon of paratroopers would have been wiped out. "I can't get rid of the thought that another 30 boys were so close to being killed," Hagai Mordechai confided to Ben-Yishai the next morning.

At the end of the war, the division conducted its own investigation and discovered that, on the night of the first flight, reservists from an elite unit identified suspicious activity in a house from where the rocket had been fired on the next day. The information was relayed to headquarters but was not dealt with thoroughly. The planners of the operation assumed that the reservists who landed the previous day had secured the drop zones. But the safety perimeter was effective only against close-range antiaircraft fire, not against missiles from greater distances. Immediately after the helicopter was downed, the brigade commander received calls on his encrypted cell phone from Eisenberg, the division commander, and Major General Eliezer Shkedi, the IAF commander. Shkeidi, in a no-nonsense tone, asked for a report on the chopper hit. As Shkeidi saw it, the flights could continue despite the downing of an aircraft. Eisenberg, who explained that the force on the ground was strong enough to protect itself and feared that another helicopter might become a statistic, decided otherwise. General Adam supported his decision to halt the operation—and the Givati and Maglan units that were supposed to land in Lebanon later that evening remained in Israel.

The original plan envisioned the paratroopers making an arduous night climb up to the village of Jabel-Amal, situated on the cliff above them, and seizing village's houses. The delay in getting started led to the plan's cancellation. Mordechai decided on an alternative course of action: The paratroops would spend Sunday's daylight hours camouflaged in vegetation in open territory. When night fell, they would proceed to their assignment. "I didn't think that at this age I'd find myself hiding in the bushes," the brigade commander confided to a journalist who was 20 years older than he. On Sunday afternoon, the paratroopers prepared for the next move: capturing observation positions that would enable them to destroy local Katyusha launchers and guide Israeli warplanes onto other Hezbollah squads. Several soldiers realized that this was the first time since the war began (33 days ago) that they were engaging in serious activity to root out the Katyushas. But just before 8:00 p.m., they were ordered to halt in their tracks. Divisional HQ recommended that the Northern Command freeze the operation on the assumption that, by the time the cease-fire went into effect Monday morning, nothing of significance would be gained. The Northern Command complied with the recommendation.

THE CHIEF OF STAFF IN
DRESS UNIFORM

On Saturday evening, around the time the chopper was hit, Peretz learned why he was not able to contact the chief of staff and discuss the feasibility of the second flight. Halutz was in middle of a television interview on TV's Channel 10, which was being broadcast live. By all accounts, this was his worst public appearance in the war. Clean-shaven and spic-and-span in dress uniform, the chief of staff seemed detached and distant from events in Saluki and Yatar. At the same time, it was obvious that his usual aura of self-confidence had begun to crack. This time the interviewers took an aggressive line, very different from the usual tone on Israeli TV toward chiefs of staff leading the army in war. The two-word expression "investigation committee" was repeated over and over in the course of the interview. "I'm not worried about a committee," Halutz said. "I wasn't born the chief of staff and I won't die the chief of staff." Then he addressed his critics with a sharp message. "Many things have to be examined. For example, how did we come to this state of affairs in the last six years? Why did the defense budget fail to provide Israel with the necessary means of defense?" He reiterated his support at the beginning of the war for postponing a ground action. If we had attacked then, he stated, "We would have found ourselves thrown out of Lebanon with our tail between our legs."

In the following hours, under the heavy impact of the Saluki casualties and the downed helicopter, the major ground operation practically faded away on its own. The illusions, nurtured since the cabinet meeting three days before, imploded. The only question that all the involved parties seemed to be asking now was how to limit the damage, end the war as quickly as possible, and let the events of the last five weeks recede into the past. By Sunday morning, the political level and the GHQ lost their appetite for further advances and gains. The forwardmost forces, to the west of the Saluki River, were still a considerable distance from the Litani. If the advance to the Litani River proceeded, it obviously would not achieve the objective in the time remaining before the cease-fire took effect and might easily end up incurring heavy losses. On Friday, at the time of the first helicopter flight, Amir Peretz, positioned in the Northern Command pit, wanted the answer to a pertinent question. "How was it," he asked the person next to him, head of the Northern Command, Major General Udi Adam, "that the IDF has big helicopters as well as small ones?" Adam was flabbergasted. Over a month had gone by since the war broke out, and Peretz still did not have a clue about the system he was in charge of.

LEBANON VOTES

On Saturday evening, the Lebanese government approved the cease-fire agreement. The decision in Beirut was unanimous; even Hezbollah ministers raised their hands in favor of the agreement. Speaking before parliament, Siniora praised the members of the Shiite organization. "The perseverance of the Hezbollah fighters has been of great importance, just as the endurance of Lebanon's citizens has been. The [UN] decision proves that the whole world supports Lebanon." That evening, Hassan Nasrallah announced that Hezbollah would fulfill its part in the decision. "If Israel ceases its acts of aggression, we will do the same. We will help the refugees to the best of our ability. As members of the Lebanese government, we agree to have the

Lebanese army deployed in the South and UNIFIL troops stationed there." However, he criticized the Security Council resolution for being neither fair nor just. "Several parts of this resolution are unacceptable to us. Many sections deal with matters related solely to Lebanon, and discussion on them must be an exclusively internal Lebanese issue. But we shall withhold our reservations till a later date, after we find out the real intentions of the Zionist and American enemies."

On Sunday night, Emily, the Beirut blogger, wrote:

There's talk about a ceasefire going into effect in seven hours and twelve minutes. What are supposed to do until the morning? What if morning comes and nothing happens? Maybe in four weeks from now I'll be sitting in the bomb shelter, trying to enliven my neighborhood with jokes about the ceasefire that was signed way back then in August? And what if this whole [catastrophe] is suddenly over, and quiet returns to the face of the land, and people crawl out of their homes and villages to check the damage, and battles are no longer on the daily agenda? We'll simply have to wait and see. In any case, the clock is ticking away.

TELL 'EM WE WON

On Sunday morning, August 13, the Israeli government approved the ceasefire agreement. The atmosphere in Jerusalem was sour. For the first time since the war broke out, Shaul Mofaz verbally took issue with the prime minister's position. He stated that he could not vote for the agreement since it lacked a guarantee that the abducted soldiers would be returned or at least transferred to a third party. But Mofaz was the only cabinet minister who dared to abstain. The rest voted in favor of the agreement and took mild solace in the upbeat picture painted by the head of MI, Amos Yadlin: Israel didn't lose the campaign and already Hezbollah is no longer what it used to be.

The day after, the civilians in the Galilee regarded the cease-fire, which was go into effect that morning, with a healthy dose of suspicion. The most obvious manifestation in the North was the quiet: no more Katyushas crashing or sirens blaring. The IDF's artillery batteries also ceased their activity, after firing close to 180,000 shells in a month. The radio broadcast birds chirping in the North, a sound that had been muffled during the war by the thunder of field artillery. In the afternoon, stores and coffee shops in Rosh Pina and Kiryat Shmona opened for business, quickly filling with civilians who wanted to taste their first break in the sun after the month-long seclusion in the shelters. Also on Monday afternoon, convoys of returnees from the center of the country could be seen. The army bases were scenes of intense activity. The reserve divisions discharged their men. Sergeant-majors began the task of reservicing the equipment, while the reservists, hauling their duffel bags, looked for a ride home. The deputy chief of staff, Moshe Kaplinsky, finally managed to contact his son, Or, a reservist in Golani's reconnaissance unit who had been in a forward position in the central sector. "What can I tell the guys, Dad?" Or asked. "Tell 'em we won" came the reply. This was probably the last time that Kaplinsky or any other general at GHQ would use such terminology.

The army, whose leaders only one day earlier had spoken of weeks in mopping up operations in South Lebanon, was quick to sense the change in public opinion. As Israel saw it, the war in the North ended with the cease-fire—and there was no reason to risk renewing hostilities in order to unearth another Katyusha bunker. Everyone wanted to get home, and fast.

Was this the end of the Katyushas? Was the hunt for rocket launchers over? On the day after the cease-fire began, a number of incidents occurred in the course of which IDF troops killed seven Hezbollah guerrillas emerging from their hideouts. But Hezbollah did not respond. It, too, seems to have preferred to lick its wounds and take stock of the damage.

The public relations battle continued full force in Jerusalem and Tel Aviv for hearts and minds of the Israeli public. Journalists and editors were invited to urgent briefings in Olmert's and Peretz's offices, where it was explained to them that the war, like the UN resolution, was actually a magnificent gain for Israel. In tune with the chief of staff's Channel 10 interview, the prime minister and defense minister also indirectly blamed the Lebanese minefield they inherited on their predecessors. A former minister who got wind of the line the political level was touting responded angrily: "With all the mud they slung on us in the last month, they should all be banished into exile, 'to a nunnery, go, and quickly too,'" he said, quoting Hamlet, no less.

Both officers and soldiers in the reserves, a large number of whom had crossed back into Israeli territory a few hours after the cease-fire, had a hard time believing the enormous gap between the story cooked up by GHQ and their own experiences on the battlefield. The bitterness reached its climax when they recalled the last two days of the fighting in which they struggled valiantly to capture territory that the IDF was now evacuating posthaste, as if the last operation of the war had been only an afterthought. Officers who attended their men's funerals heard the foreign minister on the radio explaining in a very statesmanlike manner (an approach that she would quickly drop) that the operation had been expanded in order to protect the soldiers in Lebanon. "Weren't we originally sent there to defend the civilian population?" they wondered.

The last move was a gargantuan failure. Change of Direction 11 failed to meet its objectives. The IDF did not reduce by a whit the Katyusha fire nor did the divisions reach most of the sectors that were earmarked for them. Israel's deterrent strength was not reinstituted; a victory picture was not obtained; even Olmert and Peretz failed to gain their political deliverance since they had to exhibit greater restraint in light of GHQ's pressure to widen the war. In the last 24 hours of the fighting, Hezbollah lobbed a peak number of Katyushas into the north of Israel: about 250. One person was killed and dozens wounded. On Sunday afternoon, a Channel 2 news team photographed a Katyusha rocket being launched from a Lebanese village next to Metulla, less than one kilometer from the border. A moment before the cease-fire, these photographers put the prime minister's victory pronouncements in proper perspective.

On Monday morning, the regular army and reserve paratroopers were still in South Lebanon crouching in the bushes across from Yatar and Beit Lif, when they observed guerrillas in the neighboring villages waving Hezbollah flags in the air and celebrating. The loudspeakers crackled with cries of "Allah is great!" As in the Galilee, in South Lebanon, too, convoys of refugees flowed back to their homes after a month of forced exile. That evening the paratroopers began the 12-kilometer trek in boulder-strewn territory back to the Israeli border, carrying with them the body of the female flight mechanic, Keren Tendler, which the Shaldag unit had found the previous night. (The bodies of the four other crew members had been found by the reservists and already returned to Israel.) On Tuesday morning, when the file reached the Israeli border, the point of entry appeared familiar to Ron Ben-Yishai. This was the site where Regev and Goldwasser had been abducted—the event that sparked the five-week war.

BEILINSON HOSPITAL

On Monday afternoon, about ten hours after the ceasefire took effect, Lieutenant Colonel Effie Defrin woke up in the Beilinson Hospital in Petakh Tikva (outside Tel Aviv). He hadn't the vaguest notion how he got there. The last thing he remembered was the sensation of air being sucked out of his lungs from a missile blast. In the following days he would learn that the battalion's communications officer had dragged him out of the damaged tank and removed the blood and foam from his mouth, that the reserve doctor had performed artificial respiration on him under fire, and that an air force helicopter had medivacked him at great risk straight from the front line despite the imminent threat of anti-aircraft fire and in blatant disregard of the warfare doctrine that forbade such a move in daylight. Defrin was rushed to Israel in critical condition, suffering from a severe blast wound. The medical team on board the chopper decided to bring him to the hospital in Safed, fearing that he wouldn't hang on till they reached the better-equipped Rambam Hospital in Haifa. During the night he was transferred to Beilinson, where, almost two days later, he awoke from the anesthetic, groggy but in one piece. Defrin tried to speak but discovered a pipe stuck in his throat. Around him he heard electronic beeps and somebody say, "Call his wife, he's coming to." He saw faces staring at him from a window in the room. It was all very unnerving.

Carmel Defrin gave her husband a pen and piece of paper. "What happened?" he wrote. "You're OK. You were hurt at Saluki. A missile hit you." Defrin had many more questions: "What about the crew?" Carmel replied that they were all in good condition. "Who else was hurt? What about Shai?" His wife answered that everything was OK, burst out crying, and left the room. Defrin noted that he didn't feel any pain. He began to move his toes, sort of like an inventory check to make sure that all the pieces were still in place. A few hours later Carmel told him about the casualties, including Shai Bernstein. Effie wept. "Several minutes of tears, profound sorrow. I hadn't cried like that since I was a kid and didn't want to see anyone." His last words to Bernstein kept echoing in his mind: "Move to assignment" and the thought that he, the battalion commander, had not been next to his men when they were killed. The battalion sergeant major told Defrin that a cease-fire had been declared and the brigade was already on the way out of Lebanon. From the window they lifted up Yael, his baby daughter who had been born only ten days before the war. Defrin waved "shalom" to her with a feeble hand. That night Lieutenant Colonel Lior Hochman also arrived, the battalion commander who replaced him. Defrin's spirits rose a little. He understood from Hochman's detailed report that Shai had been a real hero. He behaved exactly as was expected of him. He followed the plan and displayed leadership, maturity, and coolness under fire." He was buried in Beer Sheva's military cemetery the previous evening. Captain Shai Bernstein, twenty-four years old at the time of his death. The company commander, born on the day after the First Lebanon War, was laid to rest one day before the end of the Second Lebanon War.

CHAPTER THIRTEEN

NOT DEFEAT, FAILURE

MORE THAN A year after it ended, the second Lebanon war continues to haunt all those who fulfilled key positions in it. The interviews we conducted with these people as part of our research for this book can be compared sometimes to a visit to survivors of a multiple pileup on a foggy highway. Each and his or her own story of anger, frustration, sense of missed opportunity, and disappointment—at themselves, at their superiors, and, in some cases, also at those who were subordinate to them. For Israel, the war was not the defeat that the political opposition tried to make it out to be. But it was a stinging failure—both because of the enormous discrepancy between Israel's expectations at the beginning and the way in which it ended and because of the terrible malfunction it exposed in Israel's most crucial governing bodies, from the prime minister's office to government ministries, from the ground forces to the home front command and the local authorities.

The beginning of the cease-fire was also a signal for the start of the chief of staff's rearguard struggle for his public image. The first signal came on August 15, when *Ma'ariv* exposed Dan Halutz's decision to sell off his stock portfolio on the very day that war broke out. The stock market affair was testimony to the inconceivable incongruity between the valor of the soldiers in the field and the behavior of their commanders behind the lines. The chief of staff's friends placed heavy pressure on his colleagues to come out in his defense in interviews to the media, but even those who acquiesced did so with obvious reluctance. Ehud Olmert and Amir Peretz did not even bother to pretend. Communiqués in support of Halutz were issued embarrassingly late by the offices of the prime minister and minister of defense. The media did not fail to notice. "It wasn't I who appointed him," the prime minister pointed out to a person who came to him complaining of Halutz's function as chief of staff.

Notwithstanding the cold shoulder from politicians, Halutz decided to hold on to his job. The chief of staff, said his few remaining friends to the media, is the only one who knows what really went wrong. He is the only person capable of leading the investigation and rehabilitation process. Today, his predecessor, Moshe Ya'alon, is quite convinced that Halutz's greatest error was his refusal to resign immediately. With his stubborn intransigence, says Ya'alon, Halutz hindered the military from conducting a genuine and thorough investigation of the war and delayed by six months the essential process of rehabilitation. The generals were fed up with the chief of staff; officers in the lower ranks doubted their commanding officers. And, graver still, younger officers started asking themselves if this was the organization in which they wished to serve for the next years of their lives. Resignations were not immediate. A sense that Israel was under greater threat as a result of the war persuaded many officers to remain in the Israel Defense Forces, for a limited period at least. But the war and its aftermath brought the army's standing—among the public and, no less, among the soldiers—to an all-time low. The officers lost faith in Halutz himself, who kept providing the media with different versions of his view of the army's performance during the war. On one occasion he announced that Israel "won on points"; another time he gave the army a "mediocre" grade.

Major General Udi Adam resigned from the army in the middle of September, one month after the end of the war. The chief of staff learned of head of the Northern Command's resignation only because journalist Ben Kaspit published the news in *Ma'ariv* newspaper. Adam didn't go into detail in his letter of resignation, but it was obvious that the reason was Halutz's lack of confidence in him, which was expressed by the appointment of Moshe Kaplinsky over him a week before the end of the war. Adam did not see his resignation as accepting responsibility for any of the failures of the war. At his changeover ceremony in October (after the last of the soldiers had left Lebanese soil in accordance with Resolution 1701) when he was replaced by General Gadi Eisenkott, Adam complained that there was a lack of collegiality among the top brass in the IDF. After his resignation, he refrained from talking to the media, but, in his testimony to the Winograd Commission, he provided a broad and comprehensive outlook of the war. It was an outspoken denunciation of his former commanding officer, Halutz.

In the meantime, the army, inspired by the chief of staff, was in the throes of a glut of investigations. About 50 investigating teams were appointed to study all aspects of the war, from the chief of staff and his relationship with the Northern Command, through the neglect of the reserve system and logistical failures, to the ways in which the four divisions that took part in the war actually fought. The divisional investigations revealed the serious condition of the ground forces. But frequent leaks to the media raised suspicions that were never proven that the chief of staff was trying to place the blame for the failure in Lebanon on the division commanders, as if it were all due to the random appointment of four officers unsuitable for the jobs they were given. Tensions peaked around the investigation of the kidnapping of two reserve soldiers on July 12,[1] headed by General (Res.) Doron Almog, which ended with a recommendation to dismiss Brigadier General Gal Hirsch, commander of the 91st Division and formerly Almog's subordinate in the Paratroop Regiment; the investigation team also recommended that Hirsch be banned from holding any command position in the future. The chief of staff did not back Hirsch. On November 12, 2006, exactly four months after the abduction, Hirsch, sick of Halutz's maneuvers, announced his resignation from the army. Two months later, Chief of Staff Dan Halutz followed in the footprints of General Adam and Brigadier General Hirsch.

With all the resignations in the ranks below his, Halutz must have found it hard to muster the moral authority to determine which of his people were responsible for the failure and should be made to pay with their jobs. Even the festive announcement, in early January, that the investigations were over failed to end the bitter crisis in the army.

The chief of staff appeared to have gradually reached the realization that his officers' faith in him had been lost forever. He announced his resignation close to midnight on January 17, 2007. The letter of resignation had been sent to the prime minister two days earlier, but, by informing the defense minister at the same time as announcing it to the press, Halutz dealt Peretz one final humiliating blow. In his letter, Halutz included an in-depth study of the meaning of responsibility (eight mentions of the term in various connections), without so much as a hint of admission that he might have made mistakes. In this regard, his resignation letter had much in common with those of his angry subordinates, Adam and Hirsch. At the changeover ceremony on February 14, the chief of staff talked about "evil" and the "dangerous culture of beheading," but Olmert and Peretz were not sorry to see Halutz's back.

They clapped politely, clearly more concerned for their own heads. The audience showed more emotion and Halutz received a standing ovation. Israelis have an inherent penchant for the image of the bleeding, embittered war dog, riding off into the sunset, waving good-bye to the nation that has proven itself unworthy of his leadership.

Major General Gabi Ashkenazi, the man who lost to Halutz only two years before, in the contest for the chief of staff's job, replaced him. Ashkenazi had promptly resigned from the army; he was appointed General Director of the Defense Ministry at the height of the war. This time there was no debate as to the suitability of the new chief of staff; many believed that here was a historic restoration and that, if Ashkenazi had received the post in the first place, at least some of the blunders of the war would have been avoided. In retrospect, Ashkenazi's appointment might be seen as the best (if not the only) thing to have come out of Peretz's 13 months in the Defense Ministry.

Dan Halutz was not the last officer to resign as a result of the war. Brigadier General Erez Zuckerman, former commander of one of the divisions that fought unsuccessfully in the war, resigned from the IDF in June 2007. The sharp criticism lodged at the divisional functioning under his command is probably what precipitated his resignation. He was the first of the officers to take direct responsibility for his part in the failures of the war. In late July 2007, Vice Admiral David Ben Basat, commander in chief of the Israeli Navy, announced his resignation, after conclusions were published of an investigation into Hezbollah's guided missile attack on the Israeli Navy's corvette *Hanit* (Spear) during the Lebanon war.

THE WINOGRAD COMMISSION

The willingness of several officers to pay a personal price for the failures of the war compared out favorably to the evasiveness of senior politicians who refused to take similar responsibility. Only two government ministers—Eitan Cabel and Ophir Pines of the Labor Party, who had been constantly critical of the decision-making process throughout the war—resigned in the months thereafter. Other ministers, who had been full partners to some of the decisions, did not hesitate to attack the prime minister, conveniently failing to recognize their own part in the fiasco. Olmert and Peretz, it became obvious during the first days after the cease-fire, were absolutely determined to stay in office. Their survival—in spite of the enormous revulsion they aroused in the public opinion polls—depended on two separate issues: On the legal front, they had to block demands for an appointed state commission of inquiry in favor of one appointed by the government, whose authority would be considerably restricted. On the political front, it was necessary to extend the coalition in such a way as to weaken the united internal opposition created by such ministers as Tzipi Livni, Shaul Mofaz, and, for a short time, Avi Dichter, the minister for homeland security, too. Olmert, a political master, succeeded on both fronts. Survival is his art.

In the end, investigation of the war was entrusted to a government commission of inquiry headed by Dr. Eliyahu Winograd, former president of the Tel Aviv District Court.[2] The process of determining the commission's composition, its authority, and the issues to be examined involved a series of small but significant victories for the prime minister, whose associates worked overtime on his behalf. The Prime Minister's Office managed to thwart a state commission of inquiry; to block a proposal to appoint the soon-be-retiring president of the supreme court, Aharon Barak, to chair the commission; to include on the commission members who had been sympathetic to Olmert's interests; and to provide Winograd with a mandate to look into events that took place over the six years prior to the war.

Against this background, the commission's interim report (published in late April 2007) astonished Olmert. All the early predictions that Winograd would present a watered-down, conciliatory report vis-à-vis the prime minister were to prove false. Although the report also dealt with the years between the Israeli withdrawal from Lebanon and the outbreak of the 2006 war, it devoted itself to events between July 12 and Olmert's speech to the Knesset on July 17. Decisions surrounding going to war, said the commission, "entailed the worst kind of mistakes," the responsibility for most of which lies firmly with Olmert, Peretz, and Halutz. According to the Winograd Commission:

> The decision to respond with an immediate, intensive military strike was not based on a detailed, comprehensive and authorized military plan, based on careful study of the complex characteristics of the Lebanon arena. A meticulous examination of these characteristics would have revealed the following: the limited ability to achieve military gains having significant political-international weight; a military offensive would inevitably have led to missiles being fired at

Israel's civilian north; there was no other effective military response to such missile attacks than an extensive and prolonged ground operation to capture the areas from which the missiles were fired [. . . The high price of this] did not enjoy broad support. Cabinet support for this move was gained in part by the use of ambiguity in presenting goals and ways of achieving them, which made it easier for ministers with different or even contradictory attitudes to support them. The ministers voted for a vague decision, not understanding or knowing its nature and implications. They authorized . . . a military campaign without considering how to get out of it. . . . Some of the war's declared goals were vague and unachievable. . . .

The commission continued:

The IDF did not demonstrate creativity in proposing alternatives . . . , did not alert the political decision-makers to the discrepancy between its own scenarios and authorized activity, and did not demand—as was necessary under its own plans—early mobilization of the reserves so they could be equipped and trained in case a ground operation was required.

Even after the political leaders knew these facts, they failed to adapt the military way of operation and its goals to reality in the field. On the contrary, declared goals were too ambitious, and it was publicly stated that fighting would continue until they were achieved. But the authorized military operations did not enable their achievement.[3]

The word "failure" appeared in the report dozens of times. "The primary responsibility for these serious failings rests with the Prime Minister, the minister of defense and the (outgoing) Chief of Staff. We single out these three because it is likely that had any of them acted better—the decisions during the period in question and the ways they were made, as well as the outcome of the war, would have been significantly better."

The Winograd Commission did everything except demand the resignation of Olmert and Peretz, even though there were plenty of hints of this throughout the report. Legal experts who have spent years following Winograd's approach as a judge were not surprised. The veteran judge will leave the final move, they said, in the hands of the prime minister. Olmert knew exactly how to exploit this point. The final report, scheduled to be submitted early summer 2007, has been postponed time after time. The Winograd Commission has become embroiled in its own legal wrangles because of demands by legal representatives of high-ranking officers, whose clients might find themselves compromised by the final report and be prevented from presenting their own claims, examining documents, and interrogating witnesses. Although it may have been possible in late April to remove Olmert from office, the momentum has since died down, and the public and the media have moved on to deal with other issues. When the committee's final report was published eventually, in late January 2008, it took a moderate view of Olmert's mistakes. Politically, the prime minister had survived the storm.

To many Israelis, the Winograd Report reflects things that are much deeper and no less worrying than the question of who their prime minister will be—Olmert's victory in the first round notwithstanding. Following the publication of internal IDF investigations in November 2006, Uzi Benziman wrote in *Ha'aretz* that:

Against American professionalism, Israel has developed the ethic of improvisation. Against the Americans' stringent obeying of rules, Israel has become a slave to creativity. Rather than be "uncool" [an Israeli] will adjust to circumstances. However, over the years, these traits that Israel has attached to itself have undergone a pathological change: operational flexibility has turned into negligence and freedom of action in fulfilling assignments has become irresponsible abandon. Blunders have been revealed in GHQ that look more like the syndrome of a faulty work ethic and of a lax culture. . . . [E]very time circumstances require that the carpet be raised in an area in which government authorities are at work, hair-raising disregard, neglect and corruption are revealed. . . . It appears sometimes that there is no area of decency in the public sector and the routine in which it operates is a thin skin under which there lies an abyss. The overall impression is of a miserable management culture, based on small mindedness and dependence on external images. The thing that is important to the workers and their superiors is to appear as if work is being done. . . , rather for it to be really so. . . . [T]he overall picture is one of laxity and negligence cloaked in sleight of hand.

Politically, however, Olmert's position has never been better. He introduced Avigdor Lieberman's Israel Beitenu (Israel is our Home) right wing Party to his coalition and reduced his dependence on the Labor Party. After the Winograd interim report, Tzipi Livni considered a coup against Olmert, but changed her mind and was ridiculed by the press for not having the courage to demand the prime minister's resignation. In June 2007, Olmert said good-bye to his unwanted partner, Amir Peretz, who lost the Labor Party leadership to Ehud Barak and resigned from the government. Winograd's populist declaration that the appointment of Amir Peretz to the position of defense minister had been harmful to the country's security turned out to be harmful to Peretz himself. But more damaging still to the minister's public standing was a minor incident on the Golan Heights in February 2007, while he was observing a military exercise. Time after time, the camera caught Peretz raising his binoculars to his eyes with the lenses covered, trying unsuccessfully to view what was going on around him. Inadvertently, the defense minister had supplied the perfect image of his performance—and perhaps that of the entire government—during the second Lebanon war. It was no use his explaining that, during his own military service, he had often been called on to mend binoculars.

The second Lebanon war, which broke out a little over six years after the withdrawal from southern Lebanon that he himself orchestrated, paved the way for Ehud Barak's return to Israeli politics and the defense ministry. Israeli public opinion, it appears, is prepared to forgive Barak for his problematic performance as prime minister, if only in order to have the defense ministry headed once again by a man who is well versed in the complexities of Israeli security. Barak has declared that he would resign from the government once the final report of the Winograd Commission is published. But the repeated delays have served the two Ehuds well, especially in the face of such looming dangers as the possibility of imminent war with Iran, Syria, the religious fundamentalist state that Hamas has started establishing in the Gaza Strip—or with all of them together. The only enemy that does not appear particularly keen on renewing hostilities with Israel at this time is Hezbollah.

MISTAKES DO HAPPEN

Over the first days after the cease-fire, the Fox News channel broadcast directly from Beirut. Fox's Beirut correspondence, Shepherd Smith, interviewed commentators in the Washington studio. On one such broadcast, Smith asked David Makovsky, a researcher from the Washington Institute, "Who do you think won the war?" Makovsky began to reply, but Smith cut him off, saying "David, if you don't mind, could you raise your voice because Hezbollah people here behind me are celebrating their victory by setting off fireworks."

From the moment the cease-fire took effect on August 14, Hezbollah and its leader, Hassan Nasrallah, were racing to ensure their victory and to perpetuate their own narrative of the war. Since Nasrallah works within a totally different value system, it is difficult to get him to admit that from his point of view, too, the war was a failure. Throughout the campaign, Nasrallah adhered vehemently to the official line, according to which the war was a great success of the "resistance." Huge pictures of Nasrallah lined the streets of the Shiite neighborhoods in Beirut and southern Lebanon. Over them were the words "Nasser Allah": victory of god. Hezbollah required extra marketing efforts to overcome the grim reality in Lebanon. The total number of Lebanese casualties during the war reached 1,100[4]—Hezbollah fighters, civilians, and members of the country's security forces. About one-third of the dead were children. A further 3,628 civilians were wounded. According to estimates published in Lebanon, some 10,000 homes were destroyed by Israeli bombs, a further 22,500 buildings were badly damaged, and almost 73,000 were partially damaged. The Shiite areas in southern Lebanon and south Beirut suffered most of the damage. In the village of Maroun a-Ras, the site of fierce battles between Hezbollah and Israel's Golani and paratroop brigades, 665 of the 700 houses were hit. In the nearby village of Itaroun, 900 of the 1,500 houses were hit. The civilian infrastructure of the Hezbollah organization and its education and welfare systems were badly damaged. The IAF carried out systematic bombing of offices belonging to economic institutions identified with Hezbollah, in accordance with objectives prepared by Israeli intelligence community, causing hundreds of millions of dollars in damage. A few months after the war, the overall damage to Lebanon's economy was estimated at between $3 billion and $5 billion. The war also caused the mass migration of Lebanese villagers, mostly Shiite, from the South. According to reports from Lebanon, almost a million people left their homes as a result of the fighting; in many cases, when they returned, they found only ruins. Hezbollah was quick to send it rehabilitation units and embarked an extensive campaign to repair the bomb damage. Within a few months, rubble had been removed from the villages, and every Lebanese homeowner who could provide proof of ownership was awarded between $10,000 and $12,000 to pay for a year or more of substitute housing.

A deviation from Hezbollah's declared line was recorded on August 27, 2006, less than two weeks after the war ended. In an interview with the Lebanese TV channel NTV, Nasrallah admitted that Hezbollah would not have kidnapped the two Israeli soldiers if it had known that it would have led to war. "I certainly would not have done it, for moral, humane, military, and political reasons. After all, the prisoners in the jails and their families would not have accepted this," he said. The success of the Hezbollah leader's little attempt at penitence was only partial. Even Lebanese Shiites who were not identified with Hezbollah joined in the fierce criticism against the organization. "As for [Hezbollah's] so-called victory, I don't believe there was such a victory," said the Shiite Mufti (the leading religious figure) of Tyre, Sheikh Ali al-Amin Harshali, in an interview with the Lebanese TV channel LBC in August 2006. "I don't want to enter a debate on the significance of victory, but I do ask: were we in a position of defeat prior to July 12 that we were in need of so 'great' and 'strategic' a victory after July 12? . . . We cannot claim that the enemy has been defeated. The enemy, too, had objectives, which were not met, but there is no comparison between our pain and his. Our pain is huge, whereas the pain caused to the enemy . . . cannot be compared. There are those who said: if you suffer, you should know that they are suffering exactly like you. No, we suffered more than the enemy. The damage done to us was greater than that to our enemy." The Christian leader Samir Ja'aja', one of the leaders of the anti-Syrian March 14 camp, explained in September 2006: "We don't feel victory. Most of the Lebanese nation feels that a great tragedy has befallen it and that our present and future can be compared to a feather floating in the wind."

THE SOUTH

Hezbollah's diminished ability to move freely in southern Lebanon was the most significant change brought about by the war. About 10,000 Lebanese soldiers began deploying throughout the South just a few days after the ceasefire went into effect, alongside soldiers from the United Nations Interim Force in Lebanon (UNIFIL). Altogether, some 11,000 soldiers from foreign armies were deployed in southern Lebanon. The force, as defined in UN Resolution 1701, was authorized to open fire. "Our objective today," says a

UNIFIL officer, "is to ensure that there are no armed [people] who are not Lebanese army personnel south of the Litani. Although there are armed [people] in the Palestinian refugee camps in the south, [we] have no reports of armed Hezbollah [members]. Between the Litani and the border with Israel, there are today more than 20,000 soldiers [Lebanese and foreign], whose job it is to prevent an armed Hezbollah presence. On more than one occasion we found weapons, military equipment and bunkers . . . including rockets, grenades, ammunition, RPG launchers, and Katyushas. We have a regular routine: we secure the place and call the Lebanese army, which sends in forces, who explode the weapons and confiscate them." Israeli Military Intelligence confirmed that, at least for so long as no concentrated effort is made by Islamic organizations to expel them from Lebanon, UNIFIL is taking its assignment very seriously.[5]

Nasrallah's gamble failed. His organization, which, before the war, had been at the center of Arab consensus and enjoyed extensive support in Lebanon, had become after the war an opposition movement striving to overthrow the regime and serving the interests of Iran. "During the war," says a senior UN staff member, "Nasrallah became one of the most popular leaders in the Arab world. Today, no one is in a hurry to hang up his picture." Like Israel, Hezbollah was damaged badly from the war.

EIGHTEEN MONTHS AND NO NEWS

Throughout the spring and summer of 2007, the two families in Nahariya and Kiryat Motzkin continued to wait for news from Lebanon. No real updates were forthcoming. The fate of the two reserve soldiers, Udi Goldwasser and Eldad Regev, kidnapped on the first day of the war, remained a mystery. From time to time, reports in the Arab media confirm what Israel assumed shortly after the abduction: One of the soldiers was dead while the other was wounded and being held prisoner. The reliability of the reports is dubious. Hezbollah, for its part, has adhered stubbornly to its position that it would provide no information on the condition of the kidnapped soldiers without being significantly rewarded by Israel. As in the past, Hezbollah appears determined to draw out negotiations—and the nerves of the soldiers' families— for as long as possible.

Micky Goldwasser describes her son, Udi, as "a cynical individualist." I fear, she says, that these traits might not be to his advantage in captivity.

"I hope he's not doing or saying anything to annoy them there. I know he's good at keeping himself occupied. There's so much going on in his head, he could get through 100 years like that. But I keep asking myself what's he getting to eat. Obviously he's wounded. Does he need help using the bathroom? Can he take care of himself on his own? When the blanket falls off him at night, can he pick it back up? I am terrified that his cynicism will get him into trouble. I've spoken to others who were wounded in captivity. They said, don't worry about him, he'll manage, you should worry about yourself." Her husband, Shlomo, draws hope from family history. "My uncle opened Auschwitz and closed Auschwitz. I know that if he's alive, Udi will get through it all, even if he can't pick up his own blanket."

UNTIL THE NEXT WAR

THERE ARE MANY reasons for Israel's failure in Lebanon in the summer of 2006. The war exposed Israel's weaknesses in key areas. The trio who filled the top positions—prime minister, defense minister, and chief of staff—were all fairly new to the job, they lacked the relevant experience and, in hindsight, it can be said that they also lacked the necessary capabilities for leading Israel in a war. Olmert, Peretz, and Halutz were wrong in not taking decisions at critical crossroads; by embarking on a campaign without preparing the field for the next steps; by sidestepping the potential for ending the war at an earlier stage; by stubbornly insisting on continuing the campaign from the air, when it was obvious that such action was not going to provide the desired results; by not understanding the damage to the home front (and not dealing with it); and, of course, by embarking on the final, fruitless, extremely costly attack. Yet they were not the only ones responsible for the failure. This war exposed the weakness of Israel's land forces. The courage of the ordinary soldiers could not enough to atone for the damage of the years before. As General Yishai Beer put it so succinctly on the eve of war, the Israel Defense Forces' attempt at registering a world patent for an army without training failed. The IDF paid a high price for the drastic cuts in training budgets over the six years of the second intifada. During the war itself, untrained units received confused orders. A disturbing sloppiness revealed itself during the war at all the main stations of the command chain.

Once again it became clear that there are no shortcuts. An army that has not thoroughly trained itself for the eventuality of war in Lebanon will not function properly in real time. Reservists who have not trained for years will not suddenly remember how to operate a tank professionally. Battalion commanders who have never led their men in the dark will not exhibit a wonderful ability the first time they are required to do so, under fire. Division commanders who have not undergone training and have not seen their entire division moving together in drills cannot beat the enemy. A chief of staff whose expertise is in airborne warfare cannot be expected to know the full implications of crossing the Saluki under enemy anti-tank missiles. Nor would a prime minister and minister of defense who throughout their political careers did not show any particular interest in security issues be able to show any political and military wisdom when facing down Hezbollah. Add to all these the utter ineffectiveness of the government. One of the more troubling phenomena we encountered in researching for this book was the discrepancy between the deeply serious attitude of the field commanders regarding the war they were fighting and the almost apathetic behavior of some politicians toward the same war. Cabinet ministers who were so quick to raise their hands in favor of launching attacks are unable now to recall events in any detail. To them, Lebanon constitutes a forgettable adventure, better left to the dark reaches of their memory. After all, it was Olmert's responsibility; they were only there, at the meetings. And anyway, who is capable of remembering the details a year later?

AMERICA AND ISRAEL: DISAPPOINTMENT

Notwithstanding America's oft-repeated assurances of its commitment to Israel's security and the deep friendship between President Bush and Prime Minister Olmert, Washington, too, has noted the results of the war. "As far as our American friends are concerned, we have not delivered the goods," says Brigadier General (Res.) Giora Eiland. "America is disappointed with the way we conducted the war." Disappointment with Israel has overtaken large parts of the American establishment. American military personnel were surprised by the IDF, which, until the war, had marketed itself as the leading expert in wars against guerrilla forces and terrorist organizations. The war did not contribute to relations with the Pentagon, which were not good anyway, after Israel's arms deals with China. The secretary of state's advisors, who were well versed in Israeli affairs, became contemptuous of the IDF and spoke in terms of "[. . .] bay watch," when describing the Israeli army working on behalf of the United States. The neoconservatives, who expected good news from Lebanon after the depressing complications in Iraq, remained unsatisfied.

Steven J. Erlanger, Jerusalem bureau chief for *The New York Times*, quotes a senior White House official as saying "Bush and his deputy, Dick Cheney, believed that this was going to be another Six-Day War, two weeks at the most. That's what the Israelis told them." The American liberal-left were upset by the large number of Lebanese civilians killed in the Israeli air attacks.

Since the war, America's doubts as to the Israel's military might have reduced Olmert's political freedom of movement to a certain extent. Israel's prime minister takes care not to anger President Bush.[1] Olmert was very careful even when the issue on the agenda—the possibility of renewed negotiations with Syria—was critical to Israel's future. Bush's people, who expected Israel to attack Syria during the war with Lebanon, did not hide their objection to a possible peace process between the two countries after it. Washington would later soften its reservations, when, during the spring of 2007, tensions between Jerusalem and Damascus had risen to a level that war could have erupted. In Israel's political arena, the debate was whether to reopen negotiations with Syria over the return of the Golan Heights and if a peace agreement with Damascus would sever the Syrians from the Tehran/Hezbollah axis. In Jerusalem, it was difficult to figure out where the Syrian president was heading. Was Damascus interested in negotiations that would lead to peace with Israel, or did it see such negotiations as a means of extracting itself from its political isolation? Foreign mediators who visited Damascus returned to Jerusalem bearing messages of Bashar Assad's willingness to enter negotiations, but with no real move on his part that would prove the seriousness of his intentions. Assad continued to play a double game. While he was talking about renewing negotiations, he continued to issue public warnings against a war with Israel if his demands for the return of the Golan Heights were not met in a peace agreement. Already on August 15, 2006, one day after the cease-fire with Lebanon, Assad was threatening to take the Golan Heights by force. "I am happy to be with you in a new Middle East," he said in a speech to the Press Association in Damascus. "We are meeting today, at a time when the slogan of a new Middle East toward which Israel and the USA have been striving—this slogan has become an illusion. . . . In the past, we adopted the peace option and rejected other options. Israel thought it could receive peace for free. But, when the path of negotiations failed, the path of resistance is the way to get back our rights. It is resistance that will draft out the new Middle East. . . . We shall liberate the Golan with our own hands, through our own will and with our own determination."

In his speech, Assad claimed that Israel had been defeated in the war and its image was badly damaged. He may even have believed it. But for a year thereafter, policies he spouted were a marvel of meandering. Alongside his belligerent speeches, he took advantage of other opportunities to stress his desire for peace and political negotiations with Israel. At the same time, his army was being equipped with colossal quantities of arms from Russia, troop support, and massive reinforcements throughout the Syrian side of the Golan Heights; the army also boosted its military training. The Syrian ground-to-ground missile system was significantly larger than anything at the disposal of Hezbollah. For the first time, the antiaircraft missiles Syria had purchased and was beginning to receive from Russia seriously threatened the Israeli Air Force's freedom of movement. According to Israeli Military Intelligence, the danger of a Syrian attack had increased, with Syria striving for a strong position in renewed negotiations over the Golan Heights. The war with Lebanon had weakened Israel's deterrent factor, especially against Syria. The IDF drew some consolation from the fact that the Syrians had been given the chance to observe some of Israel's military power in Lebanon: Israel's military intelligence had completely exposed Hezbollah's top-secret Fajr rocket system and destroyed it from the air within minutes as well as the IDF's ability to move its special forces to the most vulnerable points behind enemy lines. General headquarters was convinced that Assad was quite capable of translating the significance of all this into "Syrian"—especially the fact that Syria's national infrastructures were vulnerable to a harsh blow from Israel, just as Lebanon's were during Israel's war with Hezbollah. In September 2007 the Israeli Air force attacked a military facility in Northeast Syria. According to the American press, this was actually a nuclear facility, built for Assad by North Korea. Assad did not retaliate immediately, but the danger of war between Israel and Syria will continue to hang over the region for a long time to come.

IRAN LURKS JUST AROUND THE CORNER

In the background of the troublesome developments from Israel's point of view in Syria, Lebanon, and Palestine stood one other country, Iran. Tehran was not operating a puppet theater in the Middle East. Each of its partners had its own agenda, and none of them accepted Iran's wishes as commands that had to be fulfilled unquestioningly. Still, the extreme forces at work in close proximity to Israel shared interests with Iran. The Middle East's main concern in recent years has been Iran's (and apparently Syria's, too) attempts at producing nuclear weapons. As far as Iran is concerned, the war between Israel and Hezbollah could have been premature. It exposed the extent of Hezbollah's Iran-assisted military deployment in Lebanon, which Tehran would have preferred to have used against Israel only at such a time as it (Tehran) gave the order: in the event of an American or Israeli attack on Iran's nuclear installations.[2] Still, the war had no influence whatsoever on Tehran's nuclear arms program. Indeed, the Iranians continue to disregard the sanctions imposed against them by the international community. Israeli leaders in Jerusalem are losing sleep because of the possibility that within a few years the fanatical regime of President Mahmoud Ahmadinejad will be in possession of a nuclear bomb. But this has had a similar effect not just in Washington but also in Riyadh, Cairo, and Amman. There is real fear in these capitals that Tehran will provide a nuclear umbrella to the extremists in Iraq, Lebanon, and Palestine while maintaining close ties with Assad's Allawi regime in Syria (Allawis are Muslims from a special sect in Islam. They govern Syria).

"[We] must understand how things appear in Iran," says Professor David Menashri of Tel Aviv University. "Iranians, too, feel the existential threat. They wake up every morning and see themselves surrounded by the American army and America's allies. This is a mirror image of what Washington sees. . . . Tehran has managed to quarrel with all its neighbors. It doesn't have good relations with any of them. There is in Tehran a sense of power, but it is accompanied by great fear and an understanding of the country's weak points." Menashri is skeptical about the "Shiite crescent" theory. According to him, the Shiites have indeed gained strength in certain parts of the region, "but there is no Shiite alliance . . . no strategic alliance between the Shiites in Iran and the Shiite majority in Iraq, led by Ayatollah Ali Sistani. If a Shiite state were established in southern Iraq, it is hard to say whether it would be in the Iranian or the Iraqi style. The Shiite spiritual leaders, Haminai in Iran and Sistani in Iraq, come from two different schools of thought. The current Iraqi government is controlled by Shiites and there is no similarity nor connection between it and Iran."

Iran's oil reserves have provided it with economic security. "Every one dollar increase in the price of a barrel of oil gives Iran an additional annual income of some billion dollars," says Menashri. "About five years ago, a barrel of oil cost $20. Today the price hovers around the $70 mark. But rising oil prices have not helped the Iranian citizen. The money has disappeared and

Iran is forced to import refined oil, gasoline. Someone might start asking where all this money has gone. The 1979 revolution, it should be remembered, arrived after a giant rise in oil prices. It is true that in the area of the Fertile Crescent and the Gulf, Iran's status is, in itself, firm. [Iran's] involvement in Lebanon has only increased since Syria left the country and its effect on the Israel-Palestine conflict has grown. But during the war in Lebanon, more and more voices in Iran were saying that [Iran] should focus first and foremost on its own problems. There is a Persian saying repeated often during the Lebanon war, 'If you have a light bulb that you need for your home, don't give it to the mosque.'"

Iran has a further reason for concern: a fear of a military attack aimed at halting its nuclear program. The United States and Israel, quite naturally, keep quiet on the possibility of such an attack. At the start of his tenure, Olmert did let slip a few hints as to Israel's presumed nuclear capability and its ability to take action against Iran. But he later adhered to the policies of his predecessors and refrained from detailed public utterances on the Iranian threat. Israel has continued to hold a cautious hope that Bush, despite his weak status at home and the complications caused by the war in Iraq, would still listen to his religious feelings toward Israel and strike at Iran before the end of his presidency in January 2009. In this respect, Israel's war with Hezbollah was only a campaign in the war of giants between the United States and Iran. "This is a war of cultures," says Menashri. "Between the culture of the American West and the Persian-Shiite culture. To Iran, Israel is no more than the little Satan, America's pet pooch. In some ways, Tehran sees itself as following in the footsteps of communism by providing a substitute for western culture."

RESISTANCE

The second Lebanon war came as a complete surprise to the sides involved. Hezbollah never imagined that, by abducting two Israel soldiers, it would cause so sharp and so lengthy a clash with the IDF. In spite of early intelligence, Israel was surprised once by the Hezbollah abductions and a second time by the intensity of its own reaction. More than a year later, the two sides are still studying the results of the war and trying to understand where it has left them. No less important is the question of whether the war in Lebanon has brought them closer to the possibility of further confrontation.

Ultimately, two central interdependent trends emerge, Israel's vulnerable home front and Iran's anti-Israel campaign, for the time being via intermediaries, by conducting a resistance or terror strategy (*Moqawama*).

In statistical terms only, things on the Israeli home front are not so bad. Although over 4,000 rockets were fired in the course of the war, only 53 people were killed by direct rocket hits. Compared with the first Gulf war in 1991 (when Israel was bombed by 40 Iraqi Scud rockets and 1 man was killed), the rate of direct hits was even lower. Compare the number of people killed in rocket attacks against the number in two Palestinian suicide bombings. If, for example, the Palestinians had succeeded in carrying out one or two suicide bombings during the war in the North, they might have achieved similar results.

But a statistical analysis is somewhat misleading since it cannot reflect the fear and paralysis caused by random rocket attacks or the feeling that civilians are not safe in their homes and that the state is incapable of helping them. By hurting Israel's home front and withstanding a prolonged IDF counterattack, Hezbollah succeeded where other Arab countries had failed. The neighboring states—and, especially the terrorist organizations within them—learned that Israel can be manipulated by placing pressure on its civilian population. Israel must devise immediate—even if only partial—redress for all kinds of mortar shells, Qassam, Katyusha, artillery (indeed, everything that is shot up into the sky and then lands on Israeli civilians). Israel's Arrow missile defense system can already provide the necessary response to long-range missiles such as the Scud or the Iranian Shihab 3. But Israel will have to devise ways to protect itself against "stupid" and cheap rockets, such as the Katyusha and the Qassam, without bankrupting itself every time it takes action. Defense experts believe this is possible.

The vulnerability of the Israeli home front fits in very nicely with the plans of Iran and its affiliated terrorist organizations. Terrorist leaders and President Assad make full use of the term "resistance"; Israel is still coming to terms with its meaning. According to the Reut Institute for Strategic Research in Tel Aviv, Israel must rethink the idea that terror does not pose an existential threat; instead of viewing terror as a mere nuisance requiring a local military response, it should be seen as a strategic threat, part of a "resistance structure," encompassing such countries and organizations as Iran, Syria, Hezbollah, Hamas, and others. This fairly loose, not necessarily coordinated web has a single common objective: the destruction of the State of

Israel and the establishment of an Islamic-Arab state over all of Palestine. Recognizing Israel's military supremacy, the resistance structure prefers a war of attrition to weaken Israel rather than a one-time effort to end the occupation. The fact that Israel exuded weakness in the Lebanon war increased the front's self-confidence. If it is joined in the future by Iran's nuclear capability, the danger will be much greater. For years, Israel has described itself as the safest place on earth for Jews to live in. Over time, however, it has become a dangerous place in which to live.

The Israelis shall have to learn to live with the threat of terror and with the extremist countries that encourage terror. It is going to be very difficult to reach any kind of definite resolution for terror. Not all of the countries in the region, close or farther away, are prepared to accept Israel's presence, although the occasional encouraging (mostly secret) message from one of the Arab countries does get to Israel from Saudi Arabia or the United Arab Emirates.

Veteran military analyst and *Ha'aretz* defense editor Ze'ev Schiff died less than a year after the war. In one of his last articles, Schiff made a connection between Israel's failure in Lebanon and America's complex involvement in Iraq. America has already started pulling out of Iraq, he wrote. If the Arabs interpret withdrawal as a sign of American defeat, we can look forward to a radical Arab shift that will strengthen all the extremists around Israel. In the meantime, wrote Schiff, it is hard to escape the conclusion that if Arabs and Muslims can be so cruel to one another (Shiites versus Sunnis in Iraq; Hamas versus the Palestine Liberation Organization in the occupied territories), imagine what they are capable of doing to others. Israel must learn from the cruel internal conflicts within the Arab world. According to Schiff, "The lesson is not to rely on their promises and to maintain a very wide safety zone for defense purposes."[3]

While his colleagues in GHQ were talking in diplomatic terms about the results of the war with Lebanon, Giora Eiland was voicing a rather more astute evaluation of Israel's position. The war, says Eiland, had grave, far-reaching implications. "No matter what we are telling ourselves, it does affect our environment. Something has moved in the Arab world with regard to . . . Israel's capability. Syria has held its silence for 33 years, today it can reach a conclusion that [it can] stretch the rope just a little tighter in . . . the Golan Heights. These are things that were inconceivable before the war."

It is possible, of course, that the war is only the first round in the larger campaign facing Israel. The war has left too many loose ends: Israel's wounded pride at its inability to defeat Hezbollah; Bashar Assad's hope to extract by force what he was unable to obtain with his hesitant overtures of peace; the larger clash of interests between America and Iran.

Throughout 2007, the region continued to be flammable. The potential for a conflagration on at least one of the fronts around Israel still stands. Yet according to a long-standing consensus in the Middle East, wars never erupt when everyone expects them to. Maybe that will be true this time, too. We can but hope.

ONE THE ABDUCTION

1. The investigating team headed by Major General (Res.) Doron Almog later determined that the "patrol set out without briefing, practicing or carrying out a mandatory roll call and the mission was not sent out (instructed) by a dispatching officer."

2. Typically, Hezbollah refused to provide information on the physical condition of the abducted soldiers. An examination by the IDF's Lost in Action unit revealed that the two soldiers had been badly wounded in the attack and the life of one was in danger. The conclusion is based on blood found around the abduction area (a DNA check showed that the blood was that of the abducted soldiers), on medical experts, and on experimental RPG fire on Hummers, aimed at examining potential damage. According to Ronen Bergman of Israeli newspaper *Yediot Ahronot*, these findings were presented to Prime Minister Ehud Olmert only a day before the war ended.

3. On June 15, during a visit with French president Jacques Chirac, Olmert announced that "nothing can now halt the convergence [plan]."

4. Senior IDF officers, for whom the Lebanon abduction was a harsh blow, were in full support of the line taken by the prime minister. In general headquarters, no explanation was forthcoming as to how the Beit Hanoun action could precipitate the release of Shalit, who, at the time, was probably being held in the southern part of the Gaza Strip.

5. A week after the abduction and several months after the division began demanding an observation camera, one was installed. The delay was blamed on budget limitations.

6. This is a Hebrew acronym for Pioneer Fighting Youth.

7. In the Intelligence dictionary of terms, "organization" constitutes a basic stage and is considered less grave than "alert." Both situations are

sufficient in order to take cautionary steps, especially on the northern border, where the Intelligence Branch knew in advance that the ability to obtain accurate information on Hezbollah was extremely limited.

8. On July 8, the last Saturday before the abduction, Major General Udi Adam took his wife for a drive in a civilian car along the northern road. The trip took in the red zones, where troop movement was forbidden during situations of high alert.

TWO   BARAK PROMISES

1. After the name of the town in Saudi Arabia in which the accord was negotiated and signed.

2. The Ta'if Accord, clause 5. www.Al-Bab.com.

3. In April 2002, when Hezbollah was trying to heat up the northern border, at the time of Israel's Operation Homat Magen (defensive shield) in the West Bank, Nasrallah boasted that he was not acting on Iranian orders. In Lebanon, Nasrallah was considered one of the greatest reformers in areas connected with civil and women's rights.

4. Hezbollah refrained from taking responsibility for the suicide attacks in Argentina in 1992 and 1994 against the Israel Embassy and the Jewish Community building, which it had perpetrated in retaliation to the Moussawi assassination.

5. The first Lebanese demand for Israel's withdrawal from the region was noted on April 16, 2000, when Nabih Beri insisted that resistance would continue so long as Israel refused to withdraw from all "14 farms." Israel counterclaimed that the area was Syrian in origin and that the issue would be settled as part of UN Resolution 242 (which deals with territories captured during the 1967 Six-Day War) and not in Resolution 425, which is unconnected to the Golan Heights. According to all Lebanese prime ministers, however, the territory in question is Lebanese and was handed over by Syria to Lebanon in 1951.

THREE   DENIAL

1. All armored vehicles had been removed from the area a few days previously and transferred to the occupied West Bank territories to be used in the second intifada.

2. An Israeli government-appointed commission of inquiry, chaired by retired judge Eliyahu Winograd, which investigated and drew lessons from the second Lebanon war.

3. It was the eve of his second collapse, from which he did not recover. The first collapse happened because of heart problems. The second was a major brain stroke.

4. The Finance Ministry and the military establishment conducted an annual battle over the security budget. The IDF's claims as to the damage to the system and its essential abilities are trustworthy, but the army found it hard to defend its case so long as the military establishment refused to deal with much of its unnecessary and wasteful spending, from the huge delegation in New York to the payment of "sports points" to career soldiers. ("Sports points" are a sort of annual bonus given to career soldiers to buy sports equipment and sportswear for themselves and their families. The original idea was to help them stay in shape, but it became another method to improve their financial benefits—and therefore was viewed in the media as a bit of a swindle.)

5. The quote comes from the MEMRI (The Middle East Research Institute) Web site, which follows Arabic media: www.memri.org.

6. There seems to have been another reason for Hezbollah's diminishing involvement in the territories. Six of the organization's activists who were linked to "Unit 1800" were eliminated in a series of mysterious assassinations in Lebanon. (Unit 1800's job was to assist Palestinian terror organizations in the occupied territories.) Hezbollah accused Israel of having perpetrated the murders. One of the senior figures liquidated was Raleb Alawi, the second in command of Unit 1800 and considered Nasrallah's right-hand man. When Nasrallah delivered his speech at Alawi's funeral, IDF intelligence experts watching the broadcast observed him sweating. One senior intelligence officer claimed that "Nasrallah smelled death in the yard. The message was internalized and Nasrallah has cut back on Hezbollah's assistance to Palestinian terrorists—for a while at least. He understood the rules of the game, and resumed his attacks on the Sha'aba Farms."

7. A number of Israeli Arabs were arrested during the 2006 Lebanon war on suspicion of relaying information to Hezbollah on the places where Katyusha rockets fell and the location of temporary military camps.

8. March 14 is large parliamentary faction and the strongest body in the current Lebanese government headed by Fouad Siniora. The parties making

up the faction include "The Future" Party (headed by Sa'ad Hariri); the Progressive Socialists (a nonreligious party helmed by the Druze leader Walid Jumbalat); the Lebanese Forces (a secular party mainly supported by Maronite Christians); the Phalangists (a Maronite Christian party that was under the leadership of Pierre Gemayel until his assassination); and the National Liberals (a secular party that promotes freedom of religion and whose supporters are mostly Christians). Even after the Syrian pull-out, the supporters of March 14 remained united on a number of issues: the reduction of Syrian involvement in Lebanese politics; the replacement of the pro-Syrian president Lahoud; the creation of a national consensus for defining Lebanese–Syrian relations; the prevention of Hezbollah's takeover of the Lebanese political system (which they believed would probably undermine the fragile political status quo and strengthen Iranian influence in Lebanon); and the establishment of an international tribunal that would try those responsible for Hariri's death.

9. On October 12, 2005 Syrian minister of the interior Ghazi Kanaan was found dead in his office. Two weeks earlier, the 63-year-old Kanaan had been questioned by the Mehlis Committee about his part in the Hariri murder. Kanaan was regarded as one of the stronger figures in the Syrian regime. As interior minister, he had control over a number of security mechanisms. For two decades he had been chief of Syrian intelligence in Lebanon. Opponents of Syria's presence in their country used to call him the Syrian High Commissioner for Lebanon.

10. Relations between Syria and Siniora were very tense. In November 2005, Bashar Assad disparagingly dismissed the Lebanese prime minister with the sobriquet "the slave of a slave" when Siniora filled in for Hariri junior, who had close ties to the West. In November 2006, after the second Lebanon war, Pierre Gemayel, Amin Gemayel's son and one of the most outspoken opponents of Syria's presence in Lebanon, was assassinated. Pierre's uncle, Bashar Gemayel, was also liquidated.

FOUR A NEW TRIUMVIRATE

1. The American military lost this advantage in Iraq the moment it went from triumphal conqueror to long-term occupier. It had to deal with ter-rorist and guerrilla organizations of constantly increasing sophistication and the fractured civilian population's growing opposition to its presence in the country.

2. On July 12, a few hours after the two soldiers were abducted, the GHQ's operations branch circulated the final draft of the order for Elevated Waters to commanders and units.

3. As a reserve pilot in 1982, he participated in a counterdemonstration, merely a symbolic gesture, in support of Sharon, the defense minister. At the time, 400,000 protestors demonstrated against Sharon due to his part in the Sabra and Shatila massacre.

FIVE GOING TO WAR

1. Yihiye Sakaf was one of the 11 terrorists who took part in the coastal road massacre in March 1978 in which 35 Israelis died. Nine of the terrorists were killed in the fighting with the security forces, but only 8 bodies were identified. Sakaf's body disappeared, and the case is still surrounded with mystery. The Israeli security establishment believes that slovenly record keeping led to Sakaf's body being buried in an unknown place. Israel perceives the situation as a blunder in the handling of the murderer's body; Hezbollah and the killer's family, however, have built a scenario according to which Sakaf is still alive and is being held in an Israeli prison. On several occasions, Nasrallah has promised to bring about his release. In 2002, Nissim Nasser was sentenced to six years' imprisonment in a plea bargain. Nasser was convicted of treason, spying, and willingness to sell information to Hezbollah. He was asked to acquire maps of Tel Aviv with electric and gas facilities marked on them and to hand over the names of military officers whom Hezbollah could enlist to its services. Nasser's prison term is due to end in March 2008. Israel refused to release him in a prisoner swap with Hezbollah because he is an Israeli citizen. Nasser's mother is Jewish. He moved to Israel from Lebanon in 1992, received Israeli citizenship, and even established a family in Israel.

2. At 5:00 p.m., while Chairman Nasrallah was giving a press conference, Israel's prime minister held another consultation in his office in the Kirya with heads of the security agencies. This was the first time that Nasrallah's name surfaced as a target for elimination. It was decided to set up a task force from the Mossad, Military Intelligence, and Shin Bet to draft a plan for eliminating Nasrallah. The team took up residence in the air force's pit. All of Israel's attempts to assassinate Nasrallah came to naught. Some of Olmert's advisors are convinced that the entire war was "one elimination away from victory."

SIX　THE SHIP LEAVES PORT

1. David Makovsky of the Washington Institute for Near East Policy published these figures for the first time only after the war, in October 2006. Makovsky, who is known to have strong ties with Israel's political and security establishments, obtained the data from Israeli officials.

2. Some of the principles were added to the proposal only on Sunday, July 16.

3. The source is the protocol of the "situation assessment" held in the defense minister's office on July 13 at 8:30 a.m. Two hours earlier, during GHQ's "situation assessment," Halutz said: "We're at war with Lebanon now. This is how we have to see what's happening. Wartime. This is how I define the situation and the rules we're going by." In discussions later that day, Halutz mentioned "driving Lebanon into a state of chaos." He also said that "Israel has no interest" in ending the military confrontation quickly.

4. The writer, who is identified as EDB on the blog "Anecdotes from a Banana Republic," lives in Beirut. The name Emily appears in one of the installments. The writing style and some of the texts seem to indicate that she is a journalist.

5. The Israeli intelligence community also deliberated over the same question. On Sunday, July 16, the G-8 leaders were scheduled to meet. Iran's nuclear program topped the agenda. Iran probably regarded the abduction and outbreak of war as a move that would divert attention from its nuclear plans. Israel, too, believes that Nasrallah informed Tehran's leaders on the details of the operation prior to its execution. On the day of the kidnapping, Ali Larijani, the director of Iran's nuclear program, visited Damascus. Israeli intelligence agencies now think that this was not a preplanned Iranian move because there is no proof that it was and because in many respects, the flare-up was an *ejaculatio praecox* from Iran's point of view. Certain things about Iranian capabilities were revealed during the war (especially the destruction of the Fajar layout) that Tehran would have preferred to keep in reserve (for a response against Israel in case of an American—or Israeli—attack against its nuclear facilities). In Damascus, Larijani and his hosts probably discussed Syrian aid to Hezbollah.

6. Yemen also denounced the condemnation. The Palestinian Authority and Iraq supported it.

7. Richard Armitage, the former deputy secretary of state under Colin Powell, was quoted after the war as saying that giving Israel the green light for an operation in Lebanon had been a disaster.

8. While the eight leaders were enjoying their afternoon meal, the TV crews' microphones picked up a conversation between President Bush and Tony Blair, then prime minister of Britain, without either of them aware of it. "You know," Bush said, "the irony is that now we have to make Syria force Hezbollah to end this shit." Blair, incidentally, was the senior-most leader to pay the political price for the war in Lebanon. His endorsement of the G-8's announcement in support of Israel further angered the Labour Party, which was already highly critical of his ongoing backing of U.S. moves in Iraq. Blair resigned that year.

SEVEN   THE SOLDIERS CAN WAIT

1. There is dissent among the members of the UN delegation as to Beri's part in the mediation. One described him as an extremely positive element, whereas another said he "was a bad man, who acted only in his own personal interests."
2. On July 18, France handed a nonofficial paper to the UN Security Council, which was supposed to serve as a basis to a council resolution or a call by the Secretary-General for a cease-fire. The main points of the paper were: a call for continuous and extensive cease-fire, with emphasis on the immediate need to deal with the reasons that led to the conflagration; release of the abducted Israeli soldiers; full implementation of resolutions 425, 426, 1559, and 1680, including a disarming all the militias in Lebanon; support for the Lebanese government and, especially, support for its declaration of sovereignty over all its territory; recognition of the blue line (the determined border between Israel and Lebanon according to the UN) in its entirety; and respect for the sovereignty and separateness of Israel and Lebanon. The document even called for the examination of any further steps that could contribute in the future to preventing a renewal of hostilities between Israel and Lebanon, including the possibility of reinforcing the presence of security forces and multinational supervision.

EIGHT   BINT J'BAYEL, FIRST ROUND

1. Actually the reference here is not even to the GHQ forum, which includes all the generals. Throughout the war, Chief of Staff Dan Halutz preferred to bring together and consult with small numbers of colleagues, and the

larger forum was not convened even once. The military investigation teams were very critical of the chief of staff's attitude and complained that he missed an opportunity to take advantage of the experience of some of the generals, who were left in the background with absolutely nothing to do. Combined with the inactivity of the higher command in the command pit, this approach was seen as one of the more obvious manifestations of Halutz's GHQ disorganization during the war.

2. IDF plans on the eve of the confrontation in Lebanon.

3. "What do you mean by 'major'?" Head of Central Command Yair Naveh, who, unlike Adam, appeared to be a welcome guest at the meeting, asked Halutz. Halutz replied: "[I refer to] the three divisions that have placed here in surprise, I don't approve this at this stage, although the minister of finance thinks we'll get there. So maybe we'll get there and maybe we won't. I want to try hard not to get there." The three divisions were reserve divisions, necessary for carrying out the Elevated Waters plan. Reference to the finance minister, Avraham Hirshson, touches on the repercussions on the economy of large-scale mobilization.

4. On the evening of July 12, when the paratroop headquarters moved to the north in wake of the abductions, officers of the 91st Division asked the regimental commander, Colonel Hagai Mordechai, if he could send a force to conduct arrests in the Lebanese village of Eyta a-Sha'ab, through which the kidnapped soldiers had been taken. Mordechai responded in the affirmative, but the operation was postponed in the end because a lack of intelligence. The very idea of conducting an improvised operation in Lebanese territory is proof that the IDF had still not distinguished between Hezbollah and the Palestinian organizations with which they had been in conflict over the previous years.

5. Hirsch reported to his commanding officers on 13 Hezbollah bodies. The chief of staff, who often repeated the need to take prisoners alive and to record enemy bodies as part of the war, was pleased. Halutz ordered all 13 bodies to be removed into Israeli territory, to show to the media. Major General Adam and the paratroopers who had to carry the bodies back on stretchers thought it was a waste of time. In the end and after great effort, 6 Hezbollah bodies were located and brought to Israel. The media paid little attention, but Halutz repeated the order on other occasions in the course of the war—and, under similar circumstances, aroused the anger of reserve soldiers in the Carmeli Brigade.

6. The battles at Maroun a-Ras surprised many government ministers. The chief of staff reported to the government on July 16 that the IDF was using bulldozers and security forces to destroy Hezbollah's line of fighting positions along the border. To Minister Ronny Bar-On's question if this was in preparation for a ground offensive, Halutz stressed that there was going to be no "invasive ground offensive." "How far?" asked Bar-On. Halutz replied, "A thousand meters." On Thursday, minutes before the Egoz troops attacked Maroun a-Ras, Gal Hirsch met four reporters in his office in Biranit for a briefing. The reporters were surprised to learn that, for two days, Hirsch had been simultaneously operating several regimental forces in Lebanese territory, close to the border. According to a *Ha'aretz* headline the following day: "Thousands of IDF soldiers are active in Lebanon." On Sunday, July 23, Cabinet Minister Ophir Pines asked the government for clarification. Olmert replied casually, "It's not thousands of soldiers, only a battalion." In fact, almost 2,000 soldiers were employed at that stage inside Lebanon. The number grew that evening, with the beginning of the operation in Bint J'Bayel. The exchange of words is evidence of the looseness of the political echelon's hold on the IDF and of the limited involvement of the ministers. Decisions were taken between Olmert and Halutz; in certain cases the Seven or the cabinet joined them.

7. A town south of Tel Aviv, with around 200,000 residents.

NINE   TO US, A TIE IS THE SAME AS DEFEAT

1. Even Rice, a few days before her arrival in Israel, was required to deal with the issue of arms and ammunition for the Israel Air Force. Israel's ambassador to Washington, Dani Ayalon, explained to her one night that Israel had simply run out of smart bombs. This extraordinary conversation took place after military attaché Dan Harel was unable to locate his colleague in the Defense Department and asked for Ayalon's help. Rice involved Deputy National Security Advisor Elliot Abrams and eventually signed a special order that enabled the urgent transfer of bombs to Israel.

2. The Americans presented the seven points to the Israelis before Siniora had officially published them at the Rome Conference, two days later.

3. As in the July 16 telephone conversation between Olmert and Livni on a political solution, the unofficial channel of communication serves the prime minister in his defense vis-à-vis the commission of inquiry. In the

absence of an official recording, it becomes a case of his word against hers. Here, unlike Livni, Halutz refrained from raising any claims against the prime minister. According to high-ranking staff officers, when Olmert claimed on August 7, in a visit to Northern Command, that this was the first time he had been shown plans for a broad offensive, it was a "half truth, at best." The idea had been put to him, not in detail and off the record, in a conversation with Halutz on July 24 and again on August 5.

4. Hebrew for "we've come to do reserve military service." It is also the first line of a popular song from the pre-1967 Six-Day War waiting period, when there was an across-the-board mobilization of reserve soldiers as well as buses, trucks, vans, and even private cars.

5. During the war, American neoconservatives asked Major General (res.) Amos Gilad of the Defense Ministry why Israel was not directly threatening Syria. Gilad's reply was that Israel had enough to contend with the two fronts, Lebanon and Gaza, and that a cautious attitude should be taken with Bashar Assad. "Bashar is not his father. With him, it is necessary to talk in big letters [clearly]," said Gilad. In consultations at GHQ, Deputy Chief of Staff Kaplinsky was reserved about the conciliatory attitude to Damascus. There is no reason to start a war with Syria, he said, but all the reassuring messages are superfluous. It's better to let Assad sweat.

6. At this stage, the Americans, Lebanese, and Israelis were already discussing the composition of the international force and its modus operandi. On this point, Siniora deviated from the comprehensive agreements he had reached with Hezbollah.

7. Ben-Zvi had formerly worked with President Clinton during his 1996 election campaign.

8. This number, as will be seen later, is wrong.

9. The IAF's films provide categorical proof that Hezbollah fired rockets in the near vicinity of houses. On July 28, for example, long-range 302-mm rockets were fired from the village of Habush toward the Israeli town of Afula. The long-range rocket launchers were hidden among trees in such a way as to make them difficult to locate. On August 11, a film was shot in Barasheet of a launcher from which rockets were fired. Immediately afterward the car on which the launcher was installed took cover under one of the houses.

TEN   FLOUNDERING

1. The power struggle over the publication of the announcement was a perfect example of the shoddy handling of the war by the highest offices. A
   dispute between Olmert's, Peretz's, and Halutz's staffs led to a delay in the
   publication—and exacerbated Rice's anger with Israel. At 9:00 p.m.,
   Shalom Turgeman, Welch, and Abrams finalized the draft. Turgeman
   wanted the IDF to publish it within an hour. The Prime Minister's Office
   conveyed the draft to the army, but the army spokeswoman, Miri Regev,
   said that it was a political decision and no concern of hers. Then it was
   decided that the defense ministry would make the announcement at 10:30.
   At 11:00, Peretz's office notified Gadi Shamni, Olmert's military secretary,
   that the announcement would be publicized in five minutes. But Peretz's
   office failed to keep its promise, apparently because the defense minister
   had reservations over the fact that his name would be linked to a compromise move. While waiting for the announcement, Assi Shariv, the prime
   minister's media advisor, dozed off at home. A little before midnight, news
   agencies in Beirut reported a 48-hour bombing halt. The Americans were
   fed up waiting for Olmert and Peretz to talk, so they leaked the plan to the
   Lebanese media. Shariv awoke after midnight, when Olmert called his
   house. He checked the number of unanswered calls on his cell phone and
   saw there had been over 60. Shariv finally published the announcement in
   Olmert's name at 12:40 a.m.

2. The differences of opinion were almost "all in the family." Hadley was
   Rice's deputy when she served as National Security Advisor in Bush's first
   administration. Abrams accompanied her on her travels to the Middle
   East.

3. The U.S.-French draft included the wording of the political agreement
   between Israel and Lebanon. Approval by the two countries was needed
   for another resolution to be passed regarding the dispatch of an international force. Its main points were: unconditional respect by all parties of
   Lebanon's and Israel's territorial integrity; complete respect of the blue
   line on both sides of the border; an outline of Lebanon's borders especially
   in the areas where they were disputed or uncertain, including the Sha'aba
   Farms area; security arrangements to prevent the resumption of hostilities,
   including the establishment of an area free of armed fighters, military
   assets, or ammunition between the Litani River and the blue line—except

for those belonging to the armed Lebanese forces and United Nations troops responsible for deploying the international forces in the area; full implementation of the relevant articles in the Ta'if agreement and Resolutions 1559 and 1680 that demand the total disarmament of the armed groups in Lebanon.

In accordance with the Lebanese cabinet's decisions of July 27, 2006, no groups will possess weapons or powers in Lebanon except for those in the name of Lebanon; an international force will be deployed in Lebanon; an embargo on the sale and supply of weapons in Lebanon (except for what the government approves) will go into effect; foreign forces will evacuate Lebanon; Israel will transfer of its maps of minefields in Lebanon to the United Nations.

4. The prime minister slipped again the next day in an interview with an Associated Press journalist when he stated that the results of the war in Lebanon would advance his convergence plan in the West Bank. "This will surprise you," Olmert said, "but I believe that a new arrangement will defeat the forces of terror and help create the necessary environment to enable me to generate the momentum [resume the political process] between the Palestinians and us." What his statement did manage to do was to generate an outcry. Dozens of reservists, inhabitants of the West Bank settlements, threatened to refuse to enter Lebanon if Olmert did not retract his words. "We will not put our lives in jeopardy if the war's aim is to kick us out of our homes," they swore. The Prime Minister's Office issued a clarification according to which the statements were taken out of context, and the affair died down. But at the funeral of one the reservist paratroopers killed in the August 6 Katyusha rocket at Kfar Giladi, the sister of one of the deceased soldiers screamed at them not to take part in the war because the same party that initiated the disengagement was the one that had launched the war. The public's anger toward Olmert at the end of the disastrous war was so great that the convergence plan all but disappeared from public debate. In truth, the war had an entirely different effect from what Olmert predicted: He had to place the political plan in deep freeze and, as he explained in an interview with *Ha'aretz*, "the prime minister doesn't need an agenda in order to preside over the government."

5. The former deputy chief of staff was appointed director of the Defense Ministry in July. Peretz consulted with him on a regular basis

during the war, and Olmert, too, spoke with him several times about developments in the fighting, to the displeasure of Chief of Staff Halutz.

6. About two years before the war, the IDF acquired llamas as pack animals for the infantry. The new acquisition was the subject of a bevy of colorful articles in the press. When the moment of truth came, the llamas turned out to be unsuited for combat conditions. Some froze in their tracks at the sound of gunfire; others refused to traverse the steep terraces of southern Lebanon. The soldiers, instead of the animals, had to carry a double load—and in many cases they left food and water behind in order to lug more fighting supplies.

7. Halutz informed Ganz of the plan the previous evening. Ganz told the chief of staff that he was not keen on the idea but would obey orders.

8. Gedera, a small town south of Tel Aviv, is the home of the deputy chief of staff.

9. These statements appeared for the first time in a book by Ofer Shelach and Yoav Limor, *Captives in Lebanon*.

ELEVEN   THE CABINET

1. The chief of staff did not appreciate the military secretary's opinion. In fact, Halutz was very annoyed by the independent positions that Shamni presented during the war, and their relationship chilled.

2. According to UN procedures, a draft of the resolution has to be submitted to the Security Council 24 hours before the vote.

3. For example, the unresolved dispute over Chapters 6 or 7. The references to Chapter 7 were omitted or were put in parentheses, as the United States insisted. Regarding the Sha'aba issue, it appeared in parentheses in the French proposal, which stated that the UN Secretary-General would be asked to suggest concrete steps for dealing with the farms. Regarding the international force's power to enforce its authority, the reference to its right to use all means at its disposal appeared in parentheses, as demanded by the United States. France opposed.

4. The pollster Geier, Major General (Res.) Amiram Levin, Dr. Haim Asa, and Major General (Res.) Didi Ya'ari. Another participant who was invited, Major General (Res.) Uri Sagi, did not show up.

TWELVE   CASUALTY COUNT IN SALUKI

1. During the war, the Central Command thwarted at least eight attempts by suicide bombers to cross the "Green Line" (the pre-1967 borders of Israel) from the West Bank. Hezbollah exerted pressure in the West Bank on Fatah and Islamic Jihad squads, which receive financial support and instruction from the organization, to contribute to the struggle by attacking Israel in the rear. The Central Command relied mainly on reserve battalions that were called up on emergency orders to replace the regular forces who were sent north.
2. Israel later used these photographs to prove that Syria was secretly transferring advanced Russian arms to Hezbollah.

THIRTEEN   NOT DEFEAT, FAILURE

1. General (Res.) Yoram Yair headed a separate investigating team on the performance of 91st Division throughout the war.
2. Other appointees were Professor Ruth Gavison of the Hebrew University of Jerusalem, political scientist Professor Yehezkel Dror, and retired army generals Menahem Einan and Chaim Nadel.
3. Translated in *Ha'aretz* (Herald Tribune), May 1, 2007.
4. Hezbollah made a point of hiding its real losses. At first it claimed that only 69 of its fighters were killed. A few days later, the number rose to 90. In December 2006, Hezbollah announced that 250 had been killed.
5. In June 2007, six members of the UNIFIL Spanish contingent were killed when a bomb hidden underground exploded when passed over by an armored personnel carrier near Al-Hiam. Hezbollah refrained from admitting responsibility, but the IDF suspect the involvement of the Shiite organization via a smaller, affiliated group. Israel suspects that the wave of attacks on the UN forces endanger its ability to act against Hezbollah.

EPILOGUE   UNTIL THE NEXT WAR

1. In a speech broadcast by satellite to the AIPAC (the pro-Israel lobby in Washington) Convention in March 2007, Olmert made a point of praising Bush's policies in Iraq. The declaration, which most probably was in response to a specific demand from the White House, was criticized as interference in internal U.S. affairs.

2. Some of the experts in Washington were convinced that the results of the last war with Lebanon have reinforced the view that Israel has no real military option against Iran. An army that failed in southern Lebanon, they say, will not succeed against Tehran. If this view is correct, the pressure is no longer on the United States to attack, because Israel is unable to present an alternative of its own for attack. Israeli experts disagree.

3. "The Victory won't be American," Ze'ev Schiff in *Ha'aretz*, April 20, 2007.

INDEX

34 Days